THE RISE AND GROWTH OF THE COLONIAL PORT CITIES IN ASIA

Monograph Series No. 25

Edited by

Dilip K. Basu

Center for South and Southeast Asia Studies
University of California
Berkeley, California

UNIVERSITY
PRESS OF
AMERICA

LANHAM • NEW YORK • LONDON

University Press of America,® Inc.

4720 Boston Way
Lanham, MD 20706

3 Henrietta Street
London WC2E 8LU England

Library of Congress Cataloging in Publication Data
Main entry under title:

The Rise and growth of the colonial port cities in Asia.

(Monograph series / Center for South and Southeast
Asia Studies, University of California ; no. 25)
   Bibliography: p.
   1. Cities and towns—Asia—Growth—History—
Congresses. 2. Urbanization—Asia—Congresses.
3. Urban economics—History—Congresses. 4. Asia—
Commerce—History—Congresses. 5. Colonies—Asia—
History—Congresses. I. Basu, Dilip K. II. Series:
Monograph series (University of California, Berkeley.
Center for South and Southeast Asia Studies) ; no. 25.
HT147.A2R57   1985   307.7'6095   85-11095
ISBN 0-8191-4761-3 (alk. paper)
ISBN 0-8191-4762-1 (pbk. : alk. paper)

Co-published by arrangement with
the Center for South and Southeast Asia Studies
University of California, Berkeley, California

The Center for South and Southeast Asia
Studies of the University of California
at Berkeley is the coordinating body for
research, teaching programs, outreach and
special projects relating to South and
Southeast Asia in the University of Cal-
ifornia system. The Center publishes a
Monograph Series, an Occasional Papers
Series, and a Language Teaching Materials
Series. In addition, it sponsors the pub-
lication of books on South and Southeast
Asia by the University of California Press.

Manuscripts for consideration should be
sent to: Editorial Committee, Center
for South and Southeast Asia Studies,
260 Stephens Hall, University of California, Berkeley, CA 94720.

iii

iv

TABLE OF CONTENTS

TOPIC I: RELATIONSHIP BETWEEN THE CITY AND ITS HINTERLAND

Session 1: ABSTRACTS

TOPIC II: DEVELOPMENT AND CHARACTER OF MERCANTILE ELITES

Session 2: ABSTRACTS

Topic III: The Rise, Growth, and Morphology of the Colonial Port City

vii

During the past decade we have witnessed a considerable increase in literature dealing with the genesis, economic development, morphology, and sociocultural role of towns and cities established by European settlers and sojourners during the heyday of colonialism. In the West and the Third World, both academics and popular writers are hastening to chronicle the rise of the primate city; to describe the evolution of settlement systems in individual dependencies; to identify distinguishing characteristics of urbanism in differing imperial situations; and to fashion conceptual tools for the investigation of these hybrid urban forms that always incorporated people and institutions of alien and indigenous origins. Their collective work testifies in part to the increasing legitimacy of colonial urban history. It also reflects a shared desire to effectively inaugurate the comparative study of colonial urbanism and urbanization while the record remains quite fresh and before the more vivid imprints of imperialism on society and landscape become blurred by the relentless forces of modernization and nationalism.

This long overdue flowering of research on the modern urban history of the Third World has several formative intellectual ingredients. Many scholars with common interests in colonial towns and cities have been moved by the seminal writings of Andre Gunder Frank, Immanuel Wallerstein, and Samir Amin regarding the crystallization of an interconnected world economic system in recent times and the persistent dependency relationships that bind dominant industrial nations of the Western "core" to subordinate states of a less developed "periphery." Following the lead of certain Latin Americanists, they are especially concerned with the role of embryonic primate cities and other major entrepôts as essential instruments of exploitation and spatial integration through which metropolitan authorities in Europe projected decisive politico-economic power into distant territories. Other students of colonial urbanism, who avoid a global perspective and focus instead on regional processes of social, cultural, and ecological transformation, have been content to write detailed accounts of particular towns and cities. The resulting narratives, which tend to be uneven in quality and appear in a variety of languages, often prove difficult to obtain because they are frequently geared to popular readerships in a single nation or exist only as an unpublished thesis on file in one of the world's universities. But they cannot be ignored. Indeed some studies of individual colonial cities-- such as Janet L. Abu-Lughod's recent book on Rabat, Craig A. Lockard's work on Kuching, and Pauline D. Milone's dissertation on Batavia--are instructive models of scholarship and local history that provide critical insights concerning social and economic change in diverse imperial settings.

The growing literature on non-Western cities also includes a succession of exploratory papers on theory and method by historians and social scientists who clearly recognize the inadequacy of conventional ideas based on urban experience in industrial societies. However none of these efforts to forge an adaptive model for the comparative investigation of colonial urbanism has yet received strong endorsement by concerned scholars. Though Anthony D. King in his pioneering Colonial Urban Development (London:1976) did achieve limited success in devising a framework for the investigation of urban morphogenesis and the sociopolitical uses of space in dualistic colonial cities, the quest for conceptual tools of general utility still continues.

The present volume was published five years ago by the Center for South Pacific Studies at the University of California, Santa Cruz, and already fills an important niche in the literature on Asian urbanism. It grew out of a conference on the origin and development of colonial port cities in Asia held at Santa Cruz in the middle of June, 1976. This interdisciplinary gathering--sponsored by three research units of the University of California and organized by Dilip K. Basu, Thomas R. Metcalf, and Rhoads Murphey--brought together twenty scholars from more than a dozen institutions who offered a variety of urban perspectives and had individual expertise on at least one colonial city in South Asia, China, or Southeast Asia. Almost all of these solicited papers were circulated amongst participants in advance of the meeting and each represented an original effort that dealt with one of three major themes: (1) the nature of relationships between city and hinterland, (2) the role and character of mercantile elites, and (3) urban morphology. The six sessions of the Santa Cruz conference, which revealed a considerable breadth and depth of urban knowledge, were at once informative, speculative, wide-ranging, lively, and provocative. By the same token, the abstracts and recorded discussions comprising this collection fairly reflect the spirit of the gathering and the excitement that was shared by everyone in attendance.

Dilip K. Basu, who did yeoman's service as local organizer, is to be strongly commended for his editorial work. He not only convinced all participants to reduce their often lengthy papers to abstracts of a few pages and assembled the illustrations and general bibliography, but also supervised the difficult processes of transcription and production. Furthermore, Basu successfully presented the case for reprinting to members of the Publications Committee of the Center for South and Southeast Asia Studies of the University of California, Berkeley.

Although the Center departs from usual practice in reissuing a previously published work, the arguments in favor of such a decision in the case of this volume proved especially compelling. Not only was the conference well conceived, carefully managed, and very productive, but the resulting collection of abstracts and proceedings received excellent professional reviews, continues to provoke debate, and has fostered ongoing research. In fact some of the papers presented at Santa Cruz have become the nuclei of articles in journals, chapters of books, and at least one monograph. However because of fiscal constraints, the original edition was limited in numbers and proved completely insufficient to meet

both institutional and private demands. All copies were sold within a
year and a large backlog of orders now exists. Through republication of
this important work, the Center hopes to serve a wider scholarly audience
and to foster continuing investigations of colonial urbanism.

Robert R. Reed
Department of Geography
University of California
Berkeley, CA

LIST OF PARTICIPANTS

Robert Alford,
    University of California
    Santa Cruz, California

Dilip K. Basu,
    University of California
    Santa Cruz, California

John Broomfield,
    University of Michigan
    Ann Arbor, Michigan

Frank Conlon,
    University of Washington
    Seattle, Washington

Robert Eng,
    University of California
    Berkeley, California

Sandria B. Freitag,
    University of California
    Berkeley, California

Chris Furedy,
    University of York
    Toronto, Canada

Eugene Irschick,
    University of California
    Berkeley, California

James Masselos,
    University of Sydney
    Sydney, Australia

Pauline Milone,
    Urban Consultant
    Palo Alto, California

Morris D. Morris,
    University of Washington
    Seattle, Washington

James Anderson,
    University of California
    Berkeley, California

C. A. Bayly,
    Cambridge University
    Cambridge, England

Ming Chan,
    Stanford University
    Palo Alto, California

Ashin Das Gupta
    Visva Bharati, Santiniketan
    India

Bryan H. Farrell
    University of California
    Santa Cruz, California

Robert Frykenberg,
    University of Wisconsin
    Madison, Wisconsin

Eric Gustafson,
    University of California
    Davis, California

Susan Lewandowski,
    Amherst College
    Amherst, Massachusetts

Thomas R. Metcalf,
    University of California
    Berkeley, California

Partha Mitter,
    University of Sussex
    Sussex, England

Rhoads Murphey,
    University of Michigan
    Ann Arbor, Michigan

Susan Neild,
   University of Chicago
   Chicago, Illinois

Robert Reed,
   University of California
   Berkeley, California

George Von der Muhll,
   University of California
   Santa Cruz, California

M. N. Pearson
   University of New South Wales
   Kensington, Australia

Keith Sipe
   Duke University
   Durham, North Carolina

Walter T. Vorster,
   University of California
   Berkeley, California

LIST OF ILLUSTRATIONS

*Reprinted from:

    Allom, Thomas, Esq., China, the Scenergy, Architec-
        ture, & Social Habits of that Ancient Empire,
        original and authentic sketches with Historical &
        Descriptive notices by Rev. G.N. Wright, M.A.
        Fisher, Son, & Co., London, 1843.

    Armengol, Pedro Ortiz, Intramuros de Manila, de
        1571, Hasta su Destruccion En 1445. Madrid,
        1938.

    Brown, Robert, M.A., The Countries of the World,
        Cassell & Company, Ltd., London, Paris, &
        Melbourne, n.d.

    Cummins, J. S., The Travels and Controversies of
        Friar Domingo Navarrete, 1618-1686, Vol. I,
        Cambridge, 1962.

    Sears' New and Complete History of China and India,
        New York, 1854.

    Wathen, James, Journal of a Voyage in 1811 and 1812
        to Madras and China, J. Nichols, Son, & Bentley,
        London, 1814.

It was during a luncheon meeting at Berkeley in the spring of
1975 that Thomas R. Metcalf, Rhoads Murphey, and I mooted the idea of
organizing a conference on the rise and growth of colonial port cities
in Asia. The idea impressed us as eminently worthwhile for more reasons
than one. We were aware of a burgeoning crop of monographs that pro-
mised to provide fresh perspectives on South Asia's colonial experience
in an urban setting. And we were equally aware of the need for developing interdisciplinary, cross-regional, comparative approaches to Asia's
urban history. The latter struck us as especially pertinent in the
light of the insights in studies on East Asian urbanism coming, notably,
from social scientists like G. William Skinner, Gilbert Rozman, and
Rhoads Murphey himself.

For these reasons, among others, "Colonial Port Cities" as a
heuristic device and a conference topic seemed to fit the bill. For
one thing, it could take advantage of the crop of material on South and
Southeast Asian urbanism where the "colonial" element was (and is) pro-
nounced, and compare and contrast it to East Asia's where it was less so.
For another, it seemed an important enough topic to deserve a singular
treatment in its own right.

During the fall of 1975, Metcalf and I prepared a position paper
on the conference theme, limiting the structural characteristics of the
colonial port city for the sake of convenience rather than with the intent
of inventing a new conceptual brand to three critical areas: city-hinterland
relations, the role of mercantile elites, and morphology. We then invited
some twenty scholars to contribute papers on the different phases and
stages of the growth of the colonial port city from Surat to Shanghai, with
specific foci placed on the above critical areas.

The conference was held at the Santa Cruz campus of the University
of California from June 14 through 16, 1976. Altogether six long, yet
animated, sessions were devoted to discussing the papers which we had distributed ahead of time among the participants and discussants. The proceedings were taped in their entirety. At the end of the conference, we felt
that the papers and the ensuing discussion were of such high quality as to
merit two separate major publications: (1) an edited version of the discussions with summaries of each paper, and (2) a selection of the papers on
South and Southeast Asia in a substantially revised form. The present volume
is the first in this projected two-part series.

As editor, I asked each contributor to provide me with his or her
paper and abstract, and to check and correct my edited version, based on
the proceedings tapes, of what they had said at the conference. Barring
one or two exceptions, all cooperated magnanimously and remained patient

during the long gestation period that marked the production of this volume. It was no easy task condensing the often lively and elaborate discussion panels without losing the charm and humor which are better seen and heard than read. I have, however, maintained the order according to which the conference topics proceeded--the relationship between the city and its hinterland, development and character of the mercantile elites, and rise, growth, and morphology of the colonial port city. The paper abstracts, with notes on sources, appear together before the session proceedings which include the oral presentation of the paper topic by the author, the critical evaluation by the discussant, and the general discussion that followed.

In addition, I have selected--with help from Partha Mitter, Susan Neild, and Robert Reed--several contemporary pictorial illustrations to enliven the text, and added a general bibliography at the end. At my request, Rhoads Murphey has provided a postscript for which I am grateful. The introductory essay, "Perspectives on the Colonial Port City in Asia," should be read as an attempt at sorting out the various insights that emerged in the papers and at the conference rather than as a systematic analysis of the subject.

Principal financial support for organizing and hosting the conference came from the Institute of International Studies, University of California, Berkeley, the Center for South Pacific Studies, University of California, Santa Cruz, and the Center for South and Southeast Asia Studies, University of California, Berkeley. Additional support was provided by the Center for Chinese Studies, University of California, Berkeley, the Center for South Asia Studies, University of Michigan, the Centre of South Asia Studies, University of Cambridge, Graduate Division, University of California, Berkeley, Committee on Research, University of California, Santa Cruz, and the School of African and Asian Studies, University of Sussex.

Benjamin Dunn, Sandria Freitag, and DiAnne Reid Ross were of invaluable help in planning the conference arrangements at Santa Cruz, while Paul Wrangell patiently taped the proceedings. Finally, I must express my special gratitude to two individuals: Maura Baird, who perseveringly and painstakingly typed several versions of the manuscript and saw it through press, and Bryan Farrell, Director of the Center for South Pacific Studies at Santa Cruz, who kept up his commitment to publishing this volume at a time of retrenchment.

The first edition of this volume published in January 1979 by the Center for South Pacific Studies, Santa Cruz, was sold out within a short time. Since then the Santa Cruz Center has unfortunately been shut down. I am grateful to the Publications Committee of the Center for South and Southeast Asian Studies at Berkeley for agreeing to reprint the volume.

D. K. B.

September, 1983

PERSPECTIVES ON THE COLONIAL PORT CITY IN ASIA

by

Dilip K. Basu

How often do scholars of Asian urbanism engage in a common discourse? Should one take the extant and the current corpus on Asia's long and continuous tradition of urbanization as an index, the answer is - not too often. Historians and geographers working on the same region of Asia, for instance, rarely if ever cross their disciplinary lines or establish a dialogical framework for critically examining the insights and results of their independently charted research projects. Comparative and inter-regional studies are even rarer. The main models and the substantial questions still stem from Western classics, especially those of Weber, Wirth, Sjoberg, Christaller-Lösch, or those of the Chicago School and its critics.

There are, of course, notable exceptions. During the past decade, East Asian scholars have made significant advances in their approach to premodern and modern Chinese and Japanese urban studies. Paul Wheatley's monumental study of the ancient Chinese city traces the origin and diffusion of Chinese urban life, with a focus on its ceremonial and cosmological character, and situates it in a comparative context (Wheatley, 1971). Takeo Yazaki's socio-historical study of the city in Japan from the earliest times through the industrial revolution is probably the most comprehensive, though by no means "total," account to appear to date on a single Asian region's urban history (Yazaki, 1968). Mark Elvin provides us with a brilliant if somewhat controversial study of the impact of the medieval state formation and economic revolution on market structures and urbanization in China (Elvin, 1973).

From the theoretical, empirical and interdisciplinary standpoin t, G. William Skinner's work on the traditional and contemporary Chinese market hierarchies and "central places" has been both path-breaking and trail-blazing (Skinner, 1964-65). The trail-blazing showed in his subsequent effort at organizing two major symposia and editing and publishing their results (Skinner/Elvin, 1974; Skinner, 1977). The East Asia field continues to be cast, recast and critically reformulated according to the categories and "central places" system developed by Skinner. Gilbert Rozman, for instance, has taken the concept of central place hierarchy further by applying it to urban networks that served the needs of administration and exchange in Ch'ing China (1644-1911) and Tokugawa, Japan (1601-1868). Based on the Ch'ing and Tokugawa experiences, Rozman attempts to construct a generalized, socio-historical model on the level of maturity, shape, and functions of urban areas in all pre-industrial societies in a manner that far exceeds the boundaries set by Skinner on his model (Rozman, 1973, 1976, 1981).

The South and Southeast Asian field, in contrast, has harvested fundamentally different crops. Because South and Southeast Asia were both deeply
overwhelmed by the imperialist West the works on their urban history mostly
emphasize the colonially induced and produced phenomena. Rhoads Murphey's
(1977) most recent work is of this genre. The result is an interesting
dichotomy in the contrasting empirical insights emerging from the studies on
East Asia, on the one hand, and South and Southeast Asia, on the other.
While the former emphasize the indigenous structures, hierarchies or networks
in a systematic fashion, underplaying the colonial/semi-colonial factor,
colonialism is the main motor of analysis in the latter.

Two remarkable China-derived insights dramatize this dichotomy. The
first is Elvin's hypostatized theorem of the "high-level equilibrium trap"
which he has used to explain the highly impressive economic growth in traditional China without a concomitant technological change; the second is
Skinner's hexagon-shaped solid quarries of geometrically patterned marketplace networks and urban centers that demonstrated considerable resiliency
and sturdiness even when subjected to contemporary China's revolutionary
mobilization. The logical corollary of these insights strengthen the standard argument as to imperialism's minimum negative impact on the Chinese
economy.

For instance, Dernberger and Perkins have argued that the persistence
and tenacity of the traditional economic structure along with human and institutional resources enabled China to prevent the "hypercolony" syndromes--
concessions, spheres of influence special rights--from fundamentally altering
her economic life. The reason why China, unlike Japan, failed to break out
of the high-level equilibrium trap was because the Ch'ing government was unable
"to create a favorable legal, financial, and economic environment for the
support of the emerging Chinese modern sector" that had precariously developed
along the coasts (Perkins, 1975, p. 48). Rhoads Murphey has taken this
corollary a step further in his pioneering comparative study of the Western
experience in India and China. He argues that, although the Western effort
at transformation was essentially uniform, Indian and Chinese responses
varied widely due to the internal difference between India's fragile,
segmented economy and polity, and China's sturdy, organized socio-economic
structure. Thus, while China could consistently resist the Western drive,
India was substantially remade (Murphey, 1977). Murphey has applied elsewhere the same comparative argument to the Southeast Asian countries as
well (Murphey, 1969).

This Conference brought together a group of anthropologists, economists,
historians, and sociologists in order to engage in an interdisciplinary, comparative dialogue over their recent research findings on Asian urban history. Some
twenty participants were asked to prepare substantial papers based on original
research on cities ranging from Surat to Shanghai. For obvious reasons, the
scope of the Conference had to be limited in terms of the areas covered and empirical problems posed. First, since a number of monographs on East and Southeast Asian urban studies had already appeared, a primary focus was placed on
South Asia-related questions, with a select few devoted to China and Southeast
Asia for comparative purposes. Secondly, the Conference asked to

specifically focus on the phenomenon of the colonial port city, broadly differentiated in terms of the city-hinterland relationships, morphogenesis, and the interactions between indigenous and foreign elites. Finally, the recent China-derived propositions were posed for the Conference's general consideration and evaluation. What was the nature of the indigenous economic, social, and urban structures in South and Southeast Asia before and during the Western advent? Were they as fragile and traditionally undeveloped as they have so far been considered? To what extent did the "colonial" experience transform them? Was the Western imperialist effort at "transformation" uniform throughout Asia? How does imperialism's limited impact, vis-à-vis the sturdiness of traditional Chinese socioeconomic structure thesis, hold up in the papers on Canton and Shanghai that were presented at this Conference?

One may ask why the colonial port city, and not simply colonialism, port or city? At the outset, no attempt was made to strictly define the colonial port city as an analytical or conceptual category except for its common heuristic denominators in morphogenesis, relationship to hinterland, mercantile elites on the one hand, and their considerable novelty as urban phenomena along the Asian foreshores in contrast to the traditional cities which were usually sited inland. The myriad other features of cities in general and the colonial port city in particular, including their roles as political and administrative posts, as well as centers of cultural and nationalist movements were taken for granted and purposively left outside the purview of the Conference.

However, the importance of the interrelationship between the colonial movement and the indigenous Asia elements was crucially emphasized, although no special attempt was made to go deeply into its rise and fall. It was felt that *colonialism and city* would be too broad and vague a term, while *port* was considered too narrow. By the end of the Conference some sort of complex consensus emerged as to the employment of the phrase "colonial port city in Asia" as a meaningful ideal-type that deserved further exploration and study. The role it played in the urban/economic transformation and change in Asia varied over time so that one can, perhaps, think in terms of precolonial, proto-colonial, or full-blown colonial port cities. While most of the papers deal with British colonialism, the papers dealing with the Portuguese, Spanish, and Dutch colonialism suggest a discrete variety in the pattern of impact that European expansion produced during its multiple stages.

M. N. Pearson, James Anderson/Walter Vorster, Ashin Das Gupta, Rhoads Murphey (generally) deal in their papers with the early colonial phases of Goa, Melaka, Surat, and Colombo. Two key analytical nodes emerge in their papers: colonial port city as a transplant (Goa, Colombo) and its grafting onto an indigenous base (Melaka, Surat). Pearson shows how Goa, a secondary center of seaborne trade along India's west coast with a far-flung hinterland in the interior and self-sufficient in terms of its ability to feed itself, lost its internal hinterland and self-sufficiency after the Portuguese conquest. As the centerpiece in the Portuguese empire, Goa had more contact with maritime Asia than with its immediate neighbors. Even during its height as the Portuguese capital, Goa could not outdistance Mughal Surat in terms of autonomy, sophistication, and mercantile operation. While Surat exported local products, Goa thrived on compulsion, forcing Indian merchants through armadas to call at its port.

During the sixteenth century, Goa remained a minor Indian port, a weak link in the string of precolonial port cities in Southwest India. It failed to capture the trade of Surat at one end and that of Aden at the other, and was forced to plug into the existing networks of Asian maritime trade.

Murphey's characterization of Colombo is one of total transformation written on the *tabula rasa* of a virtually collapsed Ceylonese state and society. The Western imperialist design in Colombo, therefore, succeeded remarkably in reshaping its face and structure. What the Portuguese started, the Dutch and the British continued to completion. Ceylon's largely unexplored land resources were tapped effectively to produce one of the most productive and profitable pieces of colonial real estate in Asia. Ceylon was remade in a mirror-image of Colombo as the economy thrived on coffee, tea, rubber, and coconut plantations. Murphey makes his case forcefully and effectively, but two questions remain. In the early stage, when Ceylon is described as in a state of total disarray economically, politically, socially, the cinnamon and gem trade was sufficient to draw the Portuguese to the island. While the Portuguese could easily establish their base at Colombo, they could not take over the hill state of Kandy which fell, finally, to the superior military power of the British in 1815. The second question, which Murphey also poses, relates to the post-1956 Buddhist renaissance and nativistic revivalism in Ceylon. If the colonial experience wrote indelibly on the smoothed Ceylonese tablet, then the recent cultural efflorescence seems rather oddly inexplicable. In any case, this deserves further study.

With the aid of the disciplinary tools of anthropology and geography, Anderson and Vorster have derived from historical materials a fascinating conceptual map of the indigenous trade configuration in pre-colonial Melaka. It is an important paper, not only because it successfully demolishes the standard thesis that pre-colonial Melaka had no hinterland but also because of its vivid portrayal of organized commercial activity in what they term as "equatorial ecosystem." Melaka's hinterland extended beyond its immediate unproductive surroundings to distant zones about 200 miles outward from where the products of forest, sea, and mine were extracted. A system of personal alliance based on close economic, political, and cultural relations mediated the trade in these extractables through the hierarchy ("interlap") of subordinate posts. Goods flowed from the terminal to the center, where all the parts of the trade configuration were highly interdependent. The alliance system allowed for social separateness and cultural distinctiveness of the hinterland population, and it continued well into the nineteenth century until the Dutch destroyed it by insisting on direct dealings and reducing the range of goods.

Das Gupta's paper traces the transition in Surat from the Mughal to the British times. Here again, one gets the picture of a poly-centric, delicately-balanced system of trading operation, reducing itself to a simpler form with the onset of European dominance. Mughal Surat was built around the urban focus of its castle, imitating the great inland cities.

Within its meager 400 square miles, there were no segregated residential
quarters. In this, the city was a contrast to the pre-colonial Great
Tradition cities such as Canton where foreigners were enclaved separately
as well as to the later colonial cities with their Black and White Towns.
Das Gupta attributes the decline of the city to the general decline of
the Mughal Empire. The checks and balances system, somewhat analogous
to Melaka's "alliance system," broke down, and the phenomenon of "protec-
tionism" emerged. Merchants, harrassed by rapacious local authorities,
sought and, at times, even bought, protection from the Europeans, especially the British.

    Bayly's "inland port cities" in Calcutta's hinterland conceptually
comes close to Anderson's and Vorster's trade interlap and Skinner's market
hierarchies. Although much further research ought to be done on the
question of the Mughal redistributive system between the coasts and the
interior, Bayly provides enough evidence to show that it was highly developed. Following Skinner's model to some extent, he provides an intricate analysis of the functional relationships among rural nodes--the
primary bulking centers, the major bulking centers, and the large towns
(originally court towns) in the North Indian Plains. A system of brokers,
agents, and market information networks neatly connected them. Calcutta
as a colonial port city thus did not emerge in a vacuum.

    The impact of Western trade on this hinterland was to link it,
thanks to the export markets in cotton, opium, and indigo, to the world
trade nexus. Towns like Farrukhabad, Agra, Mirzapur, and Patna were as
much port cities as the island riverine Chinese treaty ports were. The
long distance exchange trade in this part of India, however, accounted
for, in Bayly's view, a much larger proportion of total market exchange
than in nineteenth century China. The comparable sector of the Chinese
hinterland economy would be the complex overland route which brought tea
to Canton and the later Yangtze upriver trade as far as Chungking, which
had developed similar bulking centers and merchant-carrier networks.
Fluctuation in international commerce probably had a greater impact on
these Indian towns than on their Chinese counterparts. The crucial factor
was the introduction of the railways in the mid-nineteenth century. Traditional centers like Mirzapur and Farrukhabad declined, and a new township
type like Kanpur emerged in their place.

    The papers on the development and character of the mercantile
elites document how the colonial port cities were peopled and how their
businesses operated. The main emphases are on recruitment, entrepreneurship, merchant lifestyles, and commercial enterprises. Here again, questions of continuities with the indigenous traditions have surfaced. Frank
Conlon's paper on Bombay addresses the issue of ethnicity in the British
recruitment policy. The authorities offered inducements like freedom of
religion and association with groups they wished to attract to the city.
This was, indirectly, an official recognition of the corporate privilege
and internal autonomy of the communities thus invited. Such concessions
were initially made to Hindu, Muslim, Parsi, and Armenian Christians, not
as groups *per se* but as groups led by successful ("Big Men") merchants
who were allowed to bring along members of their immediate families and
their hangers-on. Such groupings were often defined or differentiated as
"castes" which came to form the basis for data on trade, wealth, and even

grain supply. Although the principle behind the freedom of religion and association was that the authorities would not interfere with the internal autonomy of the caste *panchayats*, the East India Company increasingly became involved as the arbiter in caste disputes. Western judicial proceedings thus tended to promote rather than help perish the traditional institution of caste.

Metcalf, Freitag, and Sipe, in their Karachi papers, also refer to the strong community identities and internal support structures there. Karachi was a harmonious city in the sense that the British-created community categories seemed to satisfy each community's self-perception. As a newly-opened port city, Karachi provided opportunities for many Horatio Algers. Yet these people did not seem to have been affected significantly in their social outlook and/or their occupational choices by taking up residence in the city. Sipe points to one important consideration as to why this was so. As Karachi was without its own indigenous mercantile base of any consequence, groups like Parsis, Memons, and Khojas, who had a long history of internal migration, were attracted to it. Despite its "transplant" quality, Karachi, however, did not evolve into a new sociological construct. Its dominant mercantile communities' "free-floating" characteristic was common to other Asian countries as well. Rangoon, Singapore, Kuala Lumpur, and Colombo had such free-floaters from the Coromondel coast of India. There were Cantonese merchant guilds in Shanghai, and Ningpo merchant guilds in Shanghai as well as in other parts of Southeast Asia. The best that can be said about this is that the Western-inspired settlements tapped an internal Asian tradition of spatial mobility among certain mercantile communities.

How a colonial port city acquired an indigenous personality is the subject matter of Lewandowski's paper on Madras. She specifically focuses on a fascinating form of cultural expression that also seems to have been common to other parts of Asia. The Hindu commercial elites in Madras employed the traditional Kingship model to retain and exercise power over the majority of its urban dwellers. Since much of the newly-acquired wealth went into temple building, an interesting linkage emerged between the ritual sector and the city's economic and political systems. This is not vastly dissimilar to the magnetic lifestyles, reinforced during the nineteenth century by the British policy of continuing the Mughal tradition of conferring "kingly" titles such as Raja or Maharaja on worthies deserving the Company's favor, in Calcutta, or the trend toward gentrification among the Chinese merchant classes.

The colonial port city, however, provided other emulative models for the upwardly mobile. In Calcutta, for instance, it was not sufficient for a merchant magnate to assume a kingly style and have a courtly domain, his own faction *(dal)*, it became increasingly necessary for him to play a leadership role in the various overarching secular associations, educational institution-building, and public charity.

Both Furedy and Morris raise the question of entrepreneurship. Issues centering on entrepreneurship have fortunately moved away from the tired old grounds of value systems, particularism, and conservatism of the commercial classes. Each paper in its own way breaks new grounds. Furedy has brought up a neglected subject: the development of the modern retail sector in Calcutta and the role of the small British tradesmen in it. She is justified in saying that the overwhelming emphasis in the literature on colonial entrepreneurship upon merchants and industrialists has resulted in underplaying the innovative role of the retailer. Yet Asian as well as European retail trade was an important aspect of the colonial port city. While focusing primarily on the British retailers in Calcutta, she raises some critical questions as to the relationship between the retail and the external trade sectors, movement of Indians into modern retailing, the influence of the bazaar style on European retailing, etc.

Morris, in his paper, turns away from the standard position which roundly scores the adverse effects of discriminatory colonial policy on Indian entrepreneurial colonial policy on Indian entrepreneurial choices. Adverse official policy does not sufficiently explain why the Indians succeeded in building one of the world's largest textile industries in spite of official opposition and why not others, why they did not move into jute but did go into iron and steel. Morris's main contention is that these entrepreneurial decisions were made by private investors based on their calculation of profit returns. The entrepreneurs considered the nature of the demand for the commodity, supply of raw materials, the price and cost factors, and the rate of return from one industry as compared with another. He contends that the demand side in the Indian economy was weak because of very low per capita income that was unevenly distributed. As the rich favored luxury items that could not be mass produced, there was little incentive for catering to their needs.

Large cities like Calcutta and Bombay faced foreign competition, and there was the possibility of disrupting the interests of merchant groups that imported from abroad. On the supply side, there were chronic problems with physical capital, fuel, transport, skilled labor, all of which were costly. Only human labor was cheap, but that normally works against mechanization. In addition, there were great uncertainties in demand and cost estimations which implied a higher level of risks on the part of the entrepreneurs. All these explain why the rate of investment in modern industry was quite low and why British entrepreneurs tended to invest in the foreign market sector (which explains why they developed jute but shied away from iron and steel), and the Indian industrialists tended to invest in the domestic market sector (which explains why they turned to textiles but shied away from jute).

The fact that there emerged this functional specialization raises the question as to whether the internal and external factors can be meaningfully separated. Were the private entrepreneurial choices made without reference to the colonial government's policy or non-policy? In this respect, the inherent relativism of the "Rashomon effect" should be, perhaps, extended further to include the linkages with the international division of labor that the expansion of world capitalism increasingly enforced as well as the political constraint that the colonial or semi-colonial governments imposed on Asian entrepreneurial choices. All the internal preconditions of Morris's model existed in nineteenth century Japan and China except for the fact that India probably had a lower per capita income than these two countries. Frances Moulder has recently argued that the paramount influence in the rise of industrial capitalism in Japan was not Japan's unique traditional culture but its relative political autonomy that enabled its government to plough back capital surplus to industrial ventures. In contrast, China's lack of this political autonomy led to her failure in developing industrial capitalism in the nineteenth and twentieth centuries (Moulder, 1977). The pertinent question in both the Indian and the Chinese cases is how much surplus capital was available and whether their respective governments were able to make decisive policy choices that could have spurred a self-generating industrial development spiral.

The China papers by Basu, Eng, and Chan broach this question of the impact of the expansion of the world capitalist-economy. Basu focuses on pre-colonial Canton and shows how the embedded, administratively organized and run Ch'ing commercial system was breaking down with the impact of Western trade. It is essentially a study of a port city of a great Asian empire in which the Europeans were becoming the dominant external trading group and developing relationships with the power within the city and outside of it. Basu traces the rise of the dominance of European and American interests and the growing subordination of the imperially appointed and bureaucratically ranked Hong merchants to them.

By the 1780s the British had worked out a system of trade that was reinforced by the growing political power wielded from the East India Company's territorial base in Bengal and by their critical advantage in the control over international shipping and of local capital circulating in Asian trade.

The corporate personality of traditional Hong guilds seemed extremely fragile with the galloping advance of the Hong debts, mostly incurred to the British private traders. Even the prosperous and wealthy Hong merchants became precariously dependent on the foreigners as much of their personal fortunes were pumped into the international trade. Basu uses the term "pidginization" in order to analyze the nature of this dependent relationship. Pidgin was not only the language that the Chinese and non-Chinese traders in Canton used to communicate with each other, it represented, symbolically, a commercial situation where the external factor became inevitably paramount in an indigenous Chinese context. Pidginization was a process that extended the influence of the Anglo-Indian trading system to Chinese commercial and credit operations and, at a certain level, provided the functional model for the later treaty ports.

Chan picks up the story where Basu ends. The emergence of Hong Kong did not demolish Canton's role as a port city. Gradually, a *modus vivendi* of sorts characterized their mutual relationships with Hong Kong serving, in Chan's words, as South China's "foreign trade department" while Canton became its department of purchase and collection of Chinese exports as well as redistributive center for foreign imports. In this entrepôt role, Canton continued to perform some of its traditional functions. The fact that much of Hong Kong's prosperity was predicated upon this service role was dramatically demonstrated during the joint Nationalist/ Communist-enforced blockade that followed in the wake of the Canton-Hong Kong Strike of 1925-26. Without access to Canton's services and its hinterland, the economic life of Hong Kong was virtually immobilized.

Eng's comparative study of the silk industry in Canton and
Shanghai carefully documents the conflicting relationship between the
interests of the Chinese entrepreneurs and the foreign/colonial sector.
Until the 1930s, silk was China's topmost export industry. Its importance is underscored by the fact that the Japanese silk industry developed and flourished at the expense of the Chinese industry, and the
Japanese industrialization effort to a considerable extent was financed
by the silk export profits. Eng's analysis of the Chinese silk industry,
therefore, provides a good test case for comparing and contrasting the
Chinese and Japanese industrialization at a micro-level.

From all standpoints, Shanghai was ideally suited for the expansion of the Chinese silk industry. It was located within the Kiangsu-
Chekiang silkbelt, had access to foreign expertise and technology, and it
lacked the anti-foreign ambiance of the Canton delta. Foreign entrepreneurs had grasped its export potential soon after the establishment of
the treaty port in Shanghai and had moved into silk-reeling. This certainly reinforces Morris's contention as to the tendency among foreign
investors to pick the export sector. Yet the Chinese-controlled Cantonese
filatures and silk-reelers far outstripped Shanghai's in terms of total
number, production capacity, average plan size, stability, etc.

Thanks to the great self-made entrepreneur, Ch'en Ch'i-yuan,
who had initiated the process of introducing filatures, the Cantonese
silk industry fared better, even technologically. Also, Cantonese merchants chose not to shy away from an export trade. In contrast, the
Shanghai firms languished under foreign control where the Western operators, instead of running the plans themselves, had begun to lease out
the filatures to intermediaries, encouraging speculation and discouraging
innovation and expansion.

Foreigners exerted control on the Cantonese industry indirectly
through their control over international shipping, market information,
and pricing. They conducted their own silk tests and, during slack seasons, could cancel contracts made in advance, forcing a severe price
squeeze on the Chinese filaturists. With a slender profit margin, further expansion and consolidation of the industry was not possible.
The Chinese government, harrassed internally by political strife, could
do little to support the industry with capital investment since, according to the treaty stipulation, it had to deposit the customs and salt
revenues with the foreign banks in order to contract loans to pay off the
indemnities. Eng's conclusion lends support to the Moulder thesis as to
the importance of the role of political autonomy in relation to the
Western powers in the Chinese and Japanese industrialization efforts.

The analytical node of the colonial port city as a transplant
and its grafting onto an indigenous base also surface in the papers on
morphology. Reed's paper on Manila shows how the heirs to the tradition
of Mediterranean urbanism attempted to replicate their ideal model of the
city in the widely dispersed decentralized village context of the Philippines. About two thousand colonial settlements were created after the
master plan for systematic foundation of towns and cities issued by
Phillip II in 1573. The Manila site was chosen in addition to the fact

that it provided one of the finest harbors in the world, in order to assure food supplies, a chronic problem to the early settlers. Manila, where the civil and the ecclesiastical institutions were fused together, emerged as a primate city, transforming the Christianized sectors into a clearly-defined hinterland. The commercial sector was developed by the European, Filipino, Japanese, and Chinese residents. The ideal morphological form of the city emerged during the seventeenth century, a period of rapid commercial growth.

Manila changed radically from a cluster of bamboo and thatch into a carefully planned, walled city. The central feature was Manila's grid form, a towering Catholic cathedral, stately buildings and mansions, a central plaza with hundreds of two-storied houses, and sprawling, monastic establishments surrounding it. A massive fortification of stone and brick line separated the city from the outside. Within the city, the Spanish colonists occupied the segregated quarter of Intramuros; the Chinese, the Japanese, and the Filipinos settled in separate urban quarters as well. While the different ethnic settlements developed their own personality in the course of time, the morphology of the Intramuros continued to reflect the ideal Spanish model of a city.

Mitter makes the point that the concept of the central plan of a city "with uniform layout of the houses within the walls and uniform blocks and streets that intersect at right angles" was mooted in Spain in the sixteenth century when the influence of the Renaissance there was at its height. The Portuguese attempted a centrally-planned city at Daman on India's west coast during the sixteenth century as well. When the British started to build in India, they were far removed from the Renaissance influence. He doubts whether anywhere in India the British followed a central plan model with architectural planning limited to individual buildings. The reason was not ignorance of the central plan concept (close as was the eighteenth century traditional city of Jaipur which was designed according to an indigenous central plan concept), but simply from lack of funds.

The colonial port city evolved organically according to the European needs. Security and defense considerations invariably sited them near waterfronts or near the access to the sea. The Dutch city of Batavia, with its fortified factory, provided the model. The governor's mansion was the most important building next to the fort. Two other important landmarks were the hospitals and the churches. The general segregation between the Black and White Towns was difficult to maintain.

Milone's paper further documents how a distinctive colonial port city type in the physical and morphological sense emerged with an intermeshing of European and Asian elements. A peculiar feature of the CPC* was the evolution of the concept of "entitled housing" provided to the colonial underservants. The practice seems to have derived from the Asian tradition of providing lodging for clients, employees, and relatives. European traders like the Asian merchants first lived with their merchandise in the same house; the early European factories were dormitories with mess halls, a practice continued by Canton's and Shanghai's *hongs* and the bachelor quarters for the Malay Civil Service, Chinese Maritime Customs, and by the private firms in Shanghai.

* Colonial Port City

With the building of forts, mini-towns appeared where housing and warehousing had begun to be separated. The next stage was to build outside the fort. The garden villa, another peculiarly Asian phenomenon for the upper echelon, appeared. Colonialists attempted to live out the European aristocratic lifestyle with horses, botanical gardens, and stud farms. Two-storied Neo-classical mansions with open space, parks, *maidans*, and squares started to dot cantonments, civil lines, railway junctions. Arakanese, Bengali, and Cantonese laborers were used in much of this construction and finally left their imprint in the one-storey bungalows/*indische* homes with verandahs, sloping roofs, spacious interiors that eventually replaced the two-storied mansions.

The papers by Masselos, Frykenberg, and Neild deal with the political and social dimension of the morphological aspects of Bombay and Madras. Masselos shows how the interaction between its location and colonial authority determined the growth of Bombay in its early stages, with the breakdown of its fortifications as the Indian population pressure increased, requiring the filling-up of the lowlands between its original seven islands. Even the fire of 1803, which wiped out one-third of the town, could not stem this tide.

Frykenberg shows how the segmented, indigenous polity and society in post-Vijayanagar era in Madras with their spatial diversity, separate communal interests eventually coalesced into a city where a common citizenship within the municipal government was able to preside over the diverse interest groups and weld the separate communities within an overarching institutional framework. The key was the emergence of the British as the dominant power.

Neild provides the much needed economic dynamics to Madras's spatial growth by focusing on the property relations. She shows how a relatively small, compact trading center like early Madras could no longer contain within its confines the pressures of the growing colonialist/commercial forces. The increased demand for space altered the old property relations and reorganized the spatial arrangements of the city during much of the eighteenth century. The Black Town, consisting of indigenous settlements and surrounded by the European community, was now systematically cleared, drained, divided into streets with English names while separate plots were allocated for private European residences and shops. The port site was shifted from the old fort area, typical of the early colonial era, to the more open beach area across from the overtaken Black Town in order to handle Madras's increasing participation in world trade.

If this conference did not quite come around on a commonly accepted definition of the colonial port city, it did indeed succeed in raising a series of questions that are germane to a comparative study of Asian urbanism. Precolonial Goa, Melaka, Surat, perhaps even Colombo, and certainly the riverine inland port towns like Mirzapur and Farrakhabad exhibited a kind of autonomy, indigenous trade configuration based on interlapping networks if not hierarchies that demand further inquiry.

One suspects that the sturdiness and resiliency of such phenomena were not only China-centered but extended to most of littoral Asia. The

difference was probably of degree and one that derived from the indigenous
state structures' ability to enforce and implement the imperially or roy-
ally anointed administered trade. It is remarkable for how long these
traditionally entrenched features of Asian urban commercial life persisted
and withstood the thrusts of early colonial powers, collapsing and disin-
tegrating only during the phase of full-blown colonialism. Some might
even question that they truly collapsed or disintegrated for one sees the
recrudescence and resurfacing of the precolonial structures in ethnic
recruitment, entrepreneurial roles, merchant lifestyles, and commercial
enterprises. Yet there seems to be little doubt that the colonial context,
especially the latter's visceral connections with the controlling powers
of the metropoles, shaped and reshaped them in such a way as to introduce
in the colonial port city a uniquely new form of urban entity in Asia.

References

Elvin, Mark, The Pattern of the Chinese Past. Stanford: At the University
        Press, 1973.

Murphey, Rhoads, "Traditionalism and Colonialism: Changing Urban Roles in
        Asia," Journal of Asian Studies, XXIX, November, 1969,
        pp. 67-84.

Murphey, Rhoads, The Outsiders: The Western Experience in India and China.
        Ann Arbor, The University of Michigan Press, 1977.

Perkins, Dwight H., China's Modern Economy in Historical Perspective.
        Cambridge, Harvard University Press, 1975.

Rozman, Gilbert, Urban Networks in Russia, 1750-1800. Princeton: At the
        University Press, 1973

Rozman, Gilbert, Urban Networks in Ch'ing China and Tokugawa, Japan. Princeton:
        At the University Press, 1973.

Skinner, G.William, "Marketing and Social Structure in Rural China," Parts 1 and 2.
        Journal of Asian Studies 24: 1,2 (November 1964, February 1965).

Skinner, G. William (ed.), The City in Late Imperial China. Stanford: At
        the University Press, 1977.

Skinner, G. William and Mark Elvin (eds.), The Chinese City between Two Worlds.
        Stanford: At the University Press,
        1974.

Wheatley, Paul, Pivot of the Four Squares. Edinburgh: University of Edinburgh
        Press, 1971.

Yazaki, Takeo, Social Change and the City in Japan: From Earliest Times Through
        the Industrial Revolution. Tokyo: Japan Publications, Inc.,1968.

xxx

TOPIC I: RELATIONSHIP BETWEEN THE CITY AND ITS HINTERLAND

IN SEARCH OF MELAKA'S HINTERLANDS: BEYOND THE ENTREPÔT

by

James N. Anderson
and
Walter T. Vorster

The goal of this paper is to reconsider the case of Melaka, *
one of the earliest and most important of Asia's ports, on the eve of
European penetration into Southeast Asia. Our purpose is to examine
what measure of importance pre-existing economic configurations in
Asia had in constraining the development of the colonial port during
the era of mercantile colonialism. This study undertakes a re-examina-
tion of the detailed published translations of contemporary accounts of
Melaka during the sixteenth and seventeenth century which, over the
years, have provided the foundation for analyses of the political and
economic life of the port.

Previous scholarship tended to emphasize the primacy of Melaka's
entrepôt function with the consequence that alternate or additional
roles were obscured. The impression conveyed by earlier commentators
was that, in effect, by controlling that strategic confluence of the
China and Java Seas to the north and east and the Indian Ocean to the
west, Melaka's commercial success was assured.

While not denying the importance of location and site in influen-
cing the success of emporia, such as Melaka, we suspected that other
factors, such as the indigenous organization of the port's regional trade
sphere, were fundamental to that success. Historical accounts, indeed,
suggest that, to understand fully Melaka's entrepôt function, priority
must be given to consideration of the port's role in articulating and
integrating economic potentialities of an ecologically and culturally
diverse region. In short, while its geographical advantage was the
necessary condition for the development of Melaka's commercial success,
Melaka's ability to mobilize the extraction of prized goods within a
configuration of local trade hinterlands and to structure their exchange
was the sufficient condition.

By most accounts, Melaka was at the height of its power and influence during the several decades prior to the Portuguese advent in Southeast Asia. The Portuguese conquest in 1511 in some respects marks the
beginning of Melaka's decline. Yet it took nearly three hundred years
before Melaka's role as a key entrepôt was irrevocably eclipsed. What is
surprising, and it begs explanation, is why Melaka should have dominated
so long, or, alternatively, why European colonial policies so little
altered the basic operation of the pre-colonial Melaka trade. What the

---

* Note: Standard Malay orthography is used in this paper rather
than the traditional spelling, i.e., Malacca.

1

historical documents show are not major breaks with the past following
conquest and consolidation but, rather, continuities. Indeed, despite
the inherent cultural antipathies between the Christian Portuguese and
the port's influential Muslim and Hindu traders, Melaka remained the
crucial link in the Asian interport trade throughout the sixteenth and
into the seventeenth century.

It is largely through Tome Pires's monumental compendium of
Asia's interport trade, written around 1515, that a rather detailed
reconstruction of Melaka's trade prior to the Portuguese is possible.
Prominent in that trade were bulk shipments of foodstuffs, including
large quantities of rice coming especially from Java but, also, from
Siam, Pegu, Champa, and Bengal.

The amounts and, to a certain extent, the types of foodstuffs
are surprising. The most ready explanation, and that seized on by most
studies of Melaka's trade, is that due an apparently unproductive hinterland and the population of the port (numbering anywhere from twelve to
twenty thousand inhabitants at its peak), largely dependent on food imported from abroad.

Most early European accounts of Melaka make reference to the uncul-
tivated and wild appearance of the territory immediately surrounding the
settlement. This image has given rise to the notion that Melaka, as an
entrepôt, was entirely dependent for its economic viability on the
currents of international trade that passed through the Straits. On the
basis of our research, we contend that such a judgment is insufficient
and reflects a decidedly too "Eurocentric" view of city-hinterland morphology and rural ecological adaptations. Rather than a surrounding zone
of intensive rural habitation maintaining functional ties with the port,
Melaka's hinterland corresponded to discrete zones, located within a peri-
meter having a diameter of approximately two hundred miles which encompassed
the territories on both sides of the Straits of Melaka and the intervening
archipelago where products of the sea, the forest, and the mine were extracted. These hinterlands were connected to the port via the ubiquitous
waterways that served to integrate the region.

A system of personal alliances mediated the flow of resources and
commodities between port and hinterland. This alliance system structured
and regulated the exchange of a wide range of basic commodities coveted
by hinterland populations for trade items desired by the entrepôt, including tin, camphor, resins, hardwoods, shad roe, tripang, and birds' nests.
Foodstuffs were among the basic commodities desired by these populations.
Evidence suggests that some of the foodstuffs Melaka imported were subsequently re-exported to meet this demand.

From the middle of the fifteenth century to the middle of the
seventeenth century, Melaka occupied the center of a network of alliances
that constituted its regional trade sphere. The organization and maintenance of close economic, political, and cultural relations with "tribute"
or "vassal" port principalities was one of the most essential tasks for
the continued success of Melaka's leadership. It is our view that what
remained essentially unchanged from the Sultanate through the Portuguese
and into the Dutch interregnum was the system of alliances that linked

Melaka, its subordinate ports, and their resource hinterlands. The alliance system acted as a conduit that regularized political support and the flow of goods from the termini to the center and back to the termini in a trade sphere in which all parts were highly interdependent. The mammoth East-West trade was articulated at Melaka in large measure because Melaka was able to assemble the goods that the various parties to the trade sought.

Diversity is the most striking characteristic of the equatorial ecosystems from which Melaka drew the primary products demanded by world markets. Biologically, these systems are characterized by a great variety of species distributed in low densities. Low concentration of the resource structure constituted the major constraint on ecological-economic arrangements of human populations in a large part of the Malayo-Indonesian realm prior to the nineteenth century. Where concentrations remained low in nature, population densities necessarily remained low as well, since large areas in general were required to extract valued goods.

Human economic activity and mobility substituted for non-existent natural concentrations to collect, bulk, and pass on products to intermediaries who, at bulking points downstream, amassed them further and sent them to larger trading centers. Among these human populations occupying these ecosystems who were not deeply committed to trade, highly generalized, broad spectrum subsistence economies were necessary to maintain them. Actually, few of these groups continued into historic times. Rather, historic and prehistoric evidence suggests long involvement in trade which permitted populations to maintain more specialized economies than would otherwise be possible. Imports of basic commodities, especially staple foods, released them from time that would otherwise be required for subsistence. This time was put into the extraction or production of exportables.

Melaka maintained relationships with several types of extractor populations. Most of them, although organized within very different ecosystems, shared one thing: their relatively small scale, technological simplicity and modest organizational development. These hinterland populations continued their activities only if they felt satisfied with the economic reciprocation and protection which they sought and received from the center. The terms of exchange were complex and subtle; systems of political power or authority did not exist, or could not be sustained, that could compel production. Extractors had to be cajoled into delivering commodities to the entrepôt by being provided with other goods on rather equal terms of trade.

However, the system of trade relations was mutually beneficial to all parties involved. For the port city it provided a ramifying system of political supporters who collected, processed, and concentrated the small quantities of exotic export items that lay scattered in nature. For the primary extractors who could rely on political and economic institutions of more complex societies, it permitted maintenance of more specialized socio-economic systems which substituted dependence on trade for the otherwise required commitment to more generalized, extensive subsistence arrangements.

3

An alliance system permitted localized hinterland populations to maintain their social separateness and cultural distinctiveness. The potentially disruptive impact of world trade came to focus in these hinterlands between the fifteenth and eighteenth century. But once the system of exchange via alliances was established it had the effect of enhancing many aspects of cultural integrity and conservatism. At the same time, the system of trade relations created the possibility of new socio-economic processes. The development of middleman activities which linked hinterland populations with the port acted as a buffer between the two, serving to enhance the conservative trend.

The expansion of European interests in Asia beginning in the sixteenth century acted as a stimulus to the mobilization of resources in the hinterlands of the region bounding the Straits of Melaka. Yet as long as its coveted resources remained essentially unchanged and the conditions underlying their extraction remained unaltered--which was the case until the nineteenth century--the conditions governing port-hinterland relations would remain essentially unchanged as well. If trade at Melaka was to continue at a scale commensurate with the stature of the port in former times, the types of reciprocal demands and obligations between Melaka and hinterland populations had to be maintained. The task of Albuquerque and his successors, both Portuguese and Dutch, was less a creative enterprise than a conserving one.

Although the Melaka Sultan, leader of a chain of linked dyadic bonds which radiated outward from the port, was replaced by the Portuguese Captain after 1511, the underlying economic interdependencies between Melaka and its hinterland populations would remain intact so long as no significant impediment in the organization of trade at Melaka occurred. The continuing volume of foodstuffs traded through Melaka provided one measure of the continuity of this traditional system throughout the sixteenth century.

Whether by design or by default, the Portuguese manifested a degree of flexibility that was precluded in the case of the Dutch, whose conduct of trade at Melaka and elsewhere was profoundly constrained by economic policies of the United East India Company. The open conflict of Dutch policy and traditional organization of trade at Melaka produced dramatic consequences. Both systems had as their goal to regularize and monopolize the flow of goods. The traditional approach was to articulate the inherent variety and specificity of demand by creating a complex market organization that catered to the diversity of products and tastes. By contrast, the Dutch approach was to simplify the system by operating through narrow, direct channels and reducing the range of goods--that is, economically rationalizing the system.

Wertheim has written convincingly about the inherent decentralizing tendencies operating on Southeast Asian policies. Pre-colonial and Portuguese Melaka effectively countered this process by maintaining a system of personal alliances that mediated the needs of all parties in both the regional and international spheres of trade. The seventeenth century marked the development of increasingly bitter competition among European rivals for the resources and markets of the Malayo-Indonesian realm. The consequence of this competition was that decentralizing processes were re-

4

inforced. Dutch policies within Melaka's local trade hinterlands proved to be the crucial determinant, however, which led to the ultimate demise of the entrepôt.

SOURCES

The following is a select list of works that have been consulted, among others, in writing this essay:

Abdullah bin Abdul Kadir, *The Hikayat Abdullah: Annotated Translation by A. J. Hill*. Kuala Lumpur: Oxford University Press. 1970.

Arasaratnma, S., "Some Notes on the Dutch in Malacca and the IndoMalayan Trade, 1641-1670," *Journal of Southeast Asian History*, Vol. X, No. 3: pp. 480-490.

Birch, Walter De G., ed., *The Commentaries of the Great Alfonso Dalbaquerque*, (Publications of the Hakluyt Society. Old Series, Vol. LXII and LXIII, London: Vols. III and IV.) 1880.

Boxer, C. R., *The Portuguese in the East, 1500-1800, in Portugal and Brazil, an Introduction*, edited by H. V. Livermore, (Oxford: Clarendon Press), pp. 185-247. 1953.

Bremmer, M. J., trans., *Report of Governor Malthasar Bort on Malacca, 1678*, Malay Branch of the Royal Asiastic Society 5(1): pp. 9-205. 1927.

C. C. Brown, ed., *Sejarah Melayu, or, Malay Annals*, New York: Oxford University Press (Oxford in Asia historical reprints), 1970.

Colenbrander, H. T. and W. P. Coolhaas, eds. *Jan Pietersz. Coen: Bescheiden Omtrent Zijn Bedrijf in Indie*, Seven Volumes, The Hague: Martinus Nijhoff, Vol. I; VII.

Cortesao, A., *The Suma Oriental of Tomé Pires*, London: Hakluyt Society, Second Series, 2 Vols., Vol. II, p. 287. 1944.

Dunn, F. L. "Rain-Forest Collectors and Traders: A Study of Resource Utilization," *Modern and Ancient Malaya Monographs of the Malaysian Branch of the Royal Asiatic Society*, No. 5, Kuala Lumpur: Perchetakan Mas Sdn. Bhn. 1975.

Ferrand, Gabriel, *Relations de Voyages et textes geographiques arabes, persans et turks relatifs a l'Extreme-Orient du Ville au XVII e siecles*, Paris: Erust Leroux, 2 Vols.

Gijsels, Artus (ed.), *Verhaal van cenige orrlegen in Indie, 1622 uit het Archief van Hilton*, Kroniek van het Historisch genoot schap, gevestigd te Utrecht, Sixth Series, II, 1871.

Hirth, F. and Rockhill, W. W., (trans), *Chau Ju-Kua*, New York: Paragon Book Reprint Corp., 1911 (1966).

Lach, D. F., *Southeast Asia in the Eyes of Europe, The Sixteenth Century*, Chicago: The University of Chicago Press, 1965.

Leur, J. C. van, *Indonesian Trade and Society - Essays in Asian Social and Economic History*, (Selected Studies on Indonesia by Dutch Scholars, Vol. I), The Hague: Banolung - W. van Hoeve, Ltd., 1955.

Meilink-Roelofsz, M. A. P., *Asian Trade and European Influence in the Indonesian Archipelago between 1500 and about 1630*, The Hague: Martinus Nijhof, 1962.

Mills, J. V. (trans.), "Eredia's Description of Malacca, Meridional India, and Cathay," *Journal of the Malay Branch of the Royal Asiatic Society*, 1930, VIII (1): pp. 1-288.

Teixeira, P., *The Travels of Pedro Teiseira*, translated and annotated by William F. Sinclair . . . with further notes and Introduction by Donald Ferguson, London: Printed for the Hakluyt Society, 1902.

Tibbetts, G. R., "The Malay Peninsula as known to the Arab Geographers," *Malayan Journal of Tropical Geography*, 1956, Vol. 9: pp. 21-60.

Wang, Gungwu, "The Opening of Relations Between China and Malacca, 1403-5," in *Malayan and Indonesian Studies*, J. Bastin and R. Roolvink, eds. Oxford: Clarendon Press, 1964. pp. 87-104

Wheatley, Paul, *The Golden Khersonese, Studies in the Historical Geography of the Malay Peninsula before A.D. 1500*, Kuala Lumpur: University of Malaya Press, 1961.

Walters, O. W., *Early Indonesian Commerce: A Study of the Origins of Srivijaya*. Ithaca: Cornell University Press, 1967.

GOA, FROM THE UPPER CURTAIN.

LOOKING OUTWARD:

Colonial Goa in the Sixteenth Century

by

M. N. Pearson

Sixteenth-century Goa should not be studied either in isolation or in purely economic terms. Rather, it needs to be assessed as the focus of Portugal's Asian empire, for its successes and characteristics were inextricably linked to its position in this far-flung, mostly watery domain.

In 1510, the Portuguese conquered a city that apparently traded extensively with the interior, which was able to feed itself from the surrounding countryside, and which was the center of a fairly extensive sea trade. During the sixteenth century, the first two attributes were lost. The third expanded greatly, although on a new basis, so that, while Portugal's empire was working, Goa prospered. But this prosperity was not primarily a result of economic factors. Its total trade was inferior to that of at least one other Asian port, but it received large revenues consequent on the success of the Portuguese politico-military effort in Asia.

It seems clear that Goa in the fifteenth century was not a major port, being outranked by the great Gujarati ports to the north and Calicut in Malabar, south of Goa. The city had a modest role as one of several entrepôts for the inland Muslim state of the Bahmani Kingdom and the Hindu state of Vijayanagar. The main import was horses. About one thousand of these animals, necessary for military and status reasons, came from the Persian Gulf area and south Arabia to Goa each year. The customs duty on them was a substantial contribution to Goa's revenues, but the political and military advantages of controlling this trade were even more significant. The port changed hands three times between 1356 and 1471, and the prime motive was not the customs duties on horses but the desire to control access to them.

Governor Albuquerque took Goa in 1510 because it seemed to fit excellently into his total design. The Portuguese hoped to monopolize all trade in Asian spices, dispossess all Muslim traders, and direct and tax all other Asian traders. To achieve these ends they needed a secure base from which to patrol western Indian waters. Goa's location in the middle of the coast and its relatively good harbors made it ideal for Portuguese purposes. Further, the port was protected from the potentially hostile inland state of Muslim Bijapur (which had emerged after the collapse of the Bahmani kingdom in the late fifteenth century) by the western

9

Ghats, which made up a formidable, though not impenetrable, barrier behind Goa. More immediately, the city itself was located on an island surrounded by defensible rivers and a creek. The port had still another advantage: it was surrounded by fertile land and so could function as a victualling base for Portuguese fleets. Finally, in 1510 it was controlled by Muslims, including many European Turks, and these people were especially hated by the Portuguese.

Goa's position as the focus of Portugal's whole Asian empire in the sixteenth century dictated both its prosperity and its trading activities. The latter were overwhelmingly focused outward: Goa had much more contact with seaborne Asia than with its own interior. In the later sixteenth century, goods worth about four and a half million *xerafins* (one *xerafin* was worth one and a half standard Mughal rupees) passed through Goa's customs house, while inland trade was worth about two hundred twenty-five thousand *xerafins*. This ratio between sea and land trade of 20:1 seems to be a true indication of the sixteenth century position, though in the seventeenth century Dutch and British attacks on Portuguese fleets caused a decline in sea trade. As early as 1617 the ratio had moved to 6:1. This focus on the sea is further demonstrated by figures for customs revenues. In the sixteenth century, about 60 percent of Goa's total government revenue came from customs duties.

The Portuguese were even prepared to look outward for products they could have produced locally. The Portuguese-controlled area was agriculturally productive, especially the two areas of Bardes and Salcette on the mainland, which they acquired in 1543. Yet the Portuguese preferred not to spend their time and efforts on farming. Instead, Goa imported increasing amounts of food from Kanara, to the south. In the later decades of the century three or four fleets, each of several hundred small ships, came to Goa laden with rice each year. From this one area alone, in the 1630s, Goa was importing sixty-six pounds of rice per head of total population per year.

Similarly, Portugal's efforts to attract or force sea traders into Goa seem to have precluded any encouragement for inland trade. Goa had played a real, if modest, role as an entrepôt in the fifteenth century. Under the Portuguese, this virtually ended for the Portuguese were content with the profits they made from their wider policies designed to control Asian sea trade.

Horses were the only product for which Goa continued to act as an important entrepôt. The Portuguese used naval power to control this trade and the strategic position of their fort at Hurmuz, but they also offered incentives in the form of concessions on customs duties to traders bringing in horses. From their control of this trade the Portuguese received substantial customs payments and political advantages in their dealings with the inland states, which were forced to offer bribes and concessions in return for access to these horses.

Customs duties, including those on horses, made up the bulk of Goa's sixteenth century revenue, and this revenue was ultimately derived from forcing Asian merchants to call at Portuguese forts and pay customs duties there. Goa also received profits from other Portuguese areas, these profits again being based on naval coercion. In mid-century, the fort of Hurmuz made an annual profit of over sixty thousand *xerafins* while, later in the century, Diu, in Gujarat, was able to send an even larger surplus to Goa. Similarly, voyages to some areas were declared to be Crown monopolies. Usually, the right to sail on these routes was auctioned off, resulting again in large government profits.

It is thus clear that the luxurious life of Golden Goa in the later sixteenth century was not primarily based on economic aptitude. Rather, the profits of its government and the pleasures of its citizens were founded on the relative success of Portugal's trade control policies in seaborne Asia. As Dutch and British attacks decreased the effectiveness of these policies, Goa declined precipitously. The value of her sea trade in the seventeenth century fell as follows: In 1600, about three and a half million *xerafins*; between 1616-17, less than two and a half million *xerafins*; 1635, one million eight hundred forty thousand *xerafins*; 1685, six hundred eighty thousand *xerafins*. The prosperity of the sixteenth century was, indeed, a bubble based on easy pickings from an exploitative and, inevitably, only temporarily successful, coercive policy.

Indeed, despite Goa's advantages as the lynchpin of a whole empire, even at its height it did not outrank the main Indian port of Surat, though Surat was only one (admittedly, the biggest) of several great Indian ports. In terms of organization, autonomy, and sophistication Surat's merchants were far ahead of Goa's. Surat's trade was generative, based as it was on exporting local products. Goa's trade was based on compulsion: most Indian traders called at Goa and other Portuguese forts because the armadas made them, not because the traders had any economic reason to do so. Finally, despite the absence of any compulsion, Surat's trade was still much larger than Goa's. At its height, Goa's trade was worth about four and a half million *xerafins*. In 1644, Surat's trade was over six and a half million *xerafins*, and, by the end of the century, this had risen to about ten million *xerafins*. Goa's sixteenth century prosperity was thus both unstable and, in Indian terms, relatively minor.

SOURCES

This paper is based mainly on Portuguese documents in archives in Goa, Lisbon, and London. These sources are described on pages 161-68 of my *Merchants and Rulers in Gujarat* (Berkeley and Los Angeles, 1976). For the Goa archives specifically, see my article, "The Goa Archives and Indian History," *Quarterly Review of Historical Studies*, XIII, 4, 1973-74, pp. 205-11, and other surveys of these archives cited in this article. Some of the standard sixteenth and seventeenth century travelers' accounts are useful: Most of these are listed on p. 168 of my book, cited above. By and large, the hard data available for the sixteenth century is very limited, enabling one only to talk about very general trends and even this with some hesitation.

Much more information is available for the seventeenth century, and this is usefully surveyed in T. R. de Souza, S.J., "Goa-Based Portuguese Seaborne Trade in the Early Seventeenth Century," *Indian Economic and Social History Review*, XII, 4, 1975, pp.433-42. Unfortunately, while these data are useful for investigating the decline of Goa, it tells us little about the years of her success in the sixteenth century.

12

INLAND PORT CITIES IN NORTH INDIA:

Calcutta and the Gangetic Plains, 1780-1900

by

C. A. Bayly

This paper discusses the relationship between Calcutta and the
plains of Hindustan in the nineteenth century. It is better to deal
with "processes" rather than with "city and hinterland," since Calcutta
did not represent a single, dynamic, and modern entity, nor was north
India a passive, homogenous physical region merely acted on by the city.
The relevant "processes" linking Calcutta and Gangetic north India can
be broken down into three conceptually, but not historically, separate
groups: (1) effects and opportunities induced by Calcutta as a large
and growing center of population requiring goods and services from its
surroundings, (2) links and relationships created by Calcutta's role
as an intellectual and administrative center in which social, political,
and literary behavior was being modified to confront the problems arising
from British rule, and (3) relationships created by the impact of the
"world economy" and the extractive system of the early colonial period.

In regard to (1), Calcutta inherited the earlier down-river
luxury trade to Dacca and Murshidabad. The enhanced value of north
Indian articles (shawls, horses, fruit, etc.) in Calcutta was balanced
against the cost of transport, insurance, and government duties. Generally, high-value, low-bulk goods were traded before 1860. Yet, as early
as 1820, the low cost of river transport ensured that some food grains
were brought from as far as two hundred miles distant, while bad land
transport restricted Calcutta's dealing with much nearer districts. The
same was true of labor and military service; whereas suburban Bengali
villages provided mainly service personnel (Sinha, 1965), men from the
Bhojpuri area around Benares created early links of labor migration that
later swelled the number of Hindustani workers in the cotton mills of the
Presidency. Even before the railways, the abolition of internal customs
duties in 1834 materially improved the opportunities of the small *mofussil*
trader in the city mart.

In the case of (2), the cultural impact of Calcutta on north Indian
cities came late and was of short duration. For Muslims, Bengal always
retained its "provincial" flavor, while linguistic and cultural distinctions made it harder for Bengalis to establish a leading position in
Hindustani cities than mercantile immigrants from the northwest. Except
in the two cities of Benares and Muttra, where the Bengali population was
large, their entree into north Indian society was as dependants of the
East India Company (such as commissariat contractors and clerks). It was

13

not until after 1860, with improved communications and the expansion of English education outward from the Presidencies, that Bengalis initiated their career as the leading literate clerisy and public men of Hindustan (1860-1890).

Process (3), the impact of the "colonial" economy, is most fully analysed. Here it is important to emphasize immediately that the economic and social institutions in riverine north India and Calcutta formed part of a _system_ that linked primary producers, merchants, and middlemen in India to consumers in China and Europe. Places such as Farrakhabad, Agra, and Mirzpur were as much port cities, in the sense of "bridgeheads of exogenous systems" (Murphey, 1970), as the inland riverine cities in China, which were legally designated "treaty ports." Before dealing with the emergence and institutions of the colonial trading system, it is important to try and assess the magnitude of the external and long-distance trade of north India.

All the indications from the early nineteenth century suggest that the trade in commodities such as cotton, opium, and indigo for external consumption, as also the volume of Western imports, was very small by comparison with the total volume of production and consumption within India. The bast bulk of the produce was produced, exchanged, and consumed within a single village or, at most, two or three villages. On the other hand, long-distance and export trade may have accounted for a much larger proportion of total market exchange than in nineteenth century China. Certainly, fluctuations in external trade had a much greater impact on the growth of market villages, on towns, internal migration, and the more specialized parts of society than is conceivable for China, even in the first decades of the present century.

The long distance and colonial trades in north India went through several well-defined phases: 1) Between 1650 and 1750, the commercial geography of north India changed to bring a greater volume of exchange between the Gangetic plains, central India, and the Bengal delta. Urbanization in Bengal and the growth of consuming elites in Awadh and the Mahratta territories encouraged the emigration of merchant communities and the growth of entrepôt towns. The colonial port city of Calcutta did not, therefore, develop in a vacuum but against the background of patterns of indigenous political power and consumption which were themselves in partly independent change. Such "embeddedness" of the early colonial trade in indigenous political systems proved to be a major theme of the Conference.

(2) External factors had also begun to impinge on the trade of north and central India in a substantial measure once again in the mid-1780s. The diversion of Gujarat cotton to Canton from Bengal in 1783 encouraged the growth of a major trade in raw cotton from Nagpur via Mirzapore to Bengal, along a route that had already developed as a result of the rise of Mahratta consumption. The cotton was used in the weaving marts of Dacca and Murshidabad which supplied both the Company's demand for cotton piece goods and the declining Mughal courts.

(3) In the third stage (c. 1820-60), it proved easy to switch this "proto-colonial" trade from central India to direct shipment to China.

14

The Company, private European and Indian traders, generally made use of the mercantile information and facilities, the towns, markets, and internal political alliances which had emerged in the first and second stages. The colonial import-export trades also fitted into the existing systems of banking and moneylending in upper India. Established trader-bankers (mahajans) financed the cotton trade and imported large quantities of bullion and copper for luxury consumption and investment which, in turn, facilitated up-country purchase by Calcutta-bases businesses.

The economic institutions that emerged during the peak of the cotton trade provide an example of the manner in which town-building at various levels and new social links were created. At the lowest level, the cultivator was neither an untrammelled, "rational economic man," responding to new price incentives in the production of cotton, nor a simple "debt-bonded servitor." Conditions varied from place to place, but everywhere cultivation responded to a delicate balance between familial pressures, the enhanced market value of cotton, and pressures from government revenue, the *zamindar*, or moneylender. A shift in any one of these pressures (e.g., an increase in government revenue or declining external demand) could indirectly affect the area under the crop.

The second level, or "primary marts," where the cotton was cleaned and initially bulked, were mostly "swollen" *haths,* or periodic markets. In the early nineteenth century, such marts could expand or decline with great rapidity. "Secondary marts" were larger, riverine towns such as Agra, Farrukhabad, and Kanpur, where large wholesale merchants bulked, insured, and dispatched the cotton and other goods for their journey to Calcutta.

Cities such as these may have originated as the classic Weberian "administrative city," but growth and revitalization during the early nineteenth century was closely connected with the expansion of long-distance trade and the growth of the colonial import-export trade. The European and Indian merchants who worked from these "secondary marts" were near to the source of supply, but they faced problems of market information, transport supply, trust, and credit as substantial as those of the *bhadralok* entrepreneur in Calcutta.

Bad seasons, overstocking in Mirzapur, Calcutta, and Canton were responsible for huge losses. In part, the move into local moneylending and landholding by north Indian merchant families was a rational response to these uncertainties. Moreover, while contemporaries noted the fragmented nature of the trade route and inveighed against the chains of unproductive middlemen, these complex trading and insurance arrangments had the advantage of spreading risks and employing men with local knowledge and access at every stage of the route. Even the Company found itself dependent on local traders (Kolff, 1974).

The next level of economic institutions was represented by the "colonial entrepôt mart," Mirzapur. Mirzapur's growth predated the European and China trade, but its functions in the early nineteenth century were associated with a vast wholesale market in which goods to and from Calcutta accounted for a substantial bulk of trade. In particular, the town's position on the river, and its proximity to the overland road to

15

central India gave it a decisive advantage as a forward market for the purchase of cotton. But its great dependence on two functions, transport and wholesale exchange, made Mirzpur extremely vulnerable as an urban center. Population and wealth fluctuated considerably between 1780 and 1860, when the construction of the railway and the end of the river trade destroyed its entrepôt function.

As a social organization, Mirzapur was neither a modern colonial center in which business practice and social life had been significantly modernized or Westernized, nor a traditional upper Indian "court-camp" city. Even towns with important commercial functions, such as Agra or Farrukhabad, retained some of their character and much of their population as the result of administrative and princely functions. But Mirzapur was a port city where merchants acted as rulers, and Gossain religious and trading brotherhoods held a position of leadership. The assimilation of indigenous trading institutions into the "world market" by no means presupposed considerable cultural change.

(4) The fourth stage in the emergence of the colonial import-export system in north India was influenced by the coming of the railways (or, rather, the competitive and stable freight charges offered by the railways). Bulk transport of grain, a substantial (although late) build-up of imports of European and Bengali machine-made piece-goods, and the growth of the military and European population in north India strengthened Calcutta's economic and cultural links with Hindustan. At the same time, links to Bombay and the emergence of a small industrial base in north India spelled the end of Calcutta's monopoly.

During this period, European import-export houses which had re-treated during the 1840-60 period, appeared again in greater numbers in north India, with a tighter control over the trade route from consumer to port city. Significantly, however, it was north Indian firms, particularly Marwaris and Desh Agarwals, and not Bengalis, who benefitted from the more rapid communications in the busines sphere. This was in contrast to the law and administration where the Bengalis' ability to manipulate British educational and legal forms initially enabled them to increase their hold on employment in the northwestern provinces.

During this phase, Kanpur succeeded both Mirzapur and Farrukhabad as a major entrepôt center. The presence of a consumer market in the form of the British Indian Army also facilitated the early industrialization of this city and generated processes of urbanization that were much more powerful than those of earlier entrepôt towns. Kanpur became an embryonic exchange-mart between rural produce and locally-made industrial goods; labor and supplies were drawn from a greater distance and more intensively than had been the case in Mirzapur or Farrukhabad. Kanpur, in fact, became the first transplant of the Indian industrial and capital economy in central India. Better supply factors (freight) and enhanced demand (from the army and greater urbanization) made this possible.

If it is possible to generalize about colonial port cities, how far is it possible to compare the historical geography of the trading systems that stretched into the interior? This enterprise is more difficult than it might appear.

16

Problems of river transport inhibited the development of cheap freight on the Indus, the most likely candidate for such comparison within the subcontinent, although, as an inland land mart, Shikarpur in upper Sindh bears comparison in some respects with Mirzapur. In the case of China, the complex overland route that brought tea to Canton in the early nineteenth century and the later Yangtse trade upriver as far as Chungking generated similar bulking centers and networks of merchant-carrier relationships.

But close comparisons are impossible because of a) the fundamentally different political circumstances in which these trades emerged, b) the different staple commodities shipped which determined the size and nature of mercantile facilities, and c) the different structure of merchant community kinship systems and regional organizations between the two cultures. If any general point of comparison emerges between India and China, it concerns the ultimate reassertion of the economic power of the populous, rich, and less-Westernized interiors against the more developed, more Westernized, but ultimately more vulnerable coastal regions. Paradoxically, it was the very phenomenon of "inland port cities," apparently the bridgeheads of the coastal economies, that provided outlets for the trading skills and political strength of the interior.

SOURCES

Among the secondary sources consulted, mention may be made of: P. Sinha, *Nineteenth Century Bengal* (Calcutta, 1965), R. Murphey, "Traditionalism and Colonialism: Changing Urban Roles in Asia," *Journal of Asian Studies*, XXIX, Nov. 1969, pp. 67-84; D. H. A. Kolff, "Economische ontwikelling zonder sociale verandering: de katoen van Hondoestan," *Tijdschrift voor Geschiedenis*, 87, 1974. pp. 545-553.

Primary sources include the Revenue (Customs) records of the Conquered and Ceded Provinces (NWP), Bengal Commercial Proceedings and Bengal Judicial Proceedings in the India Office Library, and the records of the same departments at district level in the Central Records Office of Uttar Pradesh, Allahabad.

There is a considerable secondary literature on trade and social conditions in Hindustan; I have also made use of the interviews, family histories, and family papers available with the descendants of commercial families in India.

VIEW OF POINT DE GALLE, CEYLON.

COLONIAL PORT CITIES AND THE RESHAPING OF ASIA:

Colombo as Prototype

by

Rhoads Murphey

Ceylon was dominated and acted on by European colonialists for longer than any other Asian country. Its smallness and easy accessibility further magnified the Western impact. At least equally important, the political and cultural traditions of Ceylon were in total disarray at the time of the Portuguese arrival and their establishment of a base at Colombo in 1505. The impressive Sinhalese kingdom and its flourishing economy centered in the Dry Zone had collapsed in the thirteenth century, to be followed by political chaos and the virtual abandonment of the Dry Zone in favor of the much less productive but more secure refuge areas in the hills of the West Zone.

Total population, which may be estimated at about four million at the height of the old kingdom, was clearly much less than one million at the opening of the sixteenth century, as it was to remain until the 1830s. There was no single political order nor even a dominant state, and the island was divided in these terms among half a dozen or more rival but ineffectual principalities. Economic activity had declined in many, perhaps most, areas to a level of bare subsistence based on a mixture of shifting cultivation, hunting, and gathering in the Wet Zone forests, and scattered pockets of rice growing. There was little surplus and only a very small trade, primarily in precious stones and in cinnamon, which was gathered wild in the forested hinterland of Colombo.

This trade, however, was enough to attract the Portuguese a few years after Da Gama's arrival on the Malabar coast and only a short distance away from those ports. Ceylon lay along the track from Malabar to the Indies, as well as to Bengal, Malacca, and Canton; its trade was seen as too profitable and too weakly defended to be by-passed.

There was already a small cluster of traders at Colombo, where the management of exports was apparently dominated by Arabs, referred to in early Portuguese accounts as "Moors," a designation that persists in Ceylon for their modern descendants. Although it was a small settlement beside a shallow and poorly-protected lagoon harbor, Colombo was already the chief base for the export trade in cinnamon and gems. The Portuguese seem to have had little difficulty in establishing themselves as the dominant power, razing the capital (at Kotte) of the small coastal state which claimed sovereignty over Colombo, and becoming themselves *de facto* sovereign over the whole of the west coastal zone. Although their repeated

19

efforts to conquer the interior hill state of Kandy failed, more as
a result of disease and topographic obstacles than of Ceylonese military
strength, they quickly acquired control of trade and, from their Colombo
base, exercised a powerful influence throughout the coastal area.

By the middle of the sixteenth century, the process of transformation was well begun which, by Independence, was to reshape virtually
the whole of Ceylon and all of its culture and economy, through the
principal agency of Colombo. Colombo accomplished what all of the colonial
ports aimed at, but none other succeeded so well. In addition to Ceylon's
small size and long history of colonial domination there was little basis
for effective resistance in almost any respect to Western pressures or to
Western modes. Alone among the Asian states and cultures of the sixteenth
and seventeenth centuries, or at least those with a Great Tradition, Ceylon
was in a parlous condition, still attempting feebly and unsuccessfully to
put together the broken pieces of its culture and economy. It was a dis-
heartened, poor, disorganized, underdeveloped, and disunified society; it
must have seen little to defend as well as no effective means of defense
against the Western colonial drive for dominance and for a new mode of
commercial and cultural development. Originally, low-caste groups in the
coastal zone were early collaborators and, as a result, became the dominant
entrepreneurs of modern Ceylon. As Dutch control replaced Portuguese in
the mid-seventeenth century and, as the Dutch subsequently yielded to the
British early in the Napoleonic Wars, Westernization and commercialization
continued to gather force.

Dutch influence was also concentrated on the coastal lowlands, but
with increasing effectiveness. But the massive transformation of modern
Ceylon as a whole came only with the British conquest of the Kandyan kingdom in 1815, their building of roads and railways, and the boom growth of
the plantation system that still dominates Ceylon's economy.

One measure of growth is provided by rising population, which
reached one million in the 1830s, 2.7 million in 188   and seven million
at Independence in 1948. Economically (as well as to some extent, culturally),
Ceylon at the beginning of British control was almost a *tabula rasa*, its
indigenous systems still a faint shadow of what they had been in their more
glorious past, with most of the island unused or only very lightly and un-
productively used, and with commercial development still relatively tiny,
including the export sector. Yet Ceylon was to prove one of the most productive and profitable pieces of colonial territory in Asia, ideally suited
in particular to plantation production of tree or bush crops, native or
suited to a wet tropical environment like that of Colombo's wet zone hinterland and indifferent to its steep slopes and low natural soil fertility.
Plantations began to grow in the 1820s, especially in the newly-opened Kandyan
kingdom, under the stimulus of newly-widened markets under Western control
and with their products for export funneled through Colombo. The first
plantation boom in coffee was wiped out by leaf fungus disease in the 1880s,
but its place was rapidly taken by tea and later importantly supplemented
by rubber at lower elevations. Coconut production for export grew concomi-
tantly but primarily from small holdings, although there was also some plantation development.

These changes required and stimlulated a massive program of road and
railway building, fed the growth of Colombo, and provided both the need and

the means for the belated provision of more nearly adequate harbor facilities. Successive breakwaters and docks were constructed between 1873 and 1906 to cope with the expanding foreign trade of Colombo, now the sole maritime link between a highly commercialized Ceylon and markets in the West. Nearly all commercial production and export crops came from the wet zone within a 75-mile radius of Colombo which also contained, by the 1920s, some 65 percent of the island's population and three-quarters of its towns and market centers.

Colombo itself was, from about 1820, the overwhelming primate among urban places and, at independence, the only real city. Ceylon's economy had been massively re-structured around the production of three main crops for export; hence, the island's economic life centered overwhelmingly on its only ocean port to which all transport networks led. And, although Ceylon outside the plantation sector was less closely tied to Colombo economically, the entire country became Colombo's hinterland and lived culturally in Colombo's shadow. Its newspapers circulated in every town, its cultural patterns, values, and ideas set the national standards. The education network, most of it English, spread from Colombo to cover the island as a whole, carrying the British colonial mode. By the time of independence, most of the Ceylonese elite, political, economic, and cultural, were more at home in English and in the colonial world of Colombo than in Sinhalese or in the indigenous village-based world, more familiar and identified with English history, literature, art, music, and values than with what once had been their own but was now largely forgotten or even moribund, lacking both creators and spokesmen. Genuinely Ceylonese culture was preserved only in what remained of the little tradition of the isolated village and in some of the Buddhist monasteries.

Ceylon could be re-made in the image of its colonial port city over some four and a half centuries, while in India, China, and Southeast Asia larger, but later established, Western bases made a much smaller proportional impact on larger, stronger, and better coordinated indigenous systems. Even in those areas where the Western hand was heavy, such as Bengal, Java, or the lower Yangtze delta, "transformation" was far from complete, and much of the indigenous traditions survived. In Ceylon, it was hard to find in the wake of a Colombo-directed transformation which was far more thoroughgoing. The nativist reaction, which has been such a prominent feature of Ceylon's "second-wave nationalism" since 1956, has attempted to identify and revive a variety of indigenous elements, but much of this is necessarily artificial, understandable though the efforts may be. What little has survived the colonial impact, or what can be identified as particularly Ceylonese--little enough, in all honesty--may, however, provide some clues to the original base on which the colonial structure was laid and suggests what may be a promising line for future research. But the legacy of the colonial port is still suffocatingly heavy. It will take time for that legacy to blend viably with the life of modern Ceylon and for Colombo to come, as the country's only real city and only conceivable capital, something that expresses and serves a new Sri Lanka.

SOURCES

The following works, among others, have been consulted in writing this essay:

Fergusson, D., ed. and transl.,"The History of Ceylon from the Earliest Times to 1600 A.D., as related by Joao de Barros and Diego do Conto," *Journal of the Royal Asiatic Society, Ceylon Branch*, Vol. 20 (1908), pp. 29-53.

Milburn, William, *Oriental Commerce*, Vol I, London, 1813.

Ryan, Bryce, *Caste in Modern Ceylon*, New Brunswick, N.J., 1953;

Pieris, Ralph, *Sinhalese Social Organization*, Colombo, 1956.

Murphey, R., "The Ruin of Ancient Ceylon," *Journal of Asian Studies*, XVI (1957), pp. 181-200; Census of Ceylon.

Wolf, Leonard, *Growing*, London, 1961.

Mendis, G. C. *Ceylon Under the British*, Colombo, 1948.

Vandendriesen, "Some Trends in the Economic History of Ceylon in the Modern Period," *Ceylon Journal of Historical and Social Studies*, 3(1960), pp. 1-17;

Rajaratnam, "The Growth of Plantation Agriculture in Ceylon," *loc cit.*, 4 (1961), pp. 1-20.

Farmer, B. H., *Pioneer Peasant Colonization in Ceylon*, London, 1957;

Perera, G. F., *The Ceylon Railway*, Colombo, 1925.

Panditharatna, B. L., "Colombo City: Its Population Growth and Increases, 1824-1854," *The Ceylon Geographer*, 14 (1960), pp. 1-16.

TOPIC I: RELATIONSHIP BETWEEN THE CITY AND ITS HINTERLAND

Session I

DISCUSSION

23

Session 1

Moderator - Bryan H. Farrell

Discussant - John Broomfield

James Anderson/Walter Vorster, *In Search of Melaka's Hinterland: on Provisioning the Emporium in the Fifteenth - Nineteenth Centuries*

M. N. Pearson [in absentia], *Looking Outward: Colonial Goa in the Sixteenth Century*

C. A. Bayly, *Inland Port Cities in North India: Calcutta and the Gangetic Plains, 1780-1900*

Rhoads Murphey, *Colonial Port Cities and the Reshaping of Asia: Colombo as Prototype*

FARRELL - We start on the business of our first day with the joint paper of James Anderson and Walter Vorster. The authors will now introduce their paper.

ANDERSON - Our paper is about the colonial city of Melaka with a special focus on its pre-colonial antecedents.

Studies of Melaka have portrayed the city, both in its pre-colonial and post-colonial phases, as a monopolizer of foreign trade, a place of trans-shipment of goods for which there was considerable demand at points far distant from Melaka. Because of its strategic position, all that was needed was for a leader to develop a fleet so as to force ships to call there and thereby monopolize the trade. The implication of this established line is that the life-blood of Melaka was in the collection of customs duties from this foreign trade.

Another line suggests that Melaka, in this role of entrepôt, didn't have a hinterland of its own and had to import its food from outside. We started with the proposition, however, that the colonial development of Melaka would have demanded

25

its ability to feed itself under seige. It was a common
concern from the beginning of the Portuguese period when
Melaka was under attack from both inside and from across
the Straits, followed by concern about attack from the
Dutch and other European sources.

So, how did Melaka feed itself? In our research
we found that not only was Melaka able to feed itself but
far more food was coming to Melaka than it needed. We traced
a significant hinterland that existed for the pre-colonial
port city continuing through the Portuguese period and then
beginning to decline during the Dutch period.

The argument that we have advanced while explaining
this decline is different from the standard interpretation.
We bring the argument to your examination. We put a good
deal of attention to the so-called "alliance system" which
tied together the trade interlaps of Melaka, areas not in
the immediate rear or to the immediate hinterland of the
city. We are using the term 'interlap' in a special sense,
meaning, an area beyond a circle extending between thirty
and two hundred miles around that city. It was necessary
for provisioning and for the extractive activity that brought
certain kinds of exotic products to the city for foreign trade
and, perhaps more importantly, which took saleable goods back
to the primary extractors.

VORSTER - Basically, our paper is devoted to a discussion of
the pre-colonial dynamics, though this is a conference on the
colonial port city. We found that the Portuguese and the
Dutch had to conform to the pre-colonial configurations. In
fact, until the turn of the nineteenth century the structure
and configuration of trade in the Straits was quite uniform.
It was only with the coming of the British that there was
any significant change in the type of commodities being traded
and, subsequently, in the organization of trade. Under the
Portuguese and the Dutch, the trade system focusing on Melaka
wasn't fundamentally altered in that the two powers had to
conform to the type of organization which had evolved under
the Melakan Sultanate.

Under the Dutch, outside forces tended to work to dis-
integrate the system somewhat. However, as we show in the
paper, the fundamental problem with the Dutch was not so much
the outside influences immobilizing the goods in the Straits,
but more due to the restraints of working under a centralized
policy of the Dutch East India Company. In order to mobilize
successfully on commodities they had to adapt to the pre-existing process of integration. Eventually, they lost interest in
extracting goods from Melaka's hinterlands as the profitability
from trade was no longer viable for the Dutch. In the end they
were reduced to extracting in the same way that the Sri Vijaya,
the precursor of Melaka, was forced to extract from the traffic
rather than from the goods in the hinterlands. The Dutch faced
the same problem as Sri Vijaya had faced. It's like a circle,
a closing circle.

26

With the British a fundamental change occurred, and that is why we end the paper at that point. In the kind of trade the British operated in this area, Melaka ceased to be the entrepôt that it once was.

ANDERSON - The finishing touch on that last point: Melaka, indeed, lost her status as the entrepôt for the Straits and the near-Straits area and became a second-rate or third-rate port principality, much as the capital of Sri Vijaya had had to come down a notch in an earlier time and much as Pase, a major port for the Indian and Arab trade before and during the earlier phases of Melaka, became a village of Melaka later on. In the same fashion, the trade of Acheh rose and fell.

FARRELL - Thank you. The next paper is by Michael Pearson. In his absence, John Broomfield has kindly offered to give us a quick summary of the paper.

BROOMFIELD - Mike Pearson's argument is that Goa is idiosyncratic among the colonial port cities. He asserts the argument broadly, although he is looking primarily at the sixteenth century. He says that the Portuguese came to Goa and found a city and a hinterland which traded extensively with the interior, was able to feed itself from the surrounding countryside, and was the center of a fairly extensive sea trade. He qualifies this somewhat later, however, pointing out that, despite Portuguese assertions to the contrary, Goa was not a great port trading city before the Portuguese era. The Portuguese exaggerated the amount of sea trade out of Goa. It was one of three middling cities on the Konkan coast. The real trading areas lay to the south and, particularly, to the north, in the Gulf of Cambay.

But the thrust of his argument in the paper is that the Portuguese successfully destroyed the first two of those features of Goa as they found it. They almost extinguished the trade with the interior, with the one very important exception of the horse trade. Trade in horseflesh was important to the Portuguese not primarily economically, although it was a large part of the actual indigenous revenues of Goa, but because it gave them the political leverage they needed to keep the Muslim states of the Deccan and Vijayanagar off their back. If they could manipulate the horse trade, forcing the Vijayanagar to come into alliance with them, then they could keep the inland virtually sealed. And that is what they wanted: a base to control the trade flowing from Melaka, the Malabar Coast, Cambay, Hurmuz, Aden. They wanted to cut that trade and divert it through their own trade routes to Europe.

Pearson argues that, although they destroyed the land trade of Goa, the Portuguese failed in the long run. Even in the sixteenth century and certainly in the seventeenth century total control of the trade of the Arabian Sea eluded them. They never conquered Aden. They had great difficulty controlling the trade up the Persian Gulf. His argument is clinched, ultimately, by a look at the comparative volumes of trade, the custom's revenues, etc., of Surat which, of course, they never

directly controlled. Surat remained a bigger trading center
than Goa despite the efforts of the Portuguese to control
the trade flowing in and out of the Gulf of Cambay, and Surat
was only one of a number of trading areas in the Gulf of Cambay. Surat, he says, grew in absolute volume; Goa declined.
The Portuguese ultimately had to compromise in the Arabian
Sea in ways that offended their ideological views, even to
the point of wheeling and dealing with a large number of
Muslims.

Goa's decline was precipitous in the seventeenth century once the Dutch and the British became important operating
a different system in collaboration, largely, with Gujarati
merchants in the Gulf of Cambay area.

FARRELL - Thank you. I understand that Ashin Das Gupta would
also like to comment on the Pearson paper.

DAS GUPTA - Pearson's strength derives from the fact that,
while working intensively on the Portuguese archives, he sees
the Indian maritime society, as well as the Portuguese in
their different levels, bringing out things we hadn't suspected before.

In this paper, he stresses the insignificance of the
Portuguese in the Indian Ocean in the sixteenth century. He
is carrying on here the heritage of the great Van Leur and
following up the work of Mrs. Meilink-Roelofsz. He has been
greatly impressed by the idea of Steensgaard that there were
several formations like the Portuguese maritime empire which
did not add anything to the productive forces in Asia. They
were redistributive enterprises.

This is a negative sort of paper in the sense that it
emphasizes the fact that the Portuguese not only did not add
to the Asian strength, in some ways they dampened Asian productive enterprises.

I suppose this conference will come back again and again
to the question: What is it that the Portuguese, the Dutch,
and the English added to what was there already? This way, it
is an important paper for all of us.

FARRELL - Thank you. I now call on Chris Bayly.

BAYLY - The title of my paper, 'Inland Port Cities,' may seem
paradoxical. My main purpose is to attempt to break down the
distinction often made between inland and coastal cities while
looking at North Indian cities as part of a complex of trading
institutions during the early colonial period. I am thinking
in terms of processes rather than hinterlands.

The first process is connected with the immediate supply
of the city of Calcutta, dependent, obviously, on such factors
as transport. The area from which Calcutta drew its grain was
extensive, even in the early nineteenth century, stretching

six hundred miles upriver. The second type of process I deal with can be described as cultural or administrative. I am interested in Calcutta as a place where British administrative forms, and Indian responses to British administrative forms, developed and, as a process, this was quite separate from the earlier one: there were colonies of Bengalis as far upcountry as Lahore by the 1860s. The third is the process of the colonial import-export system which the paper is mainly concerned with.

I suggest that the development of this system as a geographical trading entity passed through several stages. Professor Das Gupta suggested to me earlier that, in the Mughal period, the world market--if you like that term--had already penetrated far inland. During the eighteenth century the links between the Agra region and the coastal areas declined. However, during the second phase the movement of indigenous political systems in the late eighteenth century caused the development of a substantial commerce between center-upper India and Bengal, and between Bengal and the developing Maratha principalities.

Some of the trade routes that later became important in the colonial import-export trade in raw cotton, as well as mercantile facilities and town centers, developed in response to this indigenous change. The third stage saw the development of a 'proto-colonial' trade, that is, a trade in cotton between central India and Calcutta, feeding the artisan export markets of Murshidabad and Dacca which was then diverted into the high colonial trade period export to China and the import of bullion and, to some extent, English manufactured goods.

In the final stage I want to see the development between Calcutta and the interior in terms of the stage represented by the development of the railway system and the emergence in the city of Kanpur of a center of inland industrial production fixed to its hinterland.

Next, I attempt an analysis of the various levels of institutions which linked the interior with the coastal port city. I develop a rough model of the way cultivators responded to pressures from land revenue, from their familial position, and also pressures from market. I deal with the emergence of 'primary bulking centers' as a distinctive feature of long-distance trade. A small center, mainly concerned with transport and the bulking of the cash crop, was added to other small centers in north India.

I mention next the second layer of cities, that is, the major bulking centers, larger cities which were perhaps court cities in the Mughal and sub-Mughal periods and now reviving again as centers in which the major import-export merchants sat.

Then, there was the city of Mirzapore, which may or may not be terms idiosyncratic as a major funnel of trade down the river system to Calcutta. All these levels were linked by somewhat fragmented institutions of brokerage and agency and market information. It is not a question of interior merchants controlling produce, controlling traffic; the interior merchants, like the merchants of the coastal cities, were gambling against a large number of variables. In the case of the cotton trade, for instance, variables as far away as the Canton market were critical.

The final aspect of the paper concerns the analysis of Indian cities. I am suggesting that, beginning with the eighteenth century, a substantial instability connected with political authority had entered the commercial arena, and that it continued on into the early colonial period and didn't come to an end until the introduction of the railway system. The instability factor was reflected in the organization of these cities, in the type of social institutions they developed, particularly the brokerage role played by merchant communities, a contrast to the traditional Indian city where the Raja played this type of role.

FARRELL - Thank you. We will now call on Rhoads Murphey.

MURPHEY - I use the case of Colombo in Ceylon, a small place where Colombo thus played a disproportionate role as a prototype of other port cities elsewhere in Asia.

The pre-Portuguese situation of economic, cultural, and political collapse would probably have resulted in an interregnum in which the Ceylonese sorted things out, starting their own system functioning more vigorously. But they were not given a change to do that. Portuguese landed on them early, finding them demoralized and disorganized and, therefore, they and their Dutch and, more importantly, British successors were able to impose on Ceylon, almost as if it were a *tabula rasa*, a colonial design.

It was more complete in its effects in Colombo than was the case with other colonial efforts in the much larger states of Asia whose cultures and economies were not in that degree of disarray. Even a semblance of indigenous continuity in political order was lacking in Ceylon.

I would have liked to have made in the paper a more detailed comparison of the Ceylon experience with the specific experiences of other places, showing exactly in what ways these other cases fell short of the degree of transformation achieved by colonialists in Ceylon. But one must first tell the Ceylon story so that one may have something with which to compare the other experiences. By the time one does that, approaching tolerable length, one has had one's brief hour upon the stage, so to speak.

You may feel that the paper deals with Ceylon rather than with Colombo. It is certainly true, but what Colombo was doing turned out to be what Ceylon was doing, and vice versa. I therefore did not burden readers with specific remarks about Colombo itself which, in fact, is a fascinating place for the same reasons that the Ceylon experience is fascinating. Foreigners were there longer in effective possession than they were anywhere else in Asia and almost as long as they were present in Mexico. And the city of Colombo shows the marks of all of this in a very interesting way.

This paper is asking for trouble since it is casting side glances, even in its left-handed fashion, on other places. I expect people to jump on it and tell me what is wrong with it but, then, that is why one goes to conferences; at least, that is why I go.

FARRELL - Thank you. The discussant for these papers is Professor John Broomfield.

BROOMFIELD - I would start by referring to a most puzzling question raised in the Anderson/Vorster paper: "Women were becoming scarce among the Celates." Fascinating! How could that happen? I hope they'll please explain the paradox.

In looking at such disparate papers, disparate in terms of geographical area and considerable time span, a discussant can bring only a general expertise. I would attempt to put the four papers together thematically, though you may find my perspective on all four papers somewhat individualistic and idiosyncratic.

The Anderson/Vorster paper, at the opening, conveniently provides the framework for comparing the four papers. They make the point that two extreme positions have emerged in the discussion of colonial port cities. One is that the city is a transplant, diffused rather directly from the metropole, and the second is that no colonial port city started from scratch; rather, it was grafted onto an existing indigenous base.

The four papers reflect both positions, and one paper falls somewhat in between. Murphey clearly falls squarely into position one. He views Colombo as the principle determinant of the indigenous social and economic structures during the era of Western influence and domination. He represents not only the city but also the culture of colonial Ceylon's elite, rural as well as urban, as transplants from the metropole.

Murphey equates Colombo with all of the foreign impact. He is not talking as much about the port city as he is talking about foreigners coming into Ceylon. But who were the people who became the collaborators of the foreigners, and how did that change over time? I don't believe it was nearly as much a *tabula rasa* as Murphey represents it to have been. I don't believe that the foreigners had the unfettered impact that is alleged there. If they did, how could the Buddhist revival fundamentally smash the colonial elite structures of Ceylon so quickly following Independence?

31

Pearson also falls considerably under position number one of the Anderson and Vorster typology. Pearson says the Portuguese were determined to transplant their own society directly from the metropole and that they were not interested in grafting onto the existing, indigenous base. Indeed, in Goa's hinterland they were content to see that indigenous base fall apart, the horse trade excepted.

Of course, here we have a time dimension problem. Pearson is looking at one century and a half at the most. If one, however, goes on into later seventeenth, eighteenth, nineteenth century Goa, then the very interesting question arises: How much were the Portuguese taken over by the indigenous system? If would be fascinating to compare the systems that grew up in Goa with those in British Maharashtra, or Goa and the princely states, Travancore and Cochin. It would be fascinating to see what was different about the Portuguese interaction with the British and the British interactions with the systems around about them.

Position Two of the Anderson/Vorster typology is the one that Anderson and Vorster themselves take. They fall squarely into an interest in the indigenous, pre-existing system. They concentrate on the indigenous base of Melaka's economy and its political strength into the Portuguese period and the destruction of the base in the later Portuguese period and, particularly, under the Dutch when it was eroded by the short-sightedness of the foreigners.

The first thing that struck me about their paper is the point they make that when you get diverse flora and fauna with many, many different species, humans can't live in great concentration. To an anthropologist or geographer, this may be obvious, but to a historian it is new--that people have to engage in disperse settlement when flora and fauna don't have enough in concentration of the things they live on.

The second aspect of the paper that I found delightful was the indigenous, conceptual map. If one looks at Southeast Asia in that period, one has to look at the waterways, not the land. The hinterland of Melaka was along the waterways, whether it was a river, a creek, or a piece of the sea. Even though they came sailing in by the sea, the Portuguese and the Dutch did not see the waterways as crucial. They failed to observe that the waterways set up patterns of hierarchy, social status, and all the economic and political networks.

The Portuguese, partly in Southeast Asia and, as Pearson tells us, increasingly in the Arabian Sea, were forced to compromise and were quite flexible, their cruelty and destructiveness notwithstanding. The Dutch were not nearly as flexible. Anderson and Vorster tell us that they would not change their conceptual map and that in some ways they didn't have to. With military and economic power they forced a change in local trade patterns. The pre-colonial focus of the paper helps set up an interesting set of discussions about what followed in the colon-

32

ial period. They do, however, leave us with a paradox
about the Portuguese. They suggest that the Portuguese
tried to do one thing but were really quite good at doing
something else. Perhaps the Portuguese were pretending
to be doing one thing while really doing another. Some
of these interesting points become obscure in the jargon
of two disciplines, geography and anthropology, that the
authors have brought to their work.

Bayly also directs our attention to the existing
indigenous base. Let me quote:

> " . . . Company servants and private traders
> spun their webs of 'country trade' along
> existing lines of commercial activity in
> India . . . These trading patterns and the
> mercantile town-building to which they gave
> rise were not static systems merely acted
> upon by the forces from Calcutta. Like the
> regional states, they were also in the pro-
> cess of change and development which was
> independent of the growth of the colonial
> port city itself."

I applaud his opening injunction: "At the very outset there is a danger of assuming that 'Calcutta' represents
a single and uniformly dynamic entity, while its hinterland
is a passive and homogenous physical region."

Bayly points out that many of the people who lived in
Calcutta in the eighteenth century--and I would extend it into
the nineteenth and twentieth centuries as well--didn't really
see Calcutta as home. It was not their *desh* , their *adibari*,
their ancestral place, not even the place to bring the family
for a long stay. He shows that people operating in Calcutta
used different cultural and commercial modes which were not
"modern" at all. Yet some of them were indeed successful
traders and entrepreneurs.

The railways, however, "decisively altered the internal
patterns of trade." Bayly dramatically illustrates this from
the collapse of Mirzapore and the striking rise of Kanpur.
His argument confirms the classic argument that railways
caused a dramatic shift in the lines of trade, preceded by
important road-building in the pre-railway period. Let me
give one example of how much it changed relationships of
commodities:

In dry weather, during those days, from Calcutta to
Raniganj or Dhanbad was a trip of three days if you were lucky.
This was before the opening of the railroad, before the bridg-
ing, before the grand trunk road was improved. With the railroad it became a five-hour journey. Thus was radically altered
the relationship of certain areas of the hinterland with this

already sizeable city and, of course, the potential world market that lay beyond it.

John Hurd, an economic historian at Eastern Michigan University, has shown that, in most parts of India, the railways predictably lowered the differentials between districts, but this was not the case in Eastern Bengal where the rivers provided an alternative to rail transportation while themselves forming a barrier to the railways.

Finally, I would like to address two points made by Bayly, based on my own research. My current research is on rural entrepreneurship in West Bengal through the period immediately preceding and following the introduction of the railways down to 1950. I am looking at a large, extended family, its movement from peasant cultivation to a range of entrepreneurial, commercial, and some industrial activities.

At the end of his paper, Bayly points to the failure of "the entrepreneurs of the port city to penetrate the interior alongside the few European agents of imperialism." This may, he says, "at first sight appear to contrast sharply with the situation in government and administration." He goes on to say that it was an apparent contradiction because, although the Bengalis moved upcountry with the government there, ultimately they were forced out by the local people. The interesting question to me is the first part: the failure of the entrepreneurs of the port city to penetrate the interior alongside the few European agents of imperialism. Bayly is talking primarily of upper India. I'm interested in the Bengal area proper and the areas immediately to the west: Chotanagpur in Bihar.

A classic question for students of Bengal concerns the supplanting of Bengalis by Marwaris in trade and commerce. Morris raises this question in his paper, to be discussed later in this conference, and suggests that there was not one opportunity in developing colonial India but many, that potentially the economic costs for different people were different as the costs and opportunities were not the same for all groups. I don't believe the Bengalis were supplanted. "Supplant" is the wrong word. They missed some opportunities, perhaps, because they saw, as some recent research suggests, opportunities in agriculture. Opportunities in the products generated out of the land, in the trade in paddy, in the husking and milling, in transportation, in lumber, in clays, and in minerals. And one finds Bengalis in all these areas.

Marwari dominance questions still have to be answered: Why is it that entrepreneurs from the big city could not go in the countryside, and how come the Marwaris appeared to have done so well? Here Anderson's and Vorster's notion of the hinterland of Melaka as a complex of political, extractive, and market systems is helpful. In rural India one cannot make neat distinctions between the bureaucracy and the market system, between local politics and the straight-out entre-preneurial activities, or industrial enterprise. These are often bound together into patron-clientage structures. My own research suggests there was a great deal of wealth for those who could control the patron-clientage networks, link-ing village and small town. The small towns provided markets, processing facilities such as rice mills, access to legal and administrative bureaucracy, participatory access to formal political institutions when those were developed. These accesses were necessary for obtaining business licenses or for entrepreneurial endeavor in general.

The question is, why a small town and not a big city? A common myth of Bengal history is that most of Bengal was controlled by absent *zamindars* who, while neglecting their vast estates, lived it up in Calcutta with poetry, music, nautch girls, and nationalist politics. They were a scourge to the peasants and a thorn in the side of the British. This is nonsense, to say the least. These people did exist, but they were not representative of power in the countryside and, as Barney Cohn has argued, one could have title, even income, but the real power lay with people on the ground. One had to be in the locality to maintain power, even in cases of rich and powerful landholders. And what did power consist of in rural Bengal? Because of great instability of climate and flooding, the control over a source of food supply, over a *gola*, (granary) which, at times of scarcity, could enable one to manipulate prices, yielded both power and wealth, especially if one controlled processing and transportation as well.

In order to move into husking and rice-milling in Bengal, one needed access to local as well as to outside markets and, equally importantly, access to the bureaucracy, either by having a son, a cousin, a friend, or a bribed associate in the bureaucracy.

For big people in this system, this created a problem as they had to maintain contacts further off and locally. If one moved too far away, clients turned to rivals or enemies rapidly, and crops got destroyed or stolen if a close watch was slackened. Networks shifted in the way that Anderson and Vorster showed for the hinterland of Melaka. This explains why it was difficult for people from the outside to penetrate those networks beyond the small town. They could set up link-ages in the small town but, as Bayly points out, it was indeed difficult and risky to try and control the highly personalized network running from the villages through the district town to the secondary center to one of the big cities. In this sense, the colonial penetration was restrictive.

FARRELL - Thank you for a most provocative and comprehensive statement. Is there any response or rebuttal from the panel-ists to Broomfield's discussion?

ANDERSON - I would like to answer the question of why women were scarce among the so-called 'Celates.' It raises some other important points:

The Celates were a sea-faring people, living on boats. They were the rowers for Parameswara, the first leader of Melaka. They came from distant places, getting their wives from slave markets. But these are not relevant, because what we have here is a European repeat of charter association, of patron-client relationships. Celates were incorporated into the Sultanate by invitation. Diplomatic marriages were arranged, and they were given official positions, at the rank of Minister in certain cases. It is remarkable how, despite a broad spectrum of economic activity, each group maintained continuity and narrow specialization over a long period of time. I attribute the reason to economic personalism based on patron-client relationship that underlay the entire system of trade and extraction.

VORSTER - Broomfield has mentioned the importance of the *gola* in Bengal in controlling distribution of rice at key points. I found striking similarities in the power of the granary in Melaka. Not only the Sultanate but the Portuguese and the Dutch as well recognized its importance in the distribution system.

BAYLY - Two quick comments: One concerns the role of the railways. It is difficult to decide whether the railways accelerated changes already underway. Mirzapore appeared to be declining before the coming of the railway. There is a problem when we're looking at changes initiated by the railway and looking at the underlying processes as well. The important thing about the railway, however, was that it fixed networks.

The second point relates to the question of Bengal as opposed to Upper India. The merchant role must be viewed in this context at two levels: the village-controlling merchant and the state level, long-distance merchant who also might be involved in state finance. In Bengal, the long-distance merchant and state financier was destroyed in the early days of the British Empire, between 1750 and 1780, leaving a vacuum into which the Marwaris and other entrepreneurial groups could move. But in Upper India, this state-level financier and long-distance merchant became crucial to the system of extraction itself. Calcutta's impact was minimal on them.

MURPHEY - I accept the points that John Broomfield has made, but plead that it is difficult to do much about them. It is, indeed, difficult to try to deal with four and a half centuries especially when the historical record says little about the indigenous structure. Commercially and culturally, what were the Ceylonese doing in 1500? 1502? 1600? 1800? I think we have a better chance of trying to reconstruct a picture, not from historical records as they are not revealing, but based on developments in the period since 1956 when the Ceylonese,

rather than the Singhalese, renewed their search for the
indigenous and traditional elements of their culture.

Of course, something must have been going on in
indigenous Ceylon for the renewal since '56 to have happened.
The Singhalese must be drawing on cultural elements they
sense were there all along which are now, for the first time,
being pushed into the center of the stage. What these cultural elements were like during the Portuguese, the Dutch,
or the British colonial period, I don't know because nobody
talked about them then. To find them now one probably should
look in village Ceylon as an anthropologist, in a detective
way. Only then can we hope to reconstruct the interacting
role, if any, of Buddhist Ceylon with the colonial implant
pattern which dominated.

FARRELL   - The panelists have responded. It is time now for
others to comment. Dilip Basu.

BASU   - Some time ago G. William Skinner made a noted contribution to a study of market hierarchy in traditional as well as
contemporary China. Both in the Anderson/Vorster and Bayly
papers, I believe there is an implicit Skinner-type hierarchy.
I wonder whether the authors feel the Skinner model of the
central place system, of a cellular hierarchy, is appropriate
in their cases.

ANDERSON   - Skinner's classification is useful generally, but
not appropriate for the levels of Melaka's hinterland which
were quite different. Probably the port principalities, as
we call it, would fit Skinner's scheme but not the lower
levels.

METCALF   - I wonder if we might pull some chronological themes
out of structural ones? The papers of this panel have provided us with pre-, or perhaps I should say, proto-colonial
baselines of trading structures upon which we could build
more thorough transformations.

Anderson and Vorster have talked about some of the early
trading regimes. Bayly has also pointed to early trading regimes that had impinged upon and inter-mixed into indigenous
structures of trading values. These papers refer to particular
kinds of hinterland relationships. Murphey's is an exceptional
case. All the papers still indicate the need to explore the
extent of thorough-going transformations during the full-blown
colonial period. Alternately, we can ask whether the full-
blown colonial period witnessed further modifications on, plug-
gings in, or workings within the indigenous system.

The Portuguese in the Goan case, according to Pearson,
were engaging in extreme transformation. In contrast, as
Anderson says, they plugged themselves into the Melakan system,
acting within it to a substantial extent. I wonder if we can

reconcile these two views.

Insofar as the Bayly paper is concerned, there is a
note of static quality in the urban material that formed
and re-formed, often down different river-valleys. Can it
be that there was, perhaps, more transformation or growth,
even in the proto-colonial period, than Bayly is prepared
to recognize?

MILONE - I believe the Portuguese acted in Ceylon, Melaka,
   and Goa differently because of the divergent functions of the
   cities. In Goa, they conceived of themselves as being the
   capital of a vast network, with their hinterland comprised of
   trading stations throughout the world. The Dutch acted the
   same way in Batavia. In such cases there was more of a tendency toward transplant morphology since existing trade relationships with the hinterland directly behind and around the
   city were not regarded as crucial.

        Another point concerns whether they felt secure or not.
   In Goa, the Portuguese were threatened by the Kingdoms of
   Ahmadnagar and Bijapur; in Southeast Asia the Dutch were fear-
   ful of the Bantamese Sultanate, which had taken away some of
   Melaka's trade.

VORSTER - I might add that in Melaka as well--if you read
   Albuquerque's commentaries--the Portuguese held a similar
   view. They saw Melaka as part of a vast network of other
   ports without thinking much about the value of the hinterlands
   it controlled. But this was in the initial phase of the sixteenth century. By the turn of the seventeenth century the
   Portuguese had shifted their whole focus, successfully tapping
   the hinterland.

MURPHEY - I wonder whether the word 'umland' expresses better
   Melaka's role and the situation than 'hinterland' does. Hinterland implies 'in back of' and, therefore, 'on land,' whereas
   Melaka had indeed a classic 'umland,' in keeping with a number
   of other places. But Melaka is not representative of the
   colonial port cities because it never was one. It belonged in
   the same category with Atcheh, Patani, Amboina, places that
   had been important before in other hands but did not change
   much with the Portuguese as commercial agents. This was characteristic of the first three centuries of the Western presence
   in Asia, say from DaGama to Warren Hastings, when the Westerners
   were, relatively speaking, insignificant. The Portuguese certainly were. The advent of the Industrial Revolution and the
   beginnings of territorial imperialism brought about a qualitative
   change; the focus shifted away from Melaka to other places so that,
   when Raffles looked for a base in Malaya, it didn't occur to him
   to make use of Melaka. It was of no real value in the design
   that Raffles and his successors had in mind. Melaka thus belongs to the earlier period. Panikkar mislabels the whole as
   'the Age of DaGama,' implying that it began in 1498 and stretched

to 1947. The Age of DaGama actually ended around the early eighteenth century, and a different age, the Age of--what would you like to call it? Darwin? or Stevenson?--succeeded it.

ANDERSON - I agree with Murphey in essentials. I would go further and say that Melaka really never reached the same height under the Portuguese as it occupied during the Sultanate. It passed through a slow deterioration, though it is remarkable how long it survived. One should remember, however, that, despite the fact that Raffles and his ilk did not look to Melaka, they looked to Penang and Singapore. They destroyed Melaka precisely to deny it to other users.

MURPHEY - Bayly makes an important point in suggesting that exports like cotton, the big thing in the new export world, was a tiny fraction of domestic consumption. The same held true for sugar and indigo. The Jajmani system might have been responsible for the exchange of large totals of goods and services that didn't appear in commercial transactions. But the important point is that, although the inland ports would have continued anyway without the imposition of the colonial port cities, they couldn't remain entirely independent during the nineteenth century of the goings-on in Calcutta and Bombay. They responded increasingly to the effects of the port cities in enormously widening the market. The overseas and domestic systems intermatched, even though they started out separately and differently, with their own independent momentums.

BAYLY - I think the question of consumption doesn't necessarily presuppose that a great deal of goods was directed to the market. To go back to the question of central places: we may have a fragile central place system that was less cellular and where a smaller volume of commodities passed than in the traditional Chinese market networks.

I argue that the effects of governmental change, either pre-British or during the British period, and the effects of the colonial market were probably much greater than in China. I see a rapid development of standard marts, periodic markets, in the 1880s and '90s when a substantial change in local consumption occurred alongside a substantial rise in per capita income. At this point, one can begin to link them up into a kind of hierarchy that existed in China.

MURPHEY - The new market production and exports developing in India were lacking in China where commercial production remained insignificant proportionally while the colonial port cities made marginal impact on China's inland markets; in India, the impact was substantial and the inter-relationship close.

MORRIS - I would like to raise the question of transport costs which I believe to be a powerful factor affecting the way in which a hinterland existed. Water transport was so enormously

39

less costly than land transport that it wasn't only in Melaka an "umland" developed.

In Medieval Europe and early Modern Europe, water traffic was equally important. It is therefore surprising that the Portuguese missed the meaning of Melaka's hinterland. As I understand it, the Portuguese policy, beginning with Albuquerque, was to economize on force by not getting involved in land activities. The sheer burden of transport costs would have made land involvement absurd. There was, of course, a different situation in the New World where the Portuguese moved into empty space to a large extent whereas, in Asia, they had to deal with sturdy civilizations.

Now, on the question of transport costs raised by Bayly, I have two comments: one, the railroads didn't fix patterns of networks as Bayly has suggested. Because of changes in rate structures that had occurred during the later nineteenth and early twentieth centuries, there were great shifts in the importance of port cities, based on the kinds of trade they attracted. For instance, the movement of cotton out of central India to Calcutta, Bombay, or Karachi during the late nineteenth century was a function of rates. It was ultimately decided in favor of Karachi, not because of its access to inland networks but because of its lower rates.

Second, on Broomfield's point about the non-impact of the railroads in eastern Bengal due to the prevalence of waterways: This should be contrasted with the fact that the railroads did have, indeed, an impact on the Gangetic Basin which contradicts the traditional view that there was an enormous amount of commerce coming down the rivers. There was, in fact, relatively little because the monsoon affected river transport. The railroads lowered costs enormously in the Gangetic Basin, though they didn't seem to change them significantly in Eastern Bengal.

BROOMFIELD - I want to follow up Morris's point about the waterways. In his paper, he draws some basic and primary contrasts between the problems of economic development in South Asia and those that had previously been present for European economic development. One of the striking differences he alludes to is the lack of good navigable waterways in South Asia, a sub-continent approximately the size of Europe, minus European Russia. In contrast, Europe is a set of peninsulas interlaced with huge navigable waterways, improved over time by canals. Once again, this boils down to a difference in transport costs.

FRYKENBERG - I think Morris has thouched upon something important: It is not just the question of railroads; it's the rates. During the period before the railways, it wasn't a question of having roads, it was whether they were open, and how open. The flow of commodities from central India westward or eastward was partly a function of the political climate (and struc-

40

tures) insofar as centralization or decentralization of road control was concerned.

In South India, as late as the middle of the nineteenth century, in the *mofussil* hinterland, the idea that roads were "public" was an alien one. The roads were meant only for the use of certain classes, while the rest used *paddybunds* and paths through the jungle. The grand road from Bundar (Masulipatam) to Hyderabad was the Sultan's highway. Along this road there were way-stations and mosques for prayer, with fixed distances marked (in *kos*) by beautiful minaret pillars. With the breakdown of central power, these barriers and tiny townships (eventually locally-controlled) were collecting customs duties. Instead of facilitating a free flow, these customs posts exacted an accumulated *ad valorem* duty of about 200 percent, or 5 percent at each post along the road between Bandar and Hyderabad. There was a similar situation down all along the Coromandel Coast. These customs were abolished in the north in the 1830s, but they continued on in the south until 1844. So, here again, as Morris has pointed out, there was a question of rates.

CONLON - I believe another important issue is information flow. Can Bayly shed light on <u>how</u> information was flowing to the traders in the inland cities so that they could seize opportunities that would come up the road without being dependent upon intermediaries in Calcutta? The shift in the cotton trade from the Bengal markets to the West Indian markets suggests that there must have been such information flow unless the shift was entirely due to external decisions and was out of the hands of inland traders.

In his paper, Pearson is suggesting that Goa could have supplanted Surat. This doesn't seem possible, given the dimensions of space and the dimensions of the trade potential. He appears to attribute Goa's problems entirely to the Portuguese. Prior to the Portuguese arrival, Goa had experienced difficulties, including famine. It was an area that was subject to a good deal of flux caused by population growth, followed by food scarcity, migration, and the movement of trading communities up and down the coast. It is not fair to say that everything resulted from the treachery and torture that the Portuguese imposed.

The difficulty arises because of the common image of Goa as a colonial implant. This ignores the fact that the organization of the society of Goa in its immediate vicinity was not given an Iberian perfection, except for the churches. The Portuguese made desperate attempts to proselytize the existing village institutions. The published documents on the village communities by Nery Xavier suggest that the two areas that were added to Goa later were similar to the Maratha's battening onto an existing system.

Pearson's data on food leave us less convinced of the conclusions than might be otherwise the case. It is true that a lot of rice was imported into Goa, but it is not clear from the paper whether or not all of that rice imported into Goa then remained there. There was an extensive and lengthy trade in rice that went as far as the Persian Gulf. While the Portuguese never succeeded in fully capturing this trade, it nevertheless stands to reason that a certain proportion of the rice that came into Goa was trans-shipped.

BAYLY - On the question of information flow: There were two types of information--one was in connection with India, the other was export information. As regards information within India, I'm struck by the perfect system of the passage of information, even during the eighteenth century. There were large numbers of effective networks for passing information: religious networks that brought information to large cities; the Indian diplomatic state system of the eighteenth century also generated flows of information connected with the remittance of tribute between one state and another; the 'native *dak*,' an extensive system of indigenous postoffices often used by merchants and which remained much cheaper than anything the British introduced until about the 1850s. There was no difficulty with internal information dissemination among the various mercantile situations within India.

The problem was with outside information flowing into the country through the East India Company or the British private traders. In comparison, this was an imperfect system that often caused mercantile crashes in the inland ports.

ANDERSON - A comment on Morris's point about rates: One can look at transportation calculations as a matter within the macrosystem--no doubt an important economic consideration. At the microsystem level, however, pure economic calculations should be made with care because of the difficulties of determining the value of a peasant's time. How many hours should he spend going to a market, and for how much reward or profit? A peasant goes to the market for something more than pure economic transactions.

Another point: We did point out that rivers as well as seaways were communication arteries, but we also noted that some of the interflukes connecting the rivers way upstream were quite close together. In fact, people moved caravans across these, resulting in a significant trans-peninsular trade to the interior. If I may add an aside, I originally got into the paper because I worked in the Peninsula during the last two years among a people, the Makabas, who were settled in a structure that would seem odd unless you understood that they were smugglers--in our terms, traders, in theirs.

DAS GUPTA - A few words in defense of Michael Pearson: Pearson's major contribution is the attack on the Eurocentric vision, the tendency to see the Indian Ocean in terms of the Portuguese.

It is remarkable that a great Indian nationalist-historian like K. M. Panikkar had adopted the Eurocentric vision completely. Pearson is not unaware of what is being called the grafting onto the Indian systems because he has done useful studies of Goa and Diu as Indian cities with a Portuguese veneer. In this paper he is drawing attention to the fact that no great changes took place between 1500 and 1700 in the Indian Ocean.

This conference will have to come to grips with two things: One, what is a 'colonial city'? Two, how much transforming does a transformation have to be?

MASSELOS - I have a question for Bayly. One gets the impression from the trade patterns you describe that trade was invariably from Calcutta overseas. Was there not internal trade through to other Indian port cities? I know from my own work on Bombay that grain was an important item of trade from Bengal. Also, was there any movement of goods back into the *mofussil* or was it entirely one way, outwards?

BAYLY - Obviously, trade was not going in one direction only. The crucial point to remember is that it was responsive to prices and costs. Take the case of sugar. Sugar from upper India in the late eighteenth to nineteenth century was going down central India into Hyderabad, but changes in demand in Europe diverted it through the port city to Europe. Later, when the demand fell in Europe, the sugar trade resumed its usual course. I suspect this happened in other trades as well. There were considerable changes between seasons, between years, and between decades in the direction of such trade. In my paper, I've been primarily concerned with cotton trade, whose central thrust was, no doubt, to Canton.

FRYKENBERG - I would like to turn to the question of defining what is meant by the expression "colonial" port city. One way of achieving a definition might be to disaggregate and separate out all of those elements we consider to have been "colonial." In what way were they "colonial?" Was it the degree, the intensity, or the speed of transformation that mattered? Or was it the degree to which a particular port was seen as "alien" by indigenous peoples, compared to what it had been before? The Portuguese case on the one hand seems to be one of transformation but, on the other hand, as Michael Pearson has pointed out, their role seems to have been relatively insignificant in the Arabian Sea.

How much of a real change occurred in Melaka? To what degree was it a real "colonial" city? Or was it simply a further grafting on of something else to an already old and established structure?

My final question relates to the outlook of the Portuguese and the Dutch with regard to water-borne hinterlands, as opposed to dry-land hinterlands. I can see inconsistency in the Portuguese case because they committed such large numbers of soldiers so early into what turned out to be too many futile attempts at local conquest; but I find it even more difficult to see the Dutch that way simply because Holland itself was such a water-borne commercial development. I can't, therefore, understand why they should be so land conscious in Asia when they certainly weren't that way in Europe.

VORSTER - I don't believe the Dutch were 'land conscious' in Asia. They didn't have the Portuguese idea of settlement and colonialization. They had a very clear perception as to the reality of the trade. What constrained them was the policies of the Company which worked as a very centralized institution.

We have to distinguish between the Dutch in Melaka and the Dutch in Batavia and the Dutch in Amsterdam. The Dutch in Melaka were constrained in the kind of actions they could carry out by policies coming from above. They were flexible to a certain degree; yet there was a limit. They were aware, for instance, that they really should supply salt and rice in addition to textiles to get the tin, but they didn't have a good access to rice in the same way that the Javanese did. They were conscious of the fact that they couldn't simply go beyond a certain point.

ANDERSON - I would like to bring up for discussion the ethnicity-commodity relationship in entrepreneurship--why do we see a close and continual relationship between particular ethnic groups and the specificity of a commodity or commodities with which they deal?

MILONE - It seems to me that the decline of Melaka had something to do with ethnicity-commodity relationships, and not the Dutch misuse of the system. The ethnic groups that handled these commodities had departed for the cities of Java, particularly to Bantam. Melaka was starting to decline before the Dutch came.

METCALF - But that still doesn't explain the decline before the colonialists came. Bayly's point is that Mirzapore declined for reasons quite apart from the impact of the high colonial system. During the proto-colonial period or pre-colonial period these ups and downs were taking place independent of colonialism. The question should center on the kind of decline and whether it was connected to the rise of some other port city, Bombay or Singapore.

MILONE - What I was speaking about was the mobility of some of these traders. They customarily went back and forth across the Straits. It happened quite often.

METCALF - But it also happened up and down the Ganges Valley. And this wouldn't prove anything in and of itself. It was a natural, ongoing phenomenon.

44

MILONE - Yes, but I don't think that the reason the Dutch did not make use of the hinterland had to do with their acting upon a policy dictated from Holland. The traders who supplied them had left, that's all.

VORSTER - In the case of Melaka, I should correct the impression that the Dutch did make use of the hinterland. There was a more direct trade between Java and East Sumatra, for instance, where the Dutch lost out to a certain extent. However, in the case of the Peninsula, tin had become a primary concern in the trade with Melaka. Initially, the Dutch wanted to go straight to the producer, but they had trouble making them fall back on the indigenous system of extraction based on the traditional hierarchy of intermediaries. The commodities from the tin districts, coming to the various secondary collecting point ports in the Straits, were passing through the traditional system. From these points to Melaka one established contracts with the various tin states. These contracts were a way of monopolizing the trade, of regularizing the flows.

From the perspective of those individuals who stood between, who collected the material and had to supply it to Melaka in the past, there was a certain amount of flexibility which this system allowed. But the Dutch, of course, wouldn't go for it. They demanded a certain amount of tin in exchange for a certain amount of goods they had at their disposal. The result was that tin was not going to Melaka but to Acheh.

Other products, notably forest products, gradually met with the fate of tin. Melaka's place was being taken over by some Sumatran ports. It was the Dutch failure to adapt to Melaka's system that led to its decline; it wasn't due so much to the fact that the traders were leaving.

SIPE - To me, it sounds inefficient for the Dutch to have to try and get directly involved in production. On the basis of my Karachi study, I know that it was economically more efficient to deal with the middleman instead of going into production. It meant the assumption of the responsibility to meet the demands in the European markets on a regular schedule. Of course, the contract system also had its own peculiar problems.

ANDERSON - Well, the Dutch didn't get involved in production. Rather, they thought that they could collapse the chain of intermediaries through which extraction and supply of commodities bought by the extractors were obtained. It was a matter of trying to utilize contracts in a situation that simply wasn't ready for contract. It was a system operated by personalism, by statism, and by specific kinds of relationships between individuals. All these factors had a bearing on this chain of intermediaries that brought commodities out and brought commodities in. So it was not that they tried to carry out the extraction themselves, because they didn't do that. The point is that they totally failed in supplying things like foodstuffs which were an important part of the demand side required by the extractors.

Topic II: DEVELOPMENT AND CHARACTER OF MERCANTILE ELITES

Session 2

Moderator - Robert Alford
Discussant - Eric Gustafson

Frank Conlon, *Functions of Ethnicity in a Colonial
Port City: British Initiatives and Policies in
Early Bombay*

Thomas Metcalf/Sandria B. Freitag, *Karachi's
Early Merchant Families: Entrepreneurship and
Community*

Keith Sipe, *Karachi's Cotton Trade: Transitions in
Merchant Group Dominance*

ETHNICITY IN A COLONIAL PORT CITY: BOMBAY, 1665-1830

by

Frank F. Conlon

Ethnic diversity was a notable feature of the colonial port cities
of Asia. Travelers' accounts and official ethnographies publicized and
popularized the images of extensive, heterogeneous populations with distinctive economic roles and socio-cultural behaviors. Port cities were
foundation stones of the European colonial presence in Asia, serving as
bases of political, military, and economic power, and as arenas of cultural contact and confrontation.

The image of the colonial port cities' populations as congeries
of racial, religious, and linguistic communities loosely joined in
commercial endeavor under a benevolently tolerant European authority
was commonplace even in the dawn of nationalism in this century. The
existence of this ethnic diversity could and did serve as a basis for
rationalizing the continuation of colonial rule. Even when they had not
been the object of conscious "divide and rule" policies, different elements of port city populations often remained within what might be termed
a cultural division of labor that has, in turn, provided an unexpected
challenge to the full integration and development of post-colonial Asian
nations.

This essay is a preliminary result of a search for the roots of
ethnicity and ethnic diversity in a single colonial port city, Bombay, from
its founding in the seventeenth century to the early nineteenth century.
Available evidence discovered in documentation of European rule reveals
that ethnicity played a role in British policy both in the recruitment of
a useful population to Bombay and in the subsequent governance of the city.
On the other hand, the specific economic roles and capacities of the various
recruits were primarily functions of pre-modern traditions of Indian artisans and merchants.

British authorities at Bombay offered inducements to groups whom
they sought to recruit, including freedom of religion and association privileges believed to be lacking at rival ports. This offer of official recognition for corporate privilege had an obverse aspect: it conferred some
measure of internal autonomy for the group and envisioned establishment of
a degree of corporate responsibility among each group for the establishment
and maintenance of civic order. Examples of the working of this corporate
order may be found, but documentation is limited. It appears that "ethnicity" in the first half of Bombay's history was given official recognition
(not, of course, using that term); however, "Ethnicity" does not appear to
provide a sufficient description or explanation of the social and economic
life of the city.

49

The foundation of British Bombay began in 1665 when local Portuguese authorities reluctantly handed over the island on India's western coast to representatives of King Charles II to whom the port had come as a portion of his wife's dowry. After the immediate tasks of erecting defenses against hostile neighbors had been effected, Governor Humphrey Cooks set out to create a commercial activity for his fortifications to protect. Each succeeding governor acted to make Bombay "the flourishingest port in India." They did this by especially inviting merchants and artisans from other neighboring ports and provinces to relocate at Bombay. With commercial growth as his objective, an English governor was prepared to welcome merchants of any religion, language, or caste from wherever they might come. If necessary for commercial vitality, this welcome included guarantees of full freedom of religion. Such toleration had been articulated earlier by the Portuguese viceroy, Albuquerque, with considerable success, and the English anticipated benefiting from subsequent Portuguese departures from this policy.

The enterprise at Bombay was given additional force with the transfer of the island to the English East India Company in 1668. The London merchants directed their men at Bombay to strengthen the economy of the new port by inducing traders and weavers to settle there by the suspension of customs duties and with grants of freedom of religion, association, and "power for the ordering of themselves and for the hearing and determining of small controversies that arise amongst them." Such an arrangement would be familiar to the Bombay officers, for the Mughal port of Surat manifested such forms in the institution of the *mahajan*, or guild, and the *jati panchayat*, or caste council. The latter, although characteristically Hindu, was utilized also by Jain, Muslim, and Parsi communities.

Gerald Aungier, Governor of Bombay from 1669 to 1677, was acquainted with these Surat organizations and drew up a set of "Proposals Touching Bombay Island" which implicitly accepted the *mahajan* model, envisioning creation "companies or fellowships . . . for the better & more able carrying of any trade," with privileges and immunities to be officially granted. He proposed further to give recognition to the recruitees by appointing an elder for each of their castes and communities to mediate between them and the company authorities. Each caste or community was to have established a *panchayat*, or council, which could provide means of dispute resolution, avoiding the interference of the British officers.

Such offers of concessions were made to Hindu, Muslim, Parsi, and Armenian Christian merchants of Surat, Div, and other western Indian ports. In most cases, the inducements were sufficient. These "corporate" concessions were made particularly in endeavors to recruit notably famous and successful merchants. "Big men," who brought along dependents and caste-fellows, might contribute to the stable leadership of society while also practicing their considerable mercantile skills. At another social level of population recruitment, that of the Bhandaris--palm tree tappers who also served as soldiers--the authorities seem to have been prepared to come to terms with any putative leader who seemed likely to bring in a cluster of families to settle on Bombay island.

Given this recruitment strategy and Aungier's policies of encouraging a measure of semi-autonomous corporate responsibility in the
governance of Bombay, it might be expected that the forms of caste or
community organization would dominate Bombay society. Research in
available sources thus far has produced very little to document this
assumption. Little or no evidence has been found concerning the existence of *mahajans*. The materials on *panchayats* is, at best, mixed.
There are several obstacles to ready generalization: 1) It is not
certain how often concessions offered to recruit population were
taken up on a caste, community, or other ethnic basis. 2) Detailed
references to the actual existence and working of *panchayats* in Bombay
are sparse. 3) Notwithstanding the colonial authorities' stated policies of official recognition of "caste" autonomy, interference does
appear to have occurred.

"Caste" became the basis for data on trade, wealth, and even grain
supply, and "castes" were supposed to accept corporate responsibility for
defense of the island. Officials could and did interfere to settle
divisive quarrels within any given caste or community. The autonomy of
"castes" was further compromised by the principle of collective responsibility, which was invoked occasionally during the eighteenth century.
Thus, for example, a caste could be required to pay a fine to the government if one of the caste members were detected in an act of witchcraft--
or, rather, since the Honorable Company had given up a belief in witches,
of pretending to be a witch. On another level, the development of courts
of justice created fresh arenas for disputes to be acted upon, either in
original jurisdiction or on appeal from caste tribunals.

The *panchayat* system did not function smoothly, perhaps because of
the extent to which Bombay was experiencing economic growth and development which undermined the premise of compact, well-defined social units
with agreed rank and leadership. The best documented *panchayat* in the
eighteenth century was that of the Parsis, who were, in that period, under-
going considerable economic and social transformations as many of them
shifted from agricultural pursuits to those of commerce. Their council
had been constituted about 1673. Places on this *panchayat* passed heredit-
arily among several influential families whose leadership in decision-
making and adjudication was based on consensus. Consensus was most easily
attained in a stable society wherein status offered an enduring basis for
prestige and deference. Status among the mercantile population of eighteenth century Bombay, however, was not stable. Nowhere was this instability
more visible than among the Parsis. Spatial and social mobility both
undermined the *panchayat* regime. New Parsi migrants from Gujarat were not
easily put under the discipline of the older Bombay leadership, particularly
when the newcomers had achieved considerable wealth by their own endeavors.
The newly-wealthy challenged the authority of older elites. On several
occasions the East India Company authorities were obliged to intervene
to confirm and shore up the *panchayat* of the Parsis.

Such British intervention suggests that the official policy of
neutrality was eroded. In fact, the British were prepared to intervene
primarily to solidify caste *panchayats* as sources of stability and modes
of inexpensive social control for the preservation of civil order. The
Company officials were aware that a potential challenge to the caste

councils could arise in the courts. Caste issues had reached the Recorder's Court and Mayor's Court in the eighteenth century. By the early nineteenth century an Advocate-General of Bombay was prepared to argue that caste issues should be excluded from the court's jurisdiction so that authority of caste elders might not be diminished. Legislation that gave appellate jurisdiction over proceedings of caste tribunals to the Court of Petty Sessions was repealed and a specific prohibition banning judicial cognizance of caste questions was written into the new Bombay Code of 1827.

Ultimately, this effort to defend an "endangered species" proved fruitless, largely because of successful adaptations. The ethnic groups of Bombay themselves were adapting to changing political and economic circumstances, moving into arenas of public affairs, education, and opinion wherein they developed an "awareness of communal identity . . heightened by the competition of urban life."

Ethnic diversity remained and, indeed, proliferated as Bombay grew further and attracted persons from virtually every region of South Asia. The British interest in utilizing the corporate power of castes and communities faded as legal, commercial, and industrial developments created new interest groups and a more complex set of problems facing Bombay.

The perception of a heterogeneous society was utilized in the early recruitment and ordering of population in Bombay by the British. It further informed their policy in the governance of the city during the eighteenth and early nineteenth centuries, including a judicious mix of neutrality and intervention. Yet it is not clear that an "ethnic strategy," if it might be so termed, did or could serve as the sole basis for the organization of Bombay's economic and social order. Further research in the eighteenth century period is required before we may draw definite conclusions on the shape or scope of ethnicity in early Bombay. Still, the ethnic legacy of that period must be given its due--the reinforcement of corporate stereotypes, the emergence of castes and communities as the basis for new social or religious reforms, associations, and other collective endeavors, as well as the very image of Bombay as a non-melting pot, pluralistic society under benign colonial rule, all had their roots in the relations of ethnic diversity of Bombay's first British century.

SOURCES:

In addition to the Bombay Archives, the following is a select list of principal sources for this paper:

David, M D. *History of Bombay, 1661-1708,* Bombay, 1973.

Foster, Sir William, *The English Factories in India, 1665-1667,* Oxford, 1924.

Forrest, G. W., ed. *Selections from the Letters, Despatches, and other State Papers Preserved in the Bombay Secretariat. Home Series.* Bombay, 1887.

Edwards, S. M. *The Rise of Bombay: A Retrospect,* Bombay, 1902.

Malabari, P. B. M. *Bombay in the Making,* London, 1910.

The Gazetteer of the Bombay Presidency, Bombay, 1899–1901.

KARACHI'S EARLY MERCHANT FAMILIES:

Entrepreneurship and Community

by

Thomas R. Metcalf & Sandria B. Freitag

The Karachi of pre-partition India was a city of communities and commerce, of migrants and businessmen. It was very much smaller than the Karachi of Pakistan and wholly lacked the industrial sector that blossomed in the wake of partition. These same features, together with the exceptional dichotomy between city and hinterland, marked it off, too, from its neighboring colonial port cities—above all, from Bombay, until 1935 the capital of the province that included Karachi.

These features underline the distinctive characteristics of early Karachi discussed in the paper: strong community identities and internal support structures, plus a specialized entrepreneurial lifestyle that existed almost independently of its Karachi locale. Karachi was distinctive, too—perhaps because of its isolation—for its harmonious social relations. Even where no active collaboration took place, sect and community lived together in an atmosphere of amiability. There were no communal riots in Karachi before independence and only one brief spasm afterwards.

These amiable social relations may well have been the result of a sense of separateness maintained by the communities, a separateness made manifest in the earliest organization of the Karachi municipality. In 1861, when the municipal commission was first set up on an elective basis, the eleven seats were carefully apportioned among the various communities of the city. Although these seats were shifted among the various groups requesting representation, the principle held for two decades. One must, of course, beware of assuming that the categories employed by the British corresponded to any objective reality in Indian society. Uninformed, eager to comprehend and classify if not to divide and rule, the British too often created the categories they purported to discover. Yet, in Karachi, it would seem that the overwhelming emphasis on caste and community did reflect a widespread self-perception. Certainly the members of the municipality at the time thought these categories appropriate to themselves.

Cross-cutting ties and loyalties did, to be sure, grow up in Karachi. The municipality was reorganized on a ward basis by Ripon's Local Self-Government Act of 1882, although implementation was held up for three years while various plans were debated. (Objections to each proposal focused, significantly, on the lack of representation for one or more of the communities.)

55

Voluntary associations as well as politics brought together members of Karachi's urban elite on the same platform. Time and again the same individuals--two or three from each of the major communities--are found forming deputations to the Governor and heading the lists of subscribers for the city's charitable institutions. On rare occasions this cooperation took the form of joint business enterprises as well: Nagedranath Gupta founded the *Phoenix*, a newspaper, in partnership with Jaffer Fuddoo, a Khoja, who put up half the funds and ran the paper after Gupta returned to Bengal. There were even one or two joint ventures with Europeans, most notably the stevedoring firm of Brigstocke Jewanjee and Co., which remained in existence for over half a century.

Frequently, however, one community or even one individual dominated these cooperative undertakings. The Sind Sabha, a social reform body, was not, surprisingly, an affair of the educated Hindu Sindhis; while the Buyers and Shippers Chamber, an organization of firms engaged in maritime trade (although its managing committee always reflected a careful communal balance) was, in fact, held together throughout its entire existence by one man, the indefatigable Haridas Lalji. Perhaps the most effective joint body because it touched on the most important area of shared concern--the regulation of commerce--was the Karachi Indian Merchants Association. Founded initially in 1902, it had as its objective the protection and promotion of the interests of the Karachi business community "on all subjects involving their common good." But it, too, was largely controlled by one community, the Hindu Sindhis. Of the 160 members in 1924, some eighty-nine were *bhaiband*, or Shikarpuri, merchant firms. Only ten were Muslim, and one was Parsi.

The causes supported by charitable donations seem also to have varied from community to community. Muslims contributed more to education than to any other cause, while Parsis were interested in health-related projects, such as the Lady Dufferin Hospital, a maternity wing, etc. Less is available on objects of Hindu charity; the only one receiving consistent publicity was the Sind Sabba. Other occasional contributions were localized and usually specific in nature: a scholarship for learning Sanskrit, for instance. Parsis, probably because they were the most tightly-knit of the communities and well-educated, supported the largest number and widest variety of community-oriented activities, including sports teams, dramatic productions, social gatherings, and even specific Masonic Lodges. After the first decade of the twentieth century, they also built a substantial number of housing blocks for poorer Parsis. Still, members from all communities contributed to various joint memorial funds, such as the ones for Asanmal Ojha, Lorji Hari, McHinch, and the Diamond Jubilee. They also contributed to relief funds earmarked for disaster areas, including the Surat Fire Relief and local Famine and Plague Relief Funds.

Community affiliation played a large part in choice of occupation as well. Although the one did not invariably dictate the other, still community separateness in Karachi commonly involved the pursuit of different lines of enterprise. Within very broad limits, European firms, usually branches of firms headquartered in Bombay or Europe, dealt almost wholly in the overseas import/export trade. The Parsis, in Karachi as in Bombay, worked closely with the British as contractors and suppliers, controlling much of the retail trade in European-style consumer goods. Muslim firms

56

predominated in coastwise shipping of hides and skins, engineering and metal fabrication. Muslims, especially those of the Bohra and Memon sects were also active, along with the Parsis, in trade as general merchants and shopkeepers and as contractors to Government. The Hindu Sindhis of trading caste, known collectively as *bhaibands*, were the grain and cotton brokers of Karachi. Although their firms were rarely large, prominent, or found in the anglicized parts of the city, they sustained almost the whole of the commodity export trade. Apart from Ralli Brothers and Volkart, who had their own upcountry agencies, the European exporters purchased their goods from Hindu brokers. Hindus also continued active in their traditional enterprises, gold and silver smithing, Sind Work handicrafts, and the like. This Hindu mercantile predominance was reflected in their domination of the Indian Merchants Association and, after its creation in 1933, of the Karachi Cotton Association.

But what does all this mean? The paper traces the careers of the merchant families of Eduljee Dinshaw, H. J. Rustomjee, J. H. Kothari, Nusserwanjee R. Menta, Jaffer Fudoo, Ghulam Ali Chagla, and Vishindas Nihalchand. These personal histories throw light on how individual entrepreneurs operated in the mercantile milieu provided by Karachi. By looking at the ways their careers developed and how they incorporated their family members and expanded their businesses, we can discover something of Karachi business life. The histories also tell us about the causes they supported, as well as what political and other kinds of activities and rivalries surfaced in the press. And from them, at least, these generalizations may be made: Parsis, though never numerous, were among the city's earliest settlers and were the most adept at turning British rule to their own advantage. They came from Bombay, and even directly from Surat, in the wake of the British Army as it marched through Sind to Kabul in 1839. Several examples are given in the paper, and we have seen in detail how this process worked for the Kothari family.

The enterprise of single individuals lay at the heart of much of this activity. H. J. Rustomjee was a wholly self-made "merchant Prince." Eduljee Dinshaw, too, came to Karachi by himself as a youth and at once launched into business on his own. Such wealth required constant effort to preserve it. H. J. Rustomjee's five sons, as we saw, managed to squander their father's fortune in just six years. The constant effort, in turn, could only be provided by family members, for none of these merchants, regardless of community, saw his business as an entity independent of the family structure. Lacking either male members or members with the requisite business acumen, the firms and family fortunes were lost. When viewed in this light, both the Dinshaw fortune--which grew as the family diversified into other lines of business--and the Rustomjee failure give expression to a single rule. The pattern is complex, for Dinshaw's urban landholdings, rather like rural *zamindaris*, brought in a regular income with but little attention. Yet it was necessary that the family produce capable and sufficiently numerous offspring to protect the fortune. If, as with the Rustomjees, the offspring paid too much attention to spending money (even on worthwhile causes) and not enough on furthering the family firm, ruin was the result.

Behind the enterprising entrepreneur one can almost always discern the community as well as the family. Many Parsi businessmen obtained

57

financial support or training from family members, or worked for a time in other Parsi firms before striking out on their own. Family fortunes could be put back together by enterprising descendents assisted by wealthy relatives and other community members, as evidenced by the Minwallas. Such community support struc res (as we might call them) were by no means confined to the Parsis. The Kutchi Memons, deeply involved in importing and retail trade in Karachi from the mid-nineteenth century, continually encouraged the more enterprising among their number both by example and by financial support, not the least among them Abdullah Haroon.

The role of the community in encouraging entrepreneurship was thus of critical importance. It provided funds, training, networks of kin and communication and, most crucially, values--a commitment to commerce over land or the professions, an emphasis on frugality and industriousness, a sense of rootedness (reflected in language and marriage) together with great geographic mobility: in short, a distinctive entrepreneurial lifestyle.

But the community was by no means a unified whole. Factional alignments could and did exist; struggles for dominance might adversely affect the careers of individuals at times, as we saw in the case of Jaffer Fuddoo. Not all communities had an Aga Khan. But, even among the Parsis, when the community contained two such powerful individuals as Eduljee Dinshaw and H. J. Rustomjee or, later in the twentieth century, two such rival families as those of Dinshaw and Cowasjee, to be aligned with one or the other of these could make a difference.

Karachi made surprisingly little impact on these mercantile residents. The shift to Karachi meant for most businessmen simply a change of residence and did not involve any change in either occupation or social outlook. Truly innovative entrepreneurship was rare indeed among them. The Parsis alone seem to have been adept at developing new lines of business, at adding capital-intensive processing and milling to simple trading. It is striking, too, how little even prolonged residence in this bustling modern city affected the attitudes and values of these business communities. The Shikarpuri *bania*'s life was little changed--in outward appearance at any rate--from the days when he had ferried goods over the Bolan Pass on camels. Clearly, for him, as for most South Asian business communities, the traditional patterns of behavior remained advantageous in the new urban environment as in the old. This new environment was not traded for the old but added to it; as we saw with Vishindas Nihalchand, the Hindu merchant in particular seems to have maintained his rural or small town ties.

These early merchant families, then, came to Karachi as immigrants, eager to exploit the economic opportunities of the growing colonial city. But they also came as members of business communities, predisposed to certain lines of endeavor, certain styles of life and livelihood. Some of these have been explored in our paper for this conference.

SOURCES

One of the principal sources used for this paper, particularly in the personal history section, was the *Sind Gazette*. Essentially a

British-Indian paper, it was begun in 1878 as *The Civil and Military Gazette, Sind Issue,* and was published twice weekly until March, 1909 when it became a daily. It incorporated the *Sind Times* and the *Sind Advertiser* in September of that same year.

Other sources for this section included personal interviews with members of the families and firms connected with the Dinshaws, Rustomjees, Minwallas, Mehtas, Ghulamalis, and Haroons.

Directories for the period that proved most useful included Playne's *The Bombay Presidency, the United Provinces, the Punjab: Their History, People, Commerce, and Natural Resources,* (London, 1917-1920.), *The History of the Parsis,* and M. U. Abbassi's *The Colourful Personalities of Sind (Karachi: 1944).*

Certain personal histories were also used: Nagedranath Gupta's *Hormusjee Jametjee Rustomjee, a Personal Testimony* (Allahabad: 1935) and Alhai Mian Ahmad Shafi's *Haji Sir Abdoola Haroon, a Biography,* (Karachi: 1939).

Finally, the readily acquired published sources were supplemented with archival materials such as the Municipal Proceedings for relevant years and *Reports* for various years of the Karachi Indian Merchants Association.

*

City of Surat.

THE ENTRPRENEURIAL BASIS OF COMMODITY EXPLOITATION:

An Examination of Merchant Group Dominance

in Karachi's Cotton Trade

by

Keith R. Sipe

          This paper identifies the social groups that dominated Karachi's
cotton trade from the late nineteenth century to 1975. The goal of
this study is to illustrate how merchant groups evolved in the port
cities of British India. The thesis presented is that, as a colonial
port city, Karachi drew its commercial classes from the coastal regions
of western India. Karachi is viewed as the westernmost area of a cultural coastal zone ranging from Bombay City's environs to the Baluchi-
stan coastline. The zone is characterized by the use of Gujarati as a
lingua franca.

          Three periods of merchant group dominance are identified. The
first runs from approximately 1900 to 1933. This phase was marked by
the presence of local Hindu castes, mainly Lohanas. The second period,
1933 to 1947, witnessed the opening of the Sukkur Barrage and the creation of the Indus Valley Irrigation System--the world's largest canal
network. Cotton production increased greatly, and new merchant groups
were attracted to Karachi. In particular, Bombay-based firms, mainly
English and Gujarati-owned companies established branch houses in the
city during this period. The European merchants concentrated on overseas markets, while the Gujarati merchants focused their efforts on the
markets of northern and western India. Local businessmen became less
important as a consequence of the arrival of these migrants.

          The final phase analyzed covers the period from partition to 1975.
Karachi's transformation from a colonial to an independent port city is
reviewed. The termination of European and Hindu control over the cotton
trade is documented. Initially, Urdu-speaking north Indian Muslim
refugees won admission into the cotton trade because of their high level
of English language proficiency. By the mid-1960s, western Indian
trading communities began to enter cotton commerce in great numbers.
Memon and Khoja cotton traders first became prominent at this time. Both
of these groups turned to cotton trade because the Government of Pakistan
nationalized other fields of commerce they had previously controlled,
such as the rape seed and cotton seed exchanges.

          The analysis is based on interviews conducted with registered
cotton brokers at the Karachi Cotton Exchange. The evidence collected
identifies a pattern of colonial port city interaction with agricultural

hinterlands. Merchants who specialized in commodity trade migrated to Karachi because locals did not possess the expertise to establish control over export. The newcomers were members of mercantile groups that maintained well-established commercial networks, allowing them to market their goods on a wider scale than local businessmen.

Despite this advantage, the migrants were ill-equipped to deal directly with producers. They did not speak the local language and they were unfamiliar with agrarian relationships in the interior. For this reason, local busines groups were able to establish themselves as intermediaries between the migrants and the cotton producers (*zamindars*, ginners, and cleaners) up-country. As intermediaries, the locals took advantage of their knowledge of both the Sindhi and Gujerati languages. This bilingualism was important because Sindhi was the language used in the countryside, while Gujerati was the premier commercial language of the city. Thus, the locals became brokers who served as middlemen.

The existence in other South Asian cities of similar migrant commercial groups such as the Dubashis, the Marwaris, or the Chiniotis suggests that the pattern in Karachi is not unique. Although the number of *vania* groups is innumerable, only a few Indian merchant communities have historically engaged in largescale trade. These communities have a tradition of migrating to areas offering new opportunities in which they can apply their skills. Thus, many of the merchant groups found in Karachi are also present elsewhere. For example, in pre-partition India the Memons and Khojas were as prominent in Bengal as in Karachi. The contribution of migrant merchant communities to the evolution of colonial port cities was tremendous. They provided a necessary expertise, and many specialized in oceanic trade. The parsis, for instance, emerged as British India's processors of import and export merchandise.

A final topic considered is the economic impact of partition on the social groups that played a dominant role in Karachi's commerce. It is argued that, from the perspective of native Sindhis, partition brought about few changes in the cotton trade. Before partition, Gujerati-speaking Hindus dominated whereas, after 1947, Gujerati-speaking Muslim refugees performed the same role. The Muslim traders were separated from their Hindu counterparts only in religion. Both spoke the same language, engaged in the same kinds of commerce, and shared the same *weltanschauung*.

In conclusion, this paper considers the role of migrant merchant communities in spurring port city development in the colonial world. It is suggested that, in the case of Karachi, the city, insofar as it is a port city, must be viewed as a transplant. The city was populated by merchants from all parts of British India, but especially from the western Indian coastline.

SOURCES

The primary sources for this paper are the records of the Karachi Cotton Association and survey data obtained from interviews conducted with brokers during 1974. In addition, the following standard works, among others, have been consulted:

The Census of Pakistan, 1951, Vol. I.

Feldman, H. *Karachi Through a Hundred Years,* (Karachi, 1970)

Haider, A., *History of Karachi,* (Karachi, 1974)

Vakel, C. N., *Economic Consequences of a Divided India* (Bombay, 1950);

Papanek, G. F., *Pakistan's Development: Social Goals and Private Incentives* (Karachi, 1970);

"   "Pakistan's New Industrialists and Businessmen: Focus on the Memmons," in *Entrepreneurship and Modernization of Occupational Cultures in South Asia,* M. Singer, ed., (Durham, 1973).

PARSEE COTTON MERCHANTS OF BOMBAY.

TOPIC II: DEVELOPMENT AND CHARACTER OF MERCANTILE ELITES

Session 2

ALFORD   -   The first paper this afternoon is by Frank Conlon.

CONLON   -   The paper you have before you presents some thoughts
on a set of problems in the early history of Bombay. It was
stimulated not so much by a direct interest in specific problems of city founding but by a search for roots in ethnic
organization and sentiment in nineteenth century Bombay.

     I am trying to understand the function of a form of
government credited to a governor of the late seventeenth
century, Gerald Aungier, based on a series of caste *panchayats*.
The existence of this form and the complex ethnic fabric of
Bombay remained an important image and theme in the descriptive literature of the city. I have not pursued this image
in this paper. It should suffice to say that the colonial
port city tourist literature always stressed the image of
the teeming oriental metropolis, races, and nations presided
over by the firm but gentle hand of European authority. It
was a particularly gratifying image which many European
writers pursued.

     The paper points up the difficulties of the early
English rulers in Bombay in founding and sustaining the growth
of a port. They had to attract functionaries from other parts
of Western India for purposes both of trade and for production,
productions not only of goods for trade but, in addition, food
and ancillary services. They had to settle with an existing
population, particularly with respect to landed rights, property rights, and also with respect to access to certain sorts
of economic benefits such as making arrangements with toddy
tappers over who would get the monopoly of having the right
to take the toddy from the palm trees.

     The British also had to arrange a system of governance
for the inhabitants of the city and the new recruits. The
British governors, both the royal governors and then the Company governors, appeared to see "caste," or community, as
the most viable form of organization of society, both for purposes of population recruitment and for subsequent organization
of the governance of the city. It was seen as a source of
Aungier's system of giving official recognition to *panchayats*,
groups of elders, some sort of representative men of influence
for each "caste"--I put "caste" in quotes because the literature
of the time did not follow a satisfactory anthropological de-

67

finition. They simply referred to different groups as castes.
Muslims were "castes" on one occasion, and in some cases
Hindus were "castes" and, in other cases, references were
made to more specific groups that you would think of as *jatis*,
or the like.

I tried, in the limits of documentation available to
me, to pursue how far this system had, in fact, worked. And
to what extent *panchayats* had flourished in eighteenth century
Bombay, and to what extent were they protected from government interference.

It seemed that the British, in founding Bombay, had
used as one of the themes of recruitment that people would be
free to practice their own religion and to settle their own
affairs without needing a reference to higher authority. This
has been discussed by a number of writers in passing and is
often taken as being a "given" for the pre-nineteenth century
city--that castes governed themselves and there was little or
no question about their autonomy.

The available evidence, and I must emphasize that it
is incomplete evidence, suggests that "caste" might have been
a sweetener, a sort of additional benefit added to the recruitment. The concessions on matters such as house building, tax
breaks, freedom of religious practice, etc., were made not to
communities but were, for the most part, made to individual
families. But it was presumed that these families would have
dependents and retainers of the same community. Thus, it is
not wise to talk about an ethnic group always; often we are
really talking about a particular family and their dependents.
But the dependencies were within a "caste" or within a *jati*
line. In the case of Muslims, it was within the label "Muslim."
One has to be very cautious about saying that a "caste" was
brought to Bombay.

Although I haven't taken it up in the paper, it is
worth noting that the further one got from Bombay, the more
difficult it became to recruit. This is not surprising. For
instance, the merchants at the Iranian port of Bandar Abbas,
called, in those days, Gambrun, did not seem to be interested
when the East India Company tried to recruit them to Bombay
with the offer of religious freedom and special privileges
for their community. They seemed more interested in the elimination of customs charges. Ultimately, the English did
eliminate customs collections from Bombay for a short period
of time. It has to be kept in mind, however, that this recruitment of communities was not always as real as it was
apparent.

In any case, most mercantile recruits sought group
autonomy. I suspect this had to do with control of a particular group by one individual or family for economic ends rather
than for any ideological attachment to the idea of caste.

The avoidance of official interference, the avoidance of any external supervision of internal affairs of a group of merchants was desired. The discussions this morning concerning information flow suggest that one of the most efficient channels of information was an extended series of kin-relations which not only assured confidentiality but also, perhaps, social control over the reliability of the information.

The caste, *panchayats*, frequently described as all-pervasive in Bombay during the eighteenth century, do not appear to have been all-pervasive through the period from 1674 to 1805. There were many official references to caste. Such things as amounts of grain, the supplying of labor for the building of fortifications, often contain data for caste and suggestions of caste responsibility, but it is not clear that these were, in fact, followed up.

There were, however, ideas of collective responsibility. I have mentioned the matter of two Hindus being convicted for "fascination," which was a term for pretending to practice sorcery and witchcraft. Since the East India Company did not officially recognize witchcraft, one could only be convicted of pretending to practice witchcraft. A proclamation was made that if a person detected another person pretending to be a witch, that he should declare it to the authorities and receive a reward of ten rupees which would be paid by the caste to which the offender belonged. So much for collective responsibility.

The matter of non-interference by officials is not as clear as might have been assumed. Even a *panchayat* sought ultimate appeal to a court of adjudication; subsequent judicial bodies in the eighteenth century in Bombay did accept caste disputes and did determine them. There were other sorts of judicial interference, as in the case of the rape of a woman of the Agri caste. The matter came to attention because the convicted rapist petitioned the government to the effect that the small sum of twenty-five rupees would restore the victim to the bosom of her caste, (his language, not ours), that she was still in the possession of her husband's affections and, when once restored to her tribe, would be equally restored to her peace of mind. The prisoner, therefore, implored that the loss of his life was not necessary to affect all or either of these objectives.

An official investigation followed, and it was revealed that the Agris had excommunicated her because obviously she was in a state of ritual pollution, but that they would welcome her back upon payment of a fine and upon the Governor of Bombay issuing a certificate that a ceremony of readmission had taken place. The superintendent of police paid the sum, the woman was "purified" by Brahmins, she dined with her caste members assembled, a certificate confirming that all this had happened was signed by the Governor so that she could "show it to her caste" whenever and wherever she went. I regret to say that as soon as the matter reached this point it dropped from the records to which I had access.

To summarize, the system functioned sporadically and incompletely. A major difficulty emerged during the eighteenth century in that, as Bombay grew both in terms of population and economy, new elements of ostensibly the same caste or community came into Bombay. They frequently were quite independent of the existing families and elders of the community and, therefore, not immediately susceptible to control that was presumably inherent in the *panchayat* system. Also, as people in Bombay gained new wealth it was used to establish their own lines of patronage and clientage in such a way as to again find the existing--I wouldn't call them traditional-- forms of social control offensive.

It seems appropriate to think of the peopling of the colonial port city as partly the product of conscious British initiative, an ethnic strategy if you like, in which the British sought to find means of recruiting population. We don't know how many people were attracted in this fashion; we know that throughout the eighteenth century the East India authorities continued to worry about getting enough of the "right people" to Bombay. The "right people" were not identified by caste; they were identified by function. Particularly, it was thought that the more traders, the better.

As far as the caste *panchayat* scheme and the question of official support for this type of ethnic organization is concerned, we have difficulty in finding documentation. Non-intervention could be a two-edged sword. If the government did not support a *panchayat* or a group of elders, it could be tantamount to interfering in the internal affairs of the community. This is not to say that caste or community had no role in economic life; it is possible that caste, among other factors, helped promote labor market specialization, access to credit, access to training and employment, plus the indefinable comforts of a shared culture, something that became more important as Bombay and other port cities moved in the direction of becoming metropolises. We have no convincing evidence yet that these elements mattered significantly in the development of Bombay prior to the nineteenth century.

The historiography and descriptive literature on Bombay has repeatedly emphasized the chronic ethnic diversity among the Parsis, the Khojas, the Gujaratis, the Maharashtrians. These communities rose and fell, as it were, in a seesaw fashion in this literature. To me, it is not a realistic guide to economic behavior in a growing and changing metropolis. With exceptions, these communities or castes, if you will, were abstractions created by British initiatives and, in the nineteenth century, the product of community elites, those who had obtained education. The homogenity of these groups was cross-cut by heterogenity in many social and economic measures about which we need to know a great deal more. The assumption of social stability as a constant in pre-nineteenth century Bombay was based on acceptance of results of an implicit British strategy that attempted to employ ethnicity, although the British never used the term, for recruiting of population subsequent to governing it. I think we should be as cautious in translating the policy statements and administrative plans of the seventeenth century as we are skeptical of such policy statements and administrative plans of twentieth century Bombay.

ALFORD - The next paper is a joint effort by Thomas Metcalf and Sandria Freitag.

METCALF - Let me start out by re-phrasing the question that Das Gupta and Frykenberg raised this morning. How much transforming is required to make a colonial system colonial? This leads us into the general question of continuity and change. Karachi is a good test case against which we can weigh and measure out some of these changing and continuous processes. On the surface it may appear that Karachi is a splendid case for colonial systems if we define the latter as new systems, as port cities, as new cities. After all, there was basically nothing there when Karachi was founded.

It is hard to find continuities between earlier, isolated, small towns and the great metropolis that Karachi became. If one looks at the trading networks, it would seem that they are new and very different. The Bolan Pass trade to Afghanistan over and through Shikarpuri strikes me as an altogether different kind of proposition than the Indus Valley trade from the Punjab up by the railways. The two trades carried different commodities in separate directions, although out of the mouth of the same river system. Wheat and cotton were a long way from the Afghan material.

In this paper we examine the role of businessmen in Karachi's growth in the colonial context. Karachi, being a new construct, all of the people who lived there were migrants to it. We argue that a great many of these people were self-made men. We have provided several Horatio Alger-type stories. Indeed, such stories indicate that a common function of the colonial port city was to provide opportunity for rapid individual upward social mobility. With these new men there was considerable newness in the business operation and the commercial network they built up.

Of course, there were persisting old ties as well. These businessmen were organized into traditional trading communities, working different lines of enterprise and living apart in their lifestyle from the city. We had recently, in this country, a small flap over the phrase, "ethnic purity." I thought that the discussion about the import of the phrase

71

was fine but that it was applied to the wrong place. Because Karachi surely was a city where ethnic purity was the ruling concept behind community settlement.

These are the persisting continuities upon which we base our argument. In line with Conlon's comments, however, I am beginning to wonder whether these business communities themselves had this persisting traditional quality about them. Perhaps these were, as Conlon says, the creation of either Englishmen or that of the community elites trying to define themselves in a changing and complex situation. I believe at this stage the question has to be left open.

A final thought on the characteristics of Karachi and Bombay as compared to other colonial port cities in South Asia: This morning we talked about the transformations of Goa and Colombo as colonial port cities with restricted effects. Malacca and Mirzapore represented older cities and older trades persisting and declining. One could ask in this context whether the trading community syndrome, if you wish to call it that, of western India was not tied in with the special characteristics of western Indian cities. They were, perhaps, tied in with their newness in a way that was not apparent in Calcutta and Madras. I'm putting this forward as a thought that we might want to consider as we go along.

In Calcutta and Madras there was probably more continuity than in Bombay and Karachi where a disjunctive quality manifested itself in isolation from hinterland, in more migration, and the sort of business community operation that pulled people together in a new and foreign environment. In this sense, in the structure of urban development that these western port cities created, there were certain novel forms of social organization. I am not, however, certain this was indeed the case, although it seems to me that we are dealing with a fairly substantial disjuncture between the western and eastern coast of India. There is little doubt about the more cosmopolitan, open, and rapidly mobile qualities of Karachi and Bombay, compared to the more persisting village-like settled qualities of (certainly) Madras and (perhaps) Calcutta as well.

FREITAG - I would raise a specific question in regard to this apparent dichotomy between Bombay and Karachi on the one hand and Madras and Calcutta on the other. What was the role of Hindu merchants in Karachi compared to that of Hindu merchants in Madras that Lewandowski has written about? A related question will be: can we talk about Hindu merchants alone? Were there Muslim merchant groups besides the Khojas who were on the borderline? If they can be identified by labels, what was their role in other South Asian port cities? Was it similar?

ALFORD - The last paper of this session is by Keith Sipe.

SIPE - My paper deals with two separate problems. The first part discusses the role of cotton in Karachi's development,

72

and the second part deals with the social groups that dominated and controlled the cotton trade.

There are several points about Karachi that should be kept in mind. Metcalf has mentioned them already, but I wish to re-emphasize them as they play a major role in my interpretation. The first point is that the Karachi I'm dealing with is almost entirely a new city. It is the result of the partition of British India as it exists today. At the time of partition in 1947 it had, perhaps, 400,000 residents. In a matter of two years it went to over a million inhabitants. As you can imagine, there are very few linkages connecting the pre- and post-partition periods.

Given this dichotomy, I was looking for continuities and transitions that could tie the history of the two periods together. The only institution I could find that existed before and after, and that had extensive documentation, was "The Karachi Cotton Association." The Karachi Cotton Association is a place where the cotton crop from upcountry is auctioned for international and local buyers in Karachi. I attempted to look at this institution from the mid-1930s until late 1974 and identify, in numerical terms, which groups have had the largest say in what happens to the cotton crop.

The initial sector I examined is the upcountry growing of the cotton crop. The major point to keep in mind here is that, since opening the Sukkur Barrage in the mid-1930s, the amount of cottonland in the Indus River Valley and, most importantly, where long-staple American-variety cottons are grown, increased tremendously, and the short-staple *deshi* varieties were eliminated. The result of this is that Karachi emerges as the major export center for cotton of British India during the last decade. Had partition not taken place, had independence not come, it is probable that Karachi's growth would have continued unabated.

Another point I make in this part of the paper is that had partition not occurred, (partition is the focal point for most of my ideas) there would have been little difference in Karachi's position. Most of Karachi's economic hinterland extended in the areas that became part of Pakistan. The opening of the Suez Canal played a major role in making Karachi British India's closest port to Europe.

Yet, ethnographically, Karachi is completely separated from its hinterland. The upcountry crop is dominated by Sindhi producers while most of the cotton men before partition were Sikhs and Sindhi *zamindars*. I have tried to identify the cotton ginners in the interior, and their story is interesting. From what I'm able to tell, money lenders had to move into ginning and million. They were in the position of having to supply the *taccavi* (planting) loans to the *zamindars* to finance the growing of the crop and, once this happened, they were put

73

into the position where they had to develop the ginning industry. As they owned the crop, they realized they could make more money by doing their own ginning. The *haris*, landless laborers who worked in the fields, were primarily Muslim whose crop went into the hands of a regional caste called Sindhi Lohanas who dominated the crop all the way until it reached the Karachi Cotton Association.

The Karachi Cotton Association was structured into two categories: there were 'companies'--corporate bodies rather than individuals--who were called members. They founded it. But they weren't allowed to enter the auction ring. Only one group of 'brokers' handled all the technical aspects of buying, selling, hedging, etc.

In the pre-partition period, a few--three or four-- European firms vastly dominated the export of cotton, most of which went to Europe. The reason is that the long-stapled varieties were expensive in comparison with other types of cotton grown in the sub-continent. The picture that emerges is this: A few European firms dominated the export trade. A group of indigenous firms also exported cotton from Karachi to other areas of British India. These firms were predominantly Gujerati firms which had their origin in Bombay city. They had migrated to Karachi or had set up subsidiary branches there and, in turn, exported their crop back to Bombay city. Sindhi Hindus, though they existed as members, had very little control over the crop, and they were unimportant before 1947.

In the category of the brokers, the people who actually bought and sold the crop, the situation was slightly different. Brokers had to deal with the producers in the interior, had to know the quality of cotton coming. Statistics kept in British India on cotton were nothing short of phenomenal. In the canal areas, for ten to twelve acres, there were statistics on the best types of cotton with the entire area mapped out. The brokers had to maintain that kind of expertise that would enable them to tell as soon as they heard of a village what variety of cotton it produced. In other words, they were a technical group with expert knowledge.

I asked one how he got his training and he laughed. He said, "There's no such thing as training. You can join yourself as a broker if you want to, if you put up the capital." But it didn't work so easily as one wouldn't last very long without the expert knowledge of the varieties of cotton. This obviously determined who the brokers could be. They were people who migrated from the interior and maintained contacts with the interior. So, the people that were handling the buying and selling of crops were primarily indigenous. The people who then took the crop for production--to be made into cloth or exported--tended to be (a) European or (b) Gujarati firms. There were exceptions to this pattern but this was, in the main, the basic organization of the cotton trade.

In 1947, Karachi was about 50 percent Hindu, 50 percent Muslim. By 1950, there were fewer than 1 percent Hindus left in Karachi. Looking at the statistics on the surface--which is the way most scholars analyze the social consequences of partition--one would assume that the Hindu cotton traders had left Karachi with the rest of the population. But it didn't happen that way. The cotton traders stayed behind; most sent their families ahead but they remained, making a lot of money and enjoying their continued economic prosperity in Pakistan right up until the 1965 war and a few all the way to the 1971 war.

The answer to why they were able to maintain this position is, again, their expertise which Muslim refugee traders coming into Pakistan couldn't easily replace.

However, Muslims finally did penetrate the brokerage, and it turned out to be a rather simple process. The government of Pakistan said it was going to close down the Association if more Muslims weren't allowed in, and Hindus started permitting them to come in and be members and brokers. By today it is almost entirely a Muslim-dominated institution, though Sindhis still have a small role in the cotton trade, basically remaining producers. They have not been able to penetrate the Association.

I expected, if conventional wisdom about western India is any guide, that Memmons, Khojas, and possibly the Borahs would take over. What I found was just the opposite. People coming in from the U. P. and the Punjab controlled the cotton trade for the first few years. At first it didn't make any sense until I looked further. In order to be a broker one has to be fairly literate in English. The U. P. people tended to be literate; many were trained for civil service jobs. One exception is the Chiniotis, a trading community from the Punjab, who did very well. But these groups began to wane in the late 1950s and, after the 1965 war, Memmons came in and took over the Association. One now gets the pattern one would have expected to find in the first place.

Let me summarize the points I wish to make out of this: The initial point is that Karachi remains a transplant in Pakistan. The traders dominating its commerce remain groups from western India. The Memmons were originally Lohana Hindu converts. The Hindus went back to Bombay, and the Memmons came into Karachi. Most of the cotton auctioning continues to be done in Gujarati, not in Urdu or Sindhi. There is almost no change in the sense that the local population continues to play no role. This is a pattern of continuity that was established in the colonial period. What is interesting is how these groups took advantage of British rule in the area and still continue to have a sway.

I argue that perhaps the best way to interpret the phenomenon is to look at the western coast of India as a cultural

75

zone that is separated from the interior. Groups that are
predominant in this zone tend to migrate back and forth.
A particular hinterland or a particular product makes little
difference to their vocation which remains basically that
of middle men; the latter know how to deal in export and
trade.

ALFORD - The Discussant is Eric Gustafson.

GUSTAFSON - It is interesting to put Bombay and Karachi side
by side. The theme that seems to emerge out of these papers
is that these cities were *tabuli rasi* on which one could draw
with fresh chalk.

There was nothing initially to impede the introduction
of Western institutions and the colonial system. There weren't
many people locally, except Sindhi fishermen. And yet, what
is most interesting about these cities is the extent to which
they do not seem Western. This raises the issue that was
spoken of this morning in Chris Bayly's paper. It is the question of what do we mean by saying that Western institutions
"dominated"? In making such statements we refer to a fraction
in which there was an enumerator and a denominator--such and
such a percentage of the cotton trade was in such and such
hands. It seems that we have identified things in the denominator more accurately than in the enumerator.

The social groupings that persisted seemed to owe
nothing at all to the West directly. The British attempted
to use local institutions as they conceived them to be. Perhaps the locals created some institutions that the British
had imagined in order to oblige them. On the whole, most of
this was, however, froth or dusting.

The notion of the western coastal zone as different
from eastern India seems interesting. I wonder if we couldn't
push it back a little further. Let us pose a question like,
What happened to Thatta? Anyone who has seen modern Thatta
would find it hard to imagine that this was one of the principle cities in the East in its prime. It's now a dump. If
I had to define a dump, I would use an extensive description
of Thatta. Yet this was an important center of commerce at one
time. What became of its merchants? Where did they go? Where
did they set up shop? The experience of the last hundred years
would suggest to us that they probably moved somewhere else
in response to another set of opportunities. I wonder if
further investigation wouldn't bring us some confirmation of
the themes that have cropped up in Tom Metcalf's and Keith
Sipe's papers.

Some scholars have argued against the tradition that
assumes that caste councils operated and controlled eighteenth
century Bombay. We ought to bear in mind a point that Frank
Conlon didn't bring out in his presentation but which is in

his paper, a quote from an old Gujarat hand, Alexander Walker: "Most of the castes in Bombay have a permanent *panchayat* who decide petty disputes and make by-laws for its direction and governance. The extent of the interference of those *panchayats* in the concerns of their respective castes to which their interference is limited is not exactly, I believe, known, and they are afraid of exciting the jealousy of our government . . . they manage their affairs with great caution and secrecy."

We have to raise the methodological problem of how one explores the existence of the caste organizations that Keith Sipe speaks about. One can go a long time without knowing that there are Hindus in Karachi unless one looks in two places: one is the lefthand side of page 6 in the morning newspaper where the obituaries appear and where the Hindus advertise the deaths of prominent members of the community because everyone has to assemble for the ceremony. The other refers to occasional announcements of the Krishna celebrations and assorted religious occasions.

But the Hindus keep quiet; they keep to themselves. They, I suspect, settle their own disputes with relatively little reference to the courts. One can look hard in Karachi records without finding much about the existence of Hindu social organizations today. Yet we know there are several levels among them. A separate scheduled caste federation with its set of officers exists. I don't know how the caste Hindus manage their affairs, but I presume they have some way of coping, too. These organizations, as the quotation suggests, have a natural tendency--especially in a hostile environment such as the British environment--to keep submerged.

CONLON - I wish I knew how to find the data on caste *panchayats*. What I have found has come by the usual procedure of looking, skulking around neighborhoods of Bombay. One can often find a lot this way, but much depends on luck. An important aspect that deserves to be considered is the extent to which reference from *panchayat* materials come to the courts. In a static situation, I would expect relatively little. Only when the social facts of a particular community were disrupted were they likely to come to the attention of the courts. Then, again, it couldn't be a crisis generated within; it was often the result of the arrival of a new family or the sudden rise of new wealth from outside. The Parsis offer the best study of this.

I didn't give any details in my presentation; there are, however, several publications in English and a couple in Gujarati that do deal with this to some extent. I am not prepared to argue that Alexander Walker knew what he was talking about. Walker spent most of his time in Gujarat. When a reference was made to the *panchayat* in the early nineteenth century, the Parsis were cited as the example.

On a more general plane, I don't accept the idea that Karachi and Bombay were special cases. I believe Bombay was in touch with its hinterland; the Maharashtrian and Gujarati Hindu communities had maintained linkages through much of Bombay's history. The opportunities for such linkages increased further as a result of the territorial expansion of East Indian Company's domination.

The expansion of the Bombay Presidency in the early nineteenth century meant that, for the first time, there was a single administrative unit under which caste and community affairs could be conducted. It is interesting to note that when the English tried to collect caste customs in connection with their governance, the Maharashtrians resident in Gujarat for over a hundred years simply said that "whatever they say at Poona we'll abide by as far as the rules of our caste or community are concerned."

So, there was a sense of continuity, not distinctively coastal or port city but certainly a tie back into the countryside, with roots in communal or "caste" organization. Was this phenomenon that was common elsewhere? My hunch is that it was, but I would like to hear others on this.

METCALF - I might have a crack at that. There was a community aspect <u>and</u> a floating aspect to most of these business communities. On the community side the critical question is, how did people conceive of themselves as community members over different periods of time? There is no doubt that Memmons have a strong sense of identity <u>now</u>. One might, however, ask: What was the strength of this <u>identity</u>, and what cross-cutting of other kinds of identity might have existed at previous times? And what leads to the creation of newer and stronger identity?

On the question of the 'floating' business aspect, we should ask, Do these communities float up and down the western coast of India and, indeed, to the coast of East Africa, too, for that matter, rather than sticking to one trade or one region? There has to be some way of accounting for this. Perhaps the hinterland is really a waterbase, to refer back to the discussion of Melaka, rather than a land base in the minds of these people. It is a possibility that's worth exploring.

Turning to Frank Conlon's remarks about the "non-isolation quality of Bombay," I would say that that may be true <u>now</u>, but one wonders whether the hinterland itself was not, in some measure, a creation of the British. Conlon spoke about the nineteenth century pacification as making hinterland trade out of Bombay more practicable. It was just as true of Karachi, too. In addition to the pacification, the Punjab canal colonies and the railroads clearly gave Karachi a hinterland that it had not had before. In the Bombay case, the cotton districts were British-created hinterlands, something that did not exist previously.

78

In regard to the fact that some of these people still considered themselves part of other communities, one might think in terms of a social hinterland centered around their hometowns. But how was it different from an economic hinterland of a city? I believe the "social hinterland" was more of a reference point for the group or the individual and therefore really a different category. The persistence of social reference point need not be regarded as part of economic hinterland as it would stretch the term "hinterland" too far. These are not, of course, answers so much as problems that have to be dealt with as we go along in the western Indian case.

SIPE - In our discussion of communities in western India, the term "floating" has come up in reference to some who followed the British wherever the empire extended. It's hard to go to a port in the Indian Ocean basin even today that does not have either Borahs, Ismailis, or Memmons.

One aspect that we didn't get into but which can be documented is that there were cultural and social components to the types of organizations these groups created. Perhaps one can even call it an ideological component in the sense that these people most importantly conceived of themselves as trading communities which worked like a self-fulfilling prophecy. I wish to bring out an important historical fact about these communities. Most of them were originally Hindu traders dealing in sea commerce. As they faced caste expulsion for dealing in sea trade so they converted to Islam, although the conversion pattern was not uniform.

CARSTEN - I have a question. I have been to Bombay as a businessman, not a scholar. In Bombay they often referred to the textile industry in Karachi as a form of American imperialism. A great many of the up-to-date textile factories in Karachi were actually financed by the Americans. A Tata family representative speaking in Bombay referred to Karachi as "American," as "your American city," to me. In Bakersfield, about two or three hundred miles south of here in California, you often see people from Karachi buying American cotton. Now, what is the relationship between the American textile system and the Karachi system?

GUSTAFSON - Textile mills in Pakistan were constructed with United States collaboration and capital as part of its industrial expansion. Cotton was a formula that had been learned. Once you've built a dozen and see that they work, you can then build two hundred, which is roughly what Pakistan has done. But I detect that you sense something sinister in this!

CARSTEN - Oh, I never regard American expansionism as sinister. I regard it as productive for this country. (Laughter)

MORRIS - I think one of the reasons that the Pakistanis were down there in Bakersfield buying cotton was that it was a

longer staple which meant that they were producing a different kind of cloth than the Bombay mills were producing. I
don't think there was anything more than that. Also, A.I.D.
was financing it.

MASSELOS - I wish to take up a number of points. I find the
concept of a western Indian free-floating mercantile community
most interesting. I wonder, however, whether one should see
this as a mobile community as such or, rather, as a reflection
of the expansion of business interests which demanded the
movement of individual representatives.

In Karachi, for example, the initial movement would
seem to be by merchants who were subsidiary to Bombay firms,
moving from a central point to this as well as to other areas.
One might find a similar movement of merchants from Bombay to
Calcutta, at least from the 1850s. Again, from the time Bombay
was founded in the late seventeenth century, Surat had such a
central role relationship with Bombay for a number of years.
The initial pattern seems to have been a dispersion of business
interests and concurrent representation of these interests by
individuals until a critical mass for both was reached.

Take the case of the movement of Khajas: where enough
of them have gathered in a central town, they set up a *jamatkhana*.
It is only when a sufficient number of them gather that a
jamatkhana is established. Until that occurs, individuals in
surrounding or outlying towns remain in a subsidiary relationship to the central *jamatkhana*. The individuals protect business
interests and business ties; their mobility is very much there
as individuals but only at a later stage do they cohere in the
one place as a community.

Next, I believe the parallels that have been drawn
between Karachi and Bombay are strong. We've heard about
different kinds of hinterlands out of Karachi and Bombay. This,
of course, wasn't so during the founding periods. During the
seventeenth and eighteenth centuries, before the effective
conquest of Maharashtra, the Marathi areas did have some trading
link-ups with Bombay, and there was also a transfer of food from
Bombay back into Maharashtra. Yet Company policy at the turn
of the eighteenth century, for example, was geared against the
export of food into Maharashtra since the island itself had
great trouble in maintaining its own food supply. This is,
perhaps, one reason why Bombay didn't attract any large scale
immigrant Marathi population until after 1818 although there
were Marathis in Bombay, of course, before then.

Coming to the problem of caste, I'm not certain as to
the point Frank Conlon was making. One runs into problems at
the source level in trying to come to terms with the nature of
caste in India in the eighteenth century. One can make too
much of Company agreements with different families since it
made them in terms of caste and not occupation. But caste

80

was often co-existent with occupational groups. There were, for example, in eighteenth century Bombay, Christian carpenters, and there were official attempts at bringing in certain castes to promote the needs of the town. For someone who has worked on Bombay in the nineteenth century, caste dynamics are clearly important but, at the same time, there is a need to come to terms with class dynamics.

In my work on nineteenth century Bombay, I argue that a dual process occurred: an increased sense of caste identification and, at the same time, a process of integration along class/group/status lines. If one looks at elite groups, even in the eighteenth century period, one is aware of a sense of integrated group identity amongst particular castes and occupations. There was, for instance a mercantile identity reflected in those occasions when various merchants joined in affairs of common concern.

ANDERSON - I will comment on a question raised by Frank Conlon about possible parallels to indirect commercial domains. There was an interesting phenomenon in pre-colonial Melaka in the institution of *shahbandar*, who was the commercial chief of each trading group. It managed the social and economic segregation of the various trading communities.

In colonial Manila and other Philippine cities there was the institution of *capitanatina* which the Spanish found very handy. It was not the innovation of the Spaniards so much as an indigenous Chinese creation to cope with the accommodation to a new situation. The third type I wish to mention is the secret society. It was very prominent in the nineteenth and twentieth century peninsular Malaysia where tin miners and others organized themselves into special groups, often as secret societies.

LEWANDOWSKI - Bob Frykenberg and I were just talking about the question of free-floating mercantile populations as being possibly unique to the west coast of India. One can look at the Chettiyar community on the east coast, which was much involved in trading in Burma and other southeast counties, and see them in possibly a similar light. One ought to be careful, therefore, about generalizing.

Also, I agree with Jim Masselos's comment that caste was important and did indeed play a role, but I would emphasize the inter-relationship between the individual, the extended family, and the community. These entities didn't work in isolation. There were networks that linked them up, say, in the recruitment process: going out to the village in order to attract people, weavers or whatever, into the city. There is little doubt but that caste was involved in these networks among the individual, the extended family, and those people who were recruited, but there remains a question of terminology: What do you mean by "caste"? Are we talking about endogomous

81

groups or those that married among other people and ate together? I believe both these groups existed in Indian cities
during the seventeenth and eighteenth centuries, although
we have to be a bit careful when we are using these terms to
define exactly what we mean.

FRYKENBERG - I'll take the point even further. If one looks
at the free-floating of these communities eastward more than
westward one will probably find as great a flow of personnel
at all levels.

I can bring in the word "colonialization" with gusto
in regard to Rangoon and the lower Burma, to Singapore and
Malaya, and to Colombo and Ceylon. Each of them were heavily
infiltrated at several levels with different kinds of caste
communities, labor recruitment devices, the whole bit.
Rangoon was really a colonial port city creation as much of
Coromondel coasts as it was of the British. Singapore got
it coming from both sides, from South China as well as from
South India.

MURPHEY - This phenomenon of groups that are referred to as
"itinerant" or "interloper" who were drawn into these places
from other areas, functioning successfully within them, is
something that one finds in East and Southeast Asia as well.
It would be the case for every city that acquired a character
different from that of the Cathedral town of Medieval Europe.
By this I mean specifically to include cities everywhere since
that time that have been engaged in anything more than strictly
regional and/or domestic trade and local services--New York,
Buenos Aires, London.

All modern cities have this characteristic. I should
think it certainly was true in East Asia and, from what little
I know of Southeast Asia, there as well. The difference between East and Southeast was that, in cities that became something other than occasional markets in pre-European times, for
example Canton, that phenomenon was present before the Europeans
came along. Cantonese merchant guilds in Shanghai and Ningpo
merchant guilds in Tientsin continued to be common. Of course,
as I say, it seems to be true of all modern cities that are
engaged in trade, doing something other than bureaucratic paper
shuffling.

CONLON - I quite agree. The questions raised by Jim Masselos,
Susan Lewandowski, and Rhoads Murphey are all directly related
to something I was trying to pin down. I wasn't arguing that
there is no such thing as caste, regardless of definition. My
whole research thus far has been living off the Saraswat Brahmins! But, frankly, in the literature that I read I found
that people talked about "caste" or "communities" in very vague
ways. One even encounters the notion of "caste" as being an
imperialist/colonialist invention. Nobody says--and I am not
arguing now--that it took the colonial system or the presence

82

of European authority in Asia to introduce caste to cities.
As far as I can tell, every ruler who tried to build up a
city in South Asia made concessions, and I assume this to
be true elsewhere. But I would be curious to know as to
what extent is there anything distinctive about these colonial
port cities? Is there anything distinctively "colonialist"
about the way in which these populations were recruited?
Is there a functional explanation that would enable us to
talk about the colonial port city in terms other than just
pure economics?

I realize that Tom Metcalf doesn't approve of my use
of "hinterland" in terms of "social" relations. I'll concede
that it is difficult to talk about hinterland on the one hand
and trade on another, then turn around and talk about caste
rules or cultural sentiments, but the fact remains that people
do have both those things going for them at the same time.
I think that it's important to keep this in mind when we talk
about the cities. We may want, in this Conference, to carefully exclude all non-economic relationships; that would certainly simplify our task. Yet I believe that we have to keep
in mind the point that was implicit in what Susan [Lewandowski]
and Bob Frykenberg said about the social world with its relationships reaching outside the physical city.

MURPHEY - Does anyone know of a case, other than Bombay, where
the colonialists said, "We want you guys, you guys, and you
guys, this kind, that kind, to come here" and got away with it?

FRYKENBERG - Yes, Madras! To say that the caste devices were
used for recruitment of different kinds of personnel, whether
military or mercantile, is not to say that it was necessarily
an effective devise for colonialistic "divide-and-rule" practice. All one had to do was get the word out through the
castes--it was a fair game both ways. You can't have one community like the English (or, later, the British), who were a
caste or cluster of castes within that definition, employing
"dive-and-rule" without themselves being fair game for the
same kind of treatment in reverse. In other words, word went
out through the caste networks, stopping all recruitment. They
did this in Madras where different communities were able to
bring activity to a dead stop.

MURPHEY - One more illustration: A traditional Chinese case
would be the Swatow Opium Bill in the 1880s which stopped not
only all trade in opium in Swatow but way down the southeast
coast to Wuhan, Hankow, and all over central China. A couple
of foreign trading firms were ruined because the Swatow guilds
all over China took objection to things one small foreign enterprise was doing. The guild simply said, "We will stop all
trade with foreign firms," and they won. The example speaks
eloquently to the power and influence of mercantile networks
in traditional China.

METCALF - A case of the British being confounded by a Cantonese "Mafia!"

MURPHEY - Yes, though the Cantonese complained about the Ningpo Mafia!

METCALF - I'm wondering whether we might now venture toward a working definition of colonial port cities in Asia. Let me throw out the beginnings of such a definition: A colonial port city basically consisted of diverse peoples who were in some measure or another recruited, if not by the colonial power then by mercantile or other agents of the colonial power; they had, of course, to be engaged in overseas trade with a metropolis. But the question is, how many of these people had to come from how far away in order for it to be really colonial? That is to say, How many people from the immediate physical hinterland of the city can be allowed to reside in the city and let us still be able to call it a colonial city?

This goes back to the point I was making earlier about the isolation of Karachi and the extent to which people there came from quite some distance away. In Bombay we have a partially similar case, but there were a lot of Marathis there and, obviously, Madras was full of Madrasees and what not. What I'm trying to say is, how many and what kinds of people here can we incorporate within our colonial label? I just toss this out towards a working definition.

MORRIS - I am still somewhat confused. I don't go along with Frykenberg's reductionist position where everything ends up like everything else. It seems to me that one has to know what question one is asking before a term has any meaning. What is different about a colonial port city and a port city? Melcalf's three characteristics seemed to be appropriate for any number of cities, colonial or not colonial, port or not port.

BAYLY - What we ought to look at is not just the participation of Europeans in a port city but in the dominance of Europeans in certain key sectors such as shipping, the control of political institutions, the control of market information from abroad, the control of funds to indigenous entrepreneurs. Then we must look at the problems connected with the style of the setting. Often there is a confusion between a city in which the colonial style is dominant and a city where it's economic dominance of the colonial power that is at issue.

Insofar as the question of caste in the city is concerned, I'm puzzled by an apparent difference between western Indian cities and other cities. What we've got is a basic level of caste groups of an inter-actional sort, the *jati* level. In Bombay and other western Indian cities, we have a wider level, as Conlon suggests, which came about through colonial control. Lewandowski has suggested another, the question of socialization. One wonders why, in western Indian cities, socialization occurred in terms of fairly restricted caste institutions, whereas in Madras and Calcutta inter-caste groups, *dalpatis* on the one hand or left-hand or right-hand factional groupings on the other, were the dominant method of socialization. In north Indian cities a further variant of this would be the faction based around the royal power, e.g., the way that the King of Delhi attracted merchants who defined themselves in relation to him. Western India does seem to be an exception along these lines.

SIPE - One could obviously argue that colonial cities are any cities founded by a colony, but this sounds too obvious. A distinction has to be made, and I would do that by referring to the Indian Ocean basin. Before the arrival of the Europeans the basin had a series of ports that shifted frequently. If one looks at the African coast, there was first Kilwa, then Mombasa and, later, Dar. And if you look at India, you have shifting ports there as well: Cambay, Surat, finally, Bombay.

In contrast, a European port city built an institutional framework within its geographical locus that didn't allow for a port to shift. For example, it brought in railways, invested in harbor, which solidified their base. I don't know how long this colonial system or port cities in the Indian Ocean will last. Perhaps Karachi and Rangoon were the last two major ports developed. Today, some of these ports have been scheduled for elimination. Karachi will be replaced by Port Kasim, miles away, by the end of this century. Durban, the best natural port in the Indian Ocean basin, will be replaced by Richards Bay, a hundred and fifty miles to the north. But the colonial city as it exists today is clearly a creation of one particular set of circumstances, and it does continue to exist today.

DAS GUPTA - In the context of the colonial port city as it has just now been posed, there is an important question about the timing of it. European domination was established in different port cities around 1500, and the colonial system as we understand it was established much later--say, not before the middle of the eighteenth century. Many of the earlier cities were just moribund.

Secondly, the colonial port city was a structural phenomenon as well insofar as the process of extraction was concerned. Van Leur, in the 1930s, put forth the hypothesis that, before this happened, there were important changes within the traditional trade structure that involved changes in commodity composition, involved the rise and fall of cities, displacement of mercantile communities, although qualitatively the structure remained the same. This fragmented, personalized, traditional structure was displaced by something controlled from the port city after the establishment of the colonial system. It is then

85

the colonial port city emerged, not earlier. I would place
this towards the end of the eighteenth century.

MILONE - I think that in the transformation the colonial city
brought about there were differences in scale and differences
in kind. The migration of people speaking a different language, which happened along the west coast of India, also
happened in Greek imperial times. However, it is the scale
on which it occurred that was so distinct during the colonial
period. In East Africa it happened on an unprecedented scale,
starting in the nineteenth century. In Indonesia, Javanese-
speaking people had been migrating to West Java for some time.
However, it is the scale on which they started coming during
the colonial period, to Bantam and then to Batavia and to
other colonial port cities, which is unique.

     As to the difference in kind, the papers by Bayly,
Metcalf, and Freitag emphasize the provisioning of the colonial
army. In the case of Kanpur this was a unique activity, gener-
ating participation from merchant groups; in the case of Karachi,
special requirements made a lot of Parsi merchants quite wealthy.
This is a new kind of phenomenon, it seems to me.

MORRIS - A couple of points have been made thus far. First,
the question of timing, as Das Gupta puts it, which can be
marked at the late eighteenth and early nineteenth century
when migration into port cities on a large scale occurred.

     Second, the particular characteristics of provisioning
armies. The British didn't have armies out looting the country-
side--they provisioned them. What we're really saying then
is that these cities were characterized by special kinds of
organizational structures from the outside, such as military
organizations, which were quite different from what existed
in Asia or, possibly, in Europe at an earlier stage.

MILONE - Were Indian armies provisioned in the same way as
European armies? Did they need as much leather, for example?

MORRIS - It isn't a matter of what they needed; it's how they
went about getting it. And whether they got paid.

FRYKENBERG - The complete provisioning of armies in India seems
to have begun during wars with Tipu Sultan when a distinct
change seems to have occurred. The tactic was used so as to
detract attention from and undermine local support for Tipu
and to diffuse hostility against the rise of the Company's
power.

     As a result, by 1792 the Company did not allow its
armies to take provisions of booty from the countryside.
Rather, it sent out its commissariat merchants along the way,
paying a good price for what it could get. Troops caught
pillaging could be shot or court-marshalled. The logistic

support behind the last war against Mysore was really a turning point in this kind of activity. But whether or not this kind of commissariat activity can be considered "colonial" is something I'm rather dubious about, especially as this development was happening in different parts of the world at that time.

MILONE - I think the extensive use of leather was rather unique to the European-provisioned army. Their use of shoes and saddlery was more extensive than in the Indian army, wasn't it? Traditionally, only the officers in the Indian army rode, and most of the men walked barefoot. This would be a distinct difference since British patterns of provisioning must have stimulated the leather industry.

FRYKENBERG - An Indian army was an Indian army, even if you put them in uniform--

MILONE - What I mean is that more officers were riding and using saddles, probably, than in the previous armies.

FRYKENBERG -   --as the Marathas did.

MILONE - The Marathas were on horseback, of course. Nevertheless, there was more intense activity in the cantonment-type set-up than there had been previously. In a place like Kanpur, provisioning stimulated an army-catering industry.

METCALF - While all this is relevant and useful, it is a small part of the picture. It seems to me that we have to stick with the point made by Bayly, among others--that is, the question of extraction of commodities within the context of political dominance of a European power. I don't see how, otherwise, we can differentiate an Asian colonial port city from San Francisco or any number of other cities that can fall within this category.

MORRIS - I wouldn't lay stress on the fixed technology. That happens to be a phenomenon of time and not of what I believe to be a decisive factor. The social overhead required in the nineteenth and twentieth centuries was a different kind of technology but could be co-opted by any group. It was essentially the turning of the political terms of trade in favor of certain groups that we define as imperial, making a city colonial.

One can, however, ask: Where did the grouping come from? How did they operate in a system in which the imperial overlord was able to enforce control? This is a different question than is being talked about up until now. Yet I feel we must raise it: What difference did it make that there was a special kind of political power being applied?

FRYKENBERG - I am comfortable with the simple concept of "port cities" of Asia. The "colonial" concept is so fraught with stickiness that I have had to let the thing go. The concept is too muddy to be very useful. I avoid it. Also, there had always been "imperial" cities at one time or another, although the nineteenth century kind of phenomenon was, admittedly, a bit different. The simple expression "port cities of Asia" should suffice once we define the period and the kind of questions we are interested in.

REED - In cases that bring in a "colonial" element, there is invariably the projection of external authority into a given space. The city of Western foundation becomes the instrument by which the hinterland is created. Bangkok, where authority remained in the hands of the Thais, may be considered an exception. Yet even here the agents were European, though the catalysts were Thai.

MURPHEY - Buenos Aires was another kind of Bangkok. Would you call it colonial? We commonly do not. I mean nineteenth century Buenos Aires after the Spanish were kicked out in the 1820s. In Bangkok the money, at least most of it, was British as the techniques and trade links were West European. Yokohama and Osaka, especially Osaka, also fall in this category.

FRYKENBERG - But aren't we dealing with a common colonialization everywhere? In Buenos Aires there was a separate colonialization process, but weren't the people evolved of Iberian and other European derivation? We're talking about Europeans moving into an alien society and not subtracting that society.

REED - Then you're defining as "colonial" only those phenomena that were manifestations of European influence. What of a subcontinental situation such as that of India where there were "alien" peoples moving from one culture area to another within a single and major landmass? The Marwaris, for example, left their hearth in the arid realm of Rajasthan to become commercial lords in Calcutta and other port cities. What makes them any less "colonial"? And what of the role of the Chettiars in Rangoon?

GUSTAFSON - That's right. The Persian Gulf is to this day pretty much of an Indian or subcontinental "colonial" manifestation. One way or the other, the rupee has always been its coin.

CONLON - I must admit that I automatically assumed that the term "colonial" was not so much having to do with direct colonial rule, British or Portuguese, as it was having to do with one city as opposed to simply a port. Also, I believe it had something to do with the expansion of the European capitalist system during the course of the late eighteenth and early nineteenth century.

Driving down Highway I south from San Francisco to Santa Cruz, I passed place after place that were ports during

the nineteenth century, connected with the efficient extraction of commodities from the California hills. Mostly timber,
but there were other products. They weren't cities, yet they
were clearly connected with extraction. It seems, therefore,
that the extraction of a commodity wasn't necessarily a critical feature of a colonial port city. The process of extraction
generated economic growth that was not entirely under European
capitalism but was something indigenous in the sense that
indigenous elements participated in, contributed to, and perhaps
profited from, more greatly than the Europeans.

CHAN   -   If we stretch the concept of colonialism a bit and get
a little less Eurocentric, then we have to consider Japanese
control of Korea and Taiwan and, perhaps, even Vladivostok.

MILONE   -   I think we're getting too relativistic. Obviously, a
colonial city presents a difference in architecture, a difference in the official language that is used. These are European
imports that are of European origin. When one keeps on saying
no, this is something we can relate to traditional times; it
is as though one were taking the nationalist position.

FRYKENBERG   -   That's why I prefer the term "European port cities."

MILONE   -   I wouldn't go that far because the number of Europeans
that came was rather minute.

REED   -   But their institutions reigned supreme.

BROOMFIELD   -   I think Max Weber suggested the way out of the
problem we are faced with. Following his concept of an ideal
type, we can set up a typology of what a colonial port city is.
In fact, Anderson and Vorster have attempted to develop this.
Murphey has suggested this at other times in his work. We
should continue along these lines and set up some of the characteristics of the ideal type, realizing that our archetypal
colonial port cities may vary greatly in detail, but I hope
we don't get hung up on this too much.

     Basically, it will be useful to explore some interesting
ways of looking at European contacts with Asia, some of which
if not most will be economic, and others will be cultural and
so forth. At times, playing around with the term as Bayly has
done, saying "What about upcountry type port cities?" can be
very useful. A hard and fast definition is not necessary,
although a typology might be a useful way to approach it.

BASU   -   Broomfield, Das Gupta, Bayly, and Milone have said some
of the things that have come to my mind. There is obviously
a time scale: one can talk about "early colonialism" and "high
colonialism" but most important is, of course, the phenomenon
of the expansion of the world capitalist-colonialist-imperialist
system stemming from the West and the process of its integration
or interaction with Asia. The magnitude of this interaction

varied and changed according to the time scale and the particularities of the Asian country concerned. I suggest that "colonial port city" is an especially viable concept in dealing with this process of integration or interaction. These cities belong to a new genre with a good deal of Western influence, political and otherwise, and are at once Asian and non-Asian.

This dualism is no doubt most fascinating, and we can discuss endlessly how far were or are they Asian and non-Asian. We can avoid this in part by looking at specifics in their formative phases. For instance, how far and how much were the seemingly entrenched traditional networks in the hinterland changed or transformed, and how did this new genre of a city top or relate to them?

The papers by Bayly and Anderson/Vorster provide some interesting insights. I would suggest, however, that the search for the key to these relationship must begin within the structure of the port city itself where the Western traders and colonial powers by and large called the shots. To be sure, there were impressive Asian entrepreneurs and power-brokers in the port cities, but they were seldom partners in the real sense. One good explanation for this was their dependence on the Western traders for commercial intelligence and information, much of which, as we know, was neatly controlled by the Western mercantile and agency houses. In these world trade oriented port cities, such control over the flow of information was crucial.

A large number of Calcutta commercial enterprises during the early nineteenth century, for instance, collapsed partly because of a lack of premonition of what was going on in London or New York.

If these cities belonged to a new genre, one may ask to what extent the people who filled them and the indigenous entrepreneurs who dominated their economic and cultural life were new? This is tied in with "colonial" recruitment of labor and the castes and communities that responded to such recruitment efforts as well as with their social and cultural expressions in the context of the dualism of these port cities. This is a complex and difficult subject, deserving a great deal more in-depth empirical and theoretical study than we have now at hand. Let me make a brief reference to the two port cities I've studied.

Calcutta and Canton, during the early nineteenth century and certainly in the later period, were "heterogenetic" cities as opposed to the traditional "orthogenetic" type--to borrow the paired terminology that Redfield and Singer had coined some years ago. The merchant classes that were attracted to these cities were parvenus; many came from "low," in the economic sense, social origins, and many literally made it from

90

rags to riches. One doesn't come across much of a continuum between the old traditional families of the precolonial era and the new ones.

However, once the new ones were established, there was continuity. Probably because of their pedestrian origins and also because they were outsiders, as in the case of Canton merchants who came mostly from Fukien and Ningpo areas, there was a common tendency among these merchants, despite their encounter with the West, to emulate the traditional mores. Often this provided them with access to paths of social mobility and acceptance of their newly acquired status of wealth. A common form of such traditional mores was temple-building and patronizing those aspects of traditional culture that one might assume would fall into decay in an increasingly hetero-genetic framework. We have here, therefore, a phenomenon of heterogenetic cities culturally taking in the characteristics of an orthogenetic city.

MASSELOS - In terms of its hinterland, the port city can be viewed as a control transfer point. However, if one pushes this view of the role of the city as part of an extractive process too far, then the danger is that the city will be deprived of any identity of its own and that it will become just a gigantic junction.

Assuming that it is so for the moment, then the crucial question is, What kinds of linking, in economic terms, existed? Was the overall political dominance of the colonial masters reflected in the critical dominance of others who had economic power, or were all the economic relationships from the city essentially colonial? Does one talk of a "mother colony"? Can one argue that the bankruptcy in Asia in the nineteenth century was a result of imperialist economic forces? There are numerous questions that follow from this.

Finally, should one distinguish specifically between colonial and non-colonial trading patterns or, rather, argue that there was a single standard trading worldwide pattern? The emphasis on a "colonial" distribution may not get us very far.

MURPHEY - There remains a distinction between "ports" and "port cities." I cannot think of a port in any part of the world that is not also a city.

CONLON - Bixby's Landing in California was a port for extraction, but it was not a city. Apparently, it had only four or five houses. This was not uncommon before the Age of Stephenson. With its onset, the steamship, the deep draft boat, did provide for significant change.

Marc Bloch, while talking about Medieval Europe, referred to pre-modern trade patterns, using the term "capillary action."

In this paradigm, there are no large centers, nodes with interaction, but a percolation through the countryside of trade in a diverse pattern. I think this is a tenable hypothesis in the context of the sea world of Asia with its shipment of goods in shortdraft, small sailing vessels that could go into places otherwise inaccessible.

METCALF - Let's finish this discussion off by emphasizing that we are dealing with places with colonial domination. This caused the critical difference in terms of who was calling the shots at the fundamental level, although perhaps not at every level. We are talking about the extraction of commodities--an absolute must in any discussion of port cities.

Finally, we are also dealing with relatively large and diverse populations, comprising a substantial proportion of migrants who created a cosmopolitan world of some sort, a jostling of different people side by side.

TOPIC II: DEVELOPMENT AND CHARACTER OF MERCANTILE ELITES (continued)

Session 3

J. Weston del.   J. Clark dirext.

96

MERCHANTS, TEMPLES, AND POWER IN THE COLONIAL

PORT CITY OF MADRAS

by

Susan J. Lewandowski

        Research to date on the colonial port city in Asia has tended to
emphasize the Eurocentric aspects of the evolution of port cities. In
order to rectify this imbalance in the literature, one of the important
focuses of the Conference has been on the indigenous development of these
cities. In line with such an approach, this paper looks at Madras City
in southern India in terms of two themes raised by the Conference:
a) the role of the indigenous mercantile elite in the economic and political development of the city from the sixteenth through the nineteenth
centuries, and b) the impact of this elite on the morphology of the city.

        This argues that one can see a continuity between the role of the
merchant in pre-colonial India and the early port cities; that, under
East India Company rule, a Hindu commercial elite that employed a traditional model of kingship retained power over the majority of urban dwellers;
that this elite used mercantile wealth acquired through their contact with
Europeans to build temples; and that, with the emergence of the English
as the dominant political power in the port cities of India by the turn
of the nineteenth century, a number of new urban institutions were introduced from Europe that resulted in the creation of competing elites from
outside the mercantile community and new arenas for the display of urban
authority. These, however, did not replace the traditional arena of the
temple which remains today an important institution in Madras.

        This paper goes beyond political and economic issues to address
the social realities and the world view of the Hindu inhabitants who lived
within the city. What is striking in the case of the colonial port city
in India is the way in which the ritual sector is linked with the political
and economic systems, particularly in the eighteenth century.

        The paper is divided into three sections that correspond to the
chronological development of Madras and its hinterland. The first section
deals with the nature of the indigenous urbanization process prior to the
arrival of the Europeans along the Coromandel Coast. It emphasizes the
growth of urban centers in this region during the Vijayanagar Empire from
the thirteenth to the sixteenth centuries, under the patronage of *nayakas*,
Telegu warriors who expanded into much of the Tamil-speaking region to the
south of their capital, Vijayanagar. They legitimized their status in this
area, in part by building temples. The *nayakas* and, later, the Telegu
merchants they encouraged to migrate to their settlements, employed a

traditional model of kingship in their exercise of power which, it is argued, was followed by the Hindu mercantile elite initially responsible for building much of Madras. This model involved conflict arbitration, or the settling of disputes within their domain; the encouragement of trade and commerce; the preservation of the sacred order and, hence, the building of temples; the creation of a court-like environment within the settlement through the patronage of art and learning; and the use of a common pool of ceremonial elements associated with kingship and the temple in south India to delimit status, such as employing musicians and dancing girls on festive occasions.

The second section of the paper emphasizes the continuity between the role of the Hindu merchant in pre-colonial India and in the early port cities. It examines the way in which the Hindu mercantile elite, particularly those of Telegu origin, functioned as brokers in Madras City during the period from 1639, when the city was founded, to 1800. What emerges from the Conference as one of the common characteristics of the colonial port city in India is the role of powerful individuals in the maintenance of trade networks during this period.

The *dubash* in south India, and the *dewan* or *banian* in north India provided the major broker role between the producing castes on the one hand and the Europeans on the other. It was the individual supported by his extended family, rather than the caste community, that was the focal point for economic and political activity.

In the case of Madras, merchants from three Telegu-speaking castes--the Beri Chettiars, the Balijas, and the Komatis--played a crucial role in the early development of the city. They were involved in banking and minting of coins, investing in urban lands and recruiting migrants to settle in Madras. Through these roles, they exercised considerable power in the city. In the seventeenth and eighteenth centuries, *dubashes* arbitrated caste conflicts and settled disputes among multi-caste factions commonly known as the "right hand" and "left hand" castes. Caste conflicts emerged in the colonial port cities as migrants settled together from different regions of south India which each had their own local system of caste ranking. Conflicts also emerged between mercantile groups who found themselves in competition with one another in the colonial port city. In the case of Madras, this is illustrated in the conflict between the Komatis, a pan-south Indian caste belonging to the right hand faction, and the Beri Chettiars, a locally-based urban caste of the left hand division. Although the highest position in the social and political hierarchy of Madras was in the hands of the English, it was the *dubash* throughout the eighteenth century who remained a power force over the majority of urban inhabitants.

Aside from the economic and political power exercised by the Hindu mercantile elite in Madras, they were involved in affirming their status through control over ritual resources and protection of the sacred order. Like the *nayakas* and the merchants of the Vijayanagar period, the *dubashes* of eighteenth century Madras built temples. Temples not only raised the ritual status of lower caste Telegu merchants, but they provided an important urban function, for they became redistribution centers for wealth through endowments, or gifts, granted to the temples. It is suggested that the building of temples in eighteenth century Madras had an impact on the morphology of the city, for temples provided a focus for residential and cultural activity. Madras was not merely a port with an economic function but, during the eighteenth century, it particularly provided a rich social and ritual environment for its inhabitants. Although this paper stresses the building of temples, Professor Robert Eric Frykenberg's paper, "The Morphology of Madras as a City State," notes the comparable building of mosques and churches during this period, and the segmented quality of the city that emerges as a result of different interest groups such as the British, the Muslims, and the Christians, leave their own imprint on the city.

In the third section of the paper an emphasis is placed on changes in the attitude of the British in India. It is during the nineteenth century that the British became the dominant political force on the Sub-continent, and the nature of the colonial port cities began to change as Western institutions, such as law courts, schools, hospitals, and political associations, were introduced from Europe. As private merchants increasingly assumed the trade of the East India Company, agency houses were founded by European and indigenous merchants alike to compete with one another for control of overseas trade.

In the process, the role of the powerful *dubash* was considerably reduced, and he ceased to have either the economic or political resources at hand that had enabled him to exercise a king-like status in the city at an earlier period. By using the example of the Komati Chettiar community, an attempt is made to illustrate these changes and to highlight areas of continuity with an earlier period. Although the Komatis moved into the timber, sugar, cotton, and indigo trade in the nineteenth century, although they founded joint stock companies and joined modern Western political associations such as the Madras Mahajana Sabha, their status continued to be tied to the ritual sector. In the late nineteenth and early twentieth centuries, the most important modernizers of the Komati community were also trustees of the caste temple, Kanyaka Parameswari, which today as in the past, controls the largest wholesale fruit and vegetable market in the city of Madras. As such, this temple, like others in the city, continues to play an important role as a redistributive center of urban wealth and a political arena for members of the Komati community.

With the creation of new urban institutions by the British in the nineteenth century, however, an important change took place in the colonial port cities of India that made for a qualitatively different situation than had existed before. As the role of the *dubash* became less important in Madras in the course of the nineteenth century, so, too, the Telegu elite were forced to share power in the city with a growing number of castes from Tamil origins, most notably, Tamil Brahmins who, having learned English, moved into positions in government service.

Although the Telegu mercantile castes were initially slow to respond to Western education, by the early twentieth century the Komatis had founded their own Western-style association, the South India Vysia Sangam (1905) to channel money into industrial education and to create a sense of community among its members. This association, like others of its kind throughout India, provided a focus for modern associational politics in the colonial port cities. In the course of the twentieth century, Telegu merchant groups

99

were increasingly replaced by Tamilians. One of the common characteristics of colonial port cities in Asia is the replacing of merchant groups who are often perceived as "outsiders," such as the Indians in Burma and the Chinese in Malaysia, by an indigenous elite in the twentieth century, and this pattern takes place in Madras.

By looking at the indigenous urbanization process in pre-British south India, this paper raises several questions about the nature of urbanization in other colonial port cities in India such as Bombay and Calcutta, as well as cities in Southeast Asia. First of all, to what extent were temples important in the development of other North Indian port cities, and what was the relationship between the mercantile elite and the ritual sector. What are the continuities and discontinuities between north and south Indian port city development or, as the Conference has disclosed, possibly between the development of Calcutta and Madras on one hand and Bombay and the cities of western India on the other?

Secondly, are there institutions in Southeast Asian cities that were carried over from pre-colonial patterns of urbanization that had an intrinsic impact on the evolution of the colonial port city? That must be considered if we are to understand the nature of urbanization in these cities.

This paper suggests that there are a number of similarities in the overall development of the port cities of Madras and Calcutta. In the first place, Hindu merchants played a central role in the growth of both of these port cities. They acquired substantial wealth as intermediaries between the producing castes and the colonial sector and as indigenous bankers in the early years of the settlements. In both cities, individual merchants and their families were more important in maintaining trade networks than were caste groups. Similarly, the mercantile elite followed indigenous models in their exercise of power. Pradip Sinha, in his work on Calcutta, has suggested a move from a *bania* to a *raja* model of emulation among the Bengali elite around the turn of the nineteenth century. [1] I have suggested that a king-like model was adopted by the Hindu merchants of Madras who acquired wealth and power, particularly during the eighteenth century and who were involved in conflict arbitration, the protection of the sacred order, the gifting to and building of temples, and the patronage of art and learning.

In Madras, temple building was a major activity of the Hindu mercantile elite. Although, like their Calcutta counterparts, they also patronized festivals, donated funds to the poor, and celebrated lavish lifecycle ceremonies, it was the patronage and construction of temples that was most important in eighteenth century Madras. The presence of patrons of cultural and ritual activity contributed to the migration of high castes into what were initially market centers. In both cities, the concentration of commercial wealth led to a scale of competition between families that seems to have been much greater than existed in pre-colonial cities and, in Madras, is reflected in the number of temples that stand as monuments to the period. This competition in both Calcutta and Madras resulted in

---

[1] Pradip Sinha, "Approaches to Urban History: Calcutta, 1750-1850," in *Bengal, Past and Present*, 88 (January-June, 1968), p. 114.

a pattern of rival villages developing within the urban environment which had an impact on the morphology of these cities.

Politically, there were important similarities as well. In Calcutta, *dals,* or factions, established under the patronage of powerful merchants, were founded in the late eighteenth and nineteenth centuries. In many cases, these were multi-caste factions, and the role of the *dalapati* was to settle caste disputes and matters relating to the ritual sphere. In Madras, the "left and right hand" multi-caste factions were responsible for arbitrating caste matters at a time when economic rivalry took the form of encroachment on the traditional rights (often spatial rights) of competing groups.

By the early part of the nineteenth century, however, as the British emerged as the dominant political force in India and the colonial port cities began to diversify their economic base through industrialization, new migrants were increasingly attracted to these cities. In Calcutta, Bengalis were now competing commercially with north Indians who had extensive networks in the Bengal hinterland and other parts of north India and, in Madras, the Telegus were sharing trade with growing numbers of Tamil merchants. These changes paralleled developments in the political and ritual spheres. As a professional elite arose in both cities to staff a growing bureaucracy, they competed with the traditional merantile elite, and patterns of pan-urban politics emerged that cut across rival villages. Old forms of political groupings, such as *dals* and "left and right hand" caste factions, began to be replaced in the early twentieth century by caste associations based on a Western model, and more secular issues, such as the need for Western education and electoral political representation, became the concern.

These changes also had an important effect on the ritual sector. In the first place, control over temples was no longer limited to one community or one individual but became a corporate activity. Secondly, although wealth still found an outlet in lavish life-cycle ceremonies in the late nineteenth century, it was being re-channeled in the twentieth century into expenditures for secular charities and public needs. Caste associations provided a means by which money could be used to support new hospitals, schools, hostels, rest houses at railway stations, and other urban institutions. Temple endowments were also used to this end.

As Madras and Calcutta expanded in the late nineteenth century, the old residential areas could no longer incorporate migrants, and new settlement patterns developed alongside the old village structures and temple centers. Although changes have taken place in the role of the temple as an urban institution, status is still tied to the temple in Madras and it continues to function as a redistribution center for surplus wealth in the city. As such, the temple is a component of the colonial port city that has outlasted its colonists.

SOURCES

The sources for this paper include secondary works dealing with colonialism, and urban development in South and Southeast Asia, particularly comparative works on Calcutta, and primary sources on Madras, such as *The Census of India*, collections of English Factory Records; H. V. Love's *Vestiges of Old Madras*, in three volumes; a commentary on a Sanskrit text describing early eighteenth century Madras, the *Sarva-Deva-Vilasa;* the *Manual of Administration of Madras Presidency* (1886), and, for the nineteenth and twentieth centuries in particular, family histories, memoirs, and biographical data on Telegu merchants in Madras, articles from the *Madras Mail* newspaper, and souvenirs from organizations founded by the Komati community, such as *the South India Vysia Sangam.*

BRITISH TRADESMEN OF CALCUTTA, 1830-1900:

Citizens in Search of a City?

by

Chris Furedy

This paper is designed to direct attention to an overlooked aspect of the economy and social structure of the nineteenth century port cities of India, the development of a modern retail sector, and of a class of persons referred to simply as "tradesmen." The neglect of the history of retailing in the nineteenth century cities is a world-wide phenomenon: retail trading has everywhere been treated as subsidiary to large scale transactions of production and distribution. Yet the character of the retail sector bears upon some interesting issues in the understanding of the development of the port cities.

One such issue is the nature of entrepreneurship. Most studies of colonial entrepreneurship concentrate on merchants and industrial entrepreneurs; few make any reference to local traders. (Professor Morris's paper at this conference is an example.) However, by any general definition of entrepreneur appropriate to the nineteenth century (the one adopted here is that of G.H. Evans: The person or groups of persons in a firm whose function it is to determine the kind of business that is to be conducted, including the kind of goods and services, the value of them, and the clientele to be served)*, the founders and partners of retail firms must be considered entrepreneurs. A consideration of them will contribute to the understanding of the different levels and types of entrepreneurship, both British and Indian, in the colonial port city.

Then the structure of the retail sector must be explored in order to understand the relationship between the "bazaar" or "lower circuit," and the modern, or "upper circuit," of the dual economies said to characterize the colonial port cities. (The terms, "upper" and "lower" circuits are used by T. McGee in *Peasants in the Cities: A Paradox, A Paradox, a Most Ingenious Paradox,*" Human Organization, Vol. 32, No. 2, 1973, pp. 135-142.)

To what extent was the retail sector interlinked with the commercial sector, the international trade in primary commodities? When did Indians begin to move into modern retailing, and how did they learn its techniques? Did British and Indian retailers come into competition in the port cities? Was the European sector influenced by the methods of the bazaar? Did the colonial environment necessitate changes in British retailing practices?

* G.H. Evans, Jr., "Business Entrepreneurs, Their Major Functions and Related Tenets," *Journal of Economic History,* XIX, 1959, pp. 250, 252.

The social status and political role of the local tradesmen is equally of interest to the historian of the port cities. The awareness that the European tradesmen, themselves a diverse and stratified category, were treated as a distinct "interest" by the colonial administration has enhanced our understanding of the complexities of the social structure of the small European communities in these cities and the dynamics of their local politics. In this paper I argue that the British tradesmen of Calcutta may be regarded as "institutional" as well as economic entrepreneurs for the role they played in promoting the development of Western urban institutions, both voluntary (the Trades Association) and formal (the municipal corporation) in the city.

This paper brings together some preliminary data on the first two of these issues with a more detailed discussion of the last with reference to Calcutta from the 1830s to the end of the century. It is divided into two parts.

In part one I present some general information about the nature of the British tradesmen as a category and the trends in the development of the European retail sector of Calcutta in the second half of the nineteenth century. Tradesmen were a varied group containing several gradations of education, wealth, and social status. They included independent craftsmen (e.g., watchmakers, artists), skilled tradesmen (e.g., cabinet makers, bootmakers), small manufacturers, persons offering services (e.g., midwives, hairdressers, hoteliers), partners of large local trading companies, and members of the "lower professions" (chemists, engineers, and journalists). Most operated within the simple partnership company.

Post-1850 development was characterized by the decline of independent craftsmen and the expansion of the large partnership companies. Trades which showed particular development were building and engineering, pharmacies, printing, and bookselling, drapers, and tailoring. However, there was not a great proliferation of European trading firms in the later nineteenth century; expansion was expressed in an increased size of establishments and in the opening of branch stores in towns such as Simla, Lucknow, Lahore, and Allahabad. British tradesmen became predominantly managerial, employing Indian craftsmen and assistants behind the scenes, so to speak.

In the early part of the century, the small British trading community experienced little competition and made easy profits, catering especially to the Company's military and civil officers. The 1880s and 1890s were hard in comparison. Their profits and planning were seriously affected by the fluctuating value of the rupee. They began to feel the pressure of competition as Indians moved in, particularly into publishing and bookselling, pharmacies, tailoring, hardward, ironmongering, and oilman's stores. Nevertheless, the British tradesmen had carved out for themselves a secure economic niche in Calcutta, supplying the luxury needs of the urban Europeans, catering to the plantation and administrative population of the *mofussil*, and reaching out for the custom of Westernizing Indian families.

There are many aspects of the British retail companies about which we know practically nothing, for no study has been done of any one firm over time. The amount of capital necessary to start a business, the

degrees of risk, profitability, and the nature of the clientele served
all need to be explored. Another topic of interest is the recruitment
of entrepreneurs: How were partnerships formed and managers recruited?
To what extent did kinship-linking provide protection and continuity
for trading firms? Did the qualities of the entrepreneurs change with
the development of a firm--initiative, risk-taking, and capital being
necessary in the founder of a partnership, and managerial skills being
more important in the next generation? Some of these questions may be
unanswerable, for the great majority of tradesmen will always remain
shadowy figures. They were simply not important enough to receive detailed mention in contemporary documents. However, a longitudianl
study of some leading local firms (for instance, Newman and Company,
booksellers, or Burn and Company, architects) would be a useful starting
point for a better understanding of the British retail sector.

Part Two of the paper deals with the tradesmen's influence in
local affairs, particularly exercised through their association, the
Calcutta Trades Association. I argue that the tradesmen had a greater
commitment to Calcutta than to any other group of British residents.
They spent a greater part of their lives there, and their material interests were more tightly bound to the conditions of the city. There was
hardly a civic need that did not engage the tradesmen's interest: Memor-
ials went forth from the Calcutta Trades Association on railways, postal
services, port maintenance, coinage, police, drainage, and taxes.

The Trades Association played a particularly important role in
shaping demands for municipal reform, incorporating ratepayer representation between 1830 and 1875. The 1860s and early 1870s were periods of
significant interaction between trade representatives and Hindu notables
in municipal affairs, with leading tradesmen and publicists acting as the
mentors of Indians in the art of municipal management. This political relationship between Bengalis and British tradesmen was broken in the 1880s
principally by the Ilbert Bill controversy. The tradesmen of the 1880s
and 1890s sided with the majority of the British community in seeking to
restrict the power of the Bengali nationalists in local affairs and particularly in the Calcutta Corporation.

At the end of the century, the British tradesmen were a somewhat
disoriented community. Financially harrassed by the fluctuations of the
rupee, they thought they had been squeezed out of a role in local affairs
by the mobilizing Indian elites of Calcutta. They found it hard to accept
the consequences of their minority status in Calcutta's plural society,
and increasingly felt alien to the city they had tried so vigorously to
shape in previous decades. For all this, they were to prove a particularly
resilient interest in Calcutta and the major trading firms retained their
prominence in local retailing until independence.

SOURCES:

The major primary sources for this paper are the proceedings of the
Calcutta Trades Association, Calcutta; Calcutta and Bengal trade directories;
contemporary newspapers such as the *Indian Mirror*, *The Englishman*, *Bengal
Hurkaru*, *Hindoo Patriot*. In addition, relevant printed and secondary

sources have been consulted.

Standard works on the history of British retailing, such as David Alexander's *Retailing in England During the Industrial Revolution* (London, 1970) and James B. Jeffrey's *Retail Trading in Britain, 1850-1950* (Cambridge, 1954) proved useful in Calcutta's context.

THE GOVERNMENT HOUSE, FORT ST. GEORGE.

110

THE MORPHOLOGY OF MADRAS AS A CITY-STATE

by

Robert Eric Frykenberg

Madras, up through the eighteenth century, can be described as a city-state, possessing many features usually ascribed to both cities and independent states. It was a large and important town, free from external control or direction. Three levels of analysis are necessary for understanding its morphology and its development as a city-state: The first concerns the growth in Madras before and during the East India Company's early rule--a highly pluralistic or segmented polity that reflected social divisions within indigenous society, spatial complexity within the area, and varying interests within the European community itself. The second level of analysis must explain how this fragmented social order gradually developed into a city, that is, how a common municipal authority was able to assert its authority without alienating influential elites as well as to draw the many separate communities within an over-arching institutional framework. The third level requires an understanding of Madras's later role as a cosmopolitan city serving all of South India and regions much farther away.

Madras was the archetype of a segmented system. Its foundation was a clustering patchwork of villages which still remain intact, preserving links with the past. The city grew from these villages and from other indigenous elements introduced during its early years. What enabled the city-state to flourish were these very ties to the local social order, in particular to the several elite communities that dominated the various levels of social organization co-existing within the region before the Europeans arrived.

The expansion of the Company's territory, not only around Madras but also in other parts of South India during the eighteenth century can, in fact, be viewed as a culmination of complex traditional processes long at work within the clustered localities of the region. Prior to the Vijayanagar period, the area around Madras was characterized by clusters of self-contained agrarian settlements gathered into larger, loosely-structured political units. Under the umbrella of Vijayanagar rule, Telegu-speaking warbands superimposed tributary overlordships over this older system. Muslims and Marathas came later and fought for the same holdings and spoils, continuing a pattern of incessant tension, if not warfare, in the area.

Before the final establishment of the Raj, the polity of Madras might best be defined as a "tension state." Some might even call it a "stateless" society. This was based not on a developed system of sovereignty or law but on an intricate pattern of personal and communal rela-

111

tionships within and among a multitude of distinct ethnocultural and socio-political structures. Authority within these structures was exercised in a way not unlike that within a powerful extended family. Tension or "non-peace," if not actual "war," between these many units had become institutionalized and a basic fact of the society, having its own set of rituals and expectations. Absent from this scene were both any single or general common law and any sufficient intermediate structures between universal law (or *dharma*) and local communal custom (or *mamool*).

Within the area that developed into the city-state of Madras there thus existed a multiple morphology of various systems juxtaposed and superimposed on each other. From within this segmented system there emerged certain bonds and the larger formations of political consensus which permitted the establishment of the Madras city-state. Both Baniya communities and the Company skillfully forged personal and functional ties between their own members and members of virtually every community in Madras during its first century of governing. Rituals, ceremonials, festivals, etc., gave witness to the strength of these relationships and demonstrated the growing dimensions and potentialities of a larger political system. Among the earliest and most potent bonds were those formed between Company merchants and Telegu nobles and merchants. These negotiated the contract *(sasanam)* for the creation of Madras in the mid-seventeenth century; Telegu merchants also helped to make Madras renowned as the "Gentu" city.

Creating such links and adhering to local traditions, rules, and the indigenous logic of power, the Company established itself in a position of local leadership in Madras and then gradually extended the perimeters of its power. Like other local authorities who were subject to threats from stronger powers, it resorted to the same means of self-protection. It did what other local lords in the region did which enabled them to survive while larger units crumbled. By mid-eighteenth century Madras was firmly established as a local country power, a city-state fully capable of drawing substantial support from local elements within society in South India. Able to attract a steady stream of talented persons from many communities, it enjoyed a substantial advantage over its competitors. It opened its gates to all and attracted the most venturesome who were asked only to help provide for the common defense and domestic tranquility. Taxes and petty obstructions were minimal; legal redress, provided for all; no religion or customs received special advantage. If the city-state was significant for its respectful tolerance of "private" privilege and communal prejudice, it was also remarkable during its first century for its encouragement to all communities to participate in its "public" life.

A multitude of ethnically and culturally distinct communities were pulled together by the Company in Madras by the central attractions of trust, good faith, credit, confidence, and mutual profit. As practical problems arose, they were met by covenants of mutual benefit and reciprocal obligation. The city-state of Madras was founded upon a constitution of mutual respect and communal restraint in which common welfare was balanced with ritual distance. Careful not to offend against private customs and sensibilities and to play its proper role in ceremonies and rituals, the Company did no more than what was required to nurture respect for its authority.

From this secure base the Company then slowly expanded its authority without losing control over its original domains. The city-state grew until it enveloped over a hundred villages. Each village contributed to the development of Madras, either providing merchants, administrators, *dubashis*, soldiers, artisans, or laborers. All paid taxes. As personal attachments grew, various individuals served as the go-betweens, cultural interpreters, and formulators of a more general regional opinion. Members of this complex layer of intermediaries between the agrarian countryside and the commercial city were responsible for the more profound social integration of the nineteenth century.

This second level of analysis demonstrates the processes by which the morphology of Madras became metropolitan. The city-state drew the scattered settlements together, gradually superimposing its own order upon these domains. Not only spatial patterns were altered by the logic of a metropolitan center but also the conduct of local government. A municipal corporation, free associations, the formation of public opinion, were all aspects of a growing sense of Madras as a "corporate" metropolis with a distinct "corporate" style. In nineteenth century Madras a new measure of cultural synthesis had begun to emerge from the mixture of particular communities and cultures which composed the city.

It was after the Company ceased to rule that Madras, having already developed from a city-state into a metropolitan and imperial capital, became a cosmopolitan center. Serving as the political capital and cultural hub of South India, it began to reach even further. Numerous cultural and ethnic groups came to identify themselves with the city, placing their own stamp upon its character.

No satisfactory explanation has yet been formulated for the rise of the city-state of Madras from the fragmented social, spatial, and political environment of seventeenth and eighteenth century South India. To understand the growth of Madras, it is necessary to give sufficient weight to its polycentric and segmentary features and to the cross-cultural and symbiotic relationships that developed among the elites of this complicated social matrix. These relationships enabled a commonwealth of interests to be forged from among the constituent elements of the society which, on the one hand, respected the identity of each community and culture and, on the other, laid the foundation for the growth of the overarching city-state.

SOURCES

This essay is based on research among the Madras records at the India Office Library, London, and the State Archives at Madras, especially the Board of Revenue Proceedings, Public Consultations, and Madras District Records. Among the printed and secondary sources, mention may be made of H. D. Love, *Vestiges of Old Madras, 1640-1800*, 4 vols., (London, 1913), Talboy Wheeler's, *Madras in the Olden Times*, 3 vols., (Madras, 1861-62), and C. Srinivasachari, *History of the City of Madras* (Madras, 1939).

SOUTH ASIAN ENTREPRENEURSHIP AND THE RASHOMON EFFECT

by

Morris David Morris

The two general explanations of the slow industrialization of the Indian economy under British rule emphasize either the Hindu value system and social structure or the adverse effects of official policy. While these features may have contributed a frame within which economic behavior occurred, they do not explain the specific and diverse entrepreneurial choices actually made. They do not explain why Indian businessmen created the world's fourth or fifth largest cotton textile industry by 1914; they do not explain why, if they were able to develop this industry against great British opposition, they did not develop others; they also do not explain why, if the British promoted jute, they were so unsuccessful in iron and steel.

To explain these paradoxes, we must begin with the proposition that the overwhelming bulk of decisions were made by private entrepreneurs during the British period. At least 90 percent of the gross national product was allocated to consumption and investment by private entrepreneurs. Private decisionmakers were making the choices that largely determined the rates and forms by which modern mechanization was introduced into India. Obviously, those decisions were made within the framework of government policies and local values and social structure, but those who made them invariably sought to obtain the most favorable results within the bounds that the system permitted.

This meant that businessmen had to consider the nature of demand for the product, the supply of productive factors, the prices at which the product could be sold, the cost of producing it, and the rate of return that could be made in one enterprise as against another. The degree to which the combination of these was favorable or unfavorable determined the willingness of private entrepreneurs to choose those techniques of production which, when undertaken on a great scale, we call industrialization. Let me examine the characteristics of each of these elements as the businessman faced them.

First, what was the nature of demand? While India's population was very large, even in 1800, average per capita income was exceptionally low throughout the nineteenth and twentieth centuries. Moreover, much of this income was produced in non-monetized and local activities, a further discouraging factor. (This was all very much different than the situation among the North Atlantic countries when some of them began their industrialization.)

115

Not only was average per capita income low, it was quite unequally distributed. The share claimed by traditional luxury-loving groups tended to be spent on specialities that could not be mass produced but required skilled labor of the older sort. The relatively high incomes concentrated in modern urban centers did offer fairly large blocks of effective demand. But even here there were features that dampened the stimulus to industrialize. The richest and most rapidly growing urban centers after 1800 were great ports like Bombay or Calcutta and some upcountry market towns at important railway junctions. These offered the most market incentives to local businessmen, but they were also most exposed to foreign competition. Nor could foreign competition be limited by tariff protection without adversely affecting merchant groups whose incomes depended on the commerce that would be reduced.

There were also serious inhibitions on the supply side. In India's underdeveloped state, most factors were scarce and costly. This was certainly true of physical capital. Human capital in the form of skilled and technical labor had to be imported, generally, from abroad and was expensive. Fuel was costly and so was domestic transport. Only raw labor was cheap, and sometimes--as in the case of cotton and jute mills--it provided an industrial advantage. But cheap labor typically worked against mechanization. When demand for a product expanded, it did not necessarily put pressure on labor supply or on labor costs relative to other costs. Thus the businessman was not under pressure to seek new ways to produce the product. To the contrary, cheap labor and costly capital encouraged him to expand existing organization rather than shifting to techniques where capital requirements were relatively greater. This was a rational response to relative factor price relationships.

In addition to objective factors, there was a great deal of uncertainty about demand and cost estimations. A well-developed economy will have all sorts of mechanisms by which to reduce uncertainty or insure against it which a developing economy does not have. Thus, the businessmen must accept not merely a higher level of risk but also a much greater range of uncertainty. Aggregate demand is very fragile because it is highly dependent on agricultural activity which is subject to great climatic instability. Moreover, the businessman has no way of estimating the rate at which other entrepreneurs will cut into his market. There are also great uncertainties about production costs. He brought equipment from the West that had been designed to economize on labor relative to capital. He therefore had to redesign or reorganize equipment balance to allow for his very different labor/capital price ratios. The skills he needed to deal with such problems were scarce, if available at all, and the quality, if not the quantity, of his general labor force was dubious. Costs of training and turnover were hard to predict, so the businessman faced great uncertainty about the productivity he could anticipate. Typically, the pioneering businessman also had to provide his own repair shops and power plants as well as maintain larger inventories of raw materials and replacement parts. In effect, he had to allow for greater amounts of fixed and working capital while operating in an underdeveloped credit system which could produce capital only in a most fitful fashion.

These clusters of incalculability combined with the objective inhibitions earlier described to serve as very considerable obstacles to

116

the rapid expansion of mechanized industry. An enterprise had to give promise of a very high rate of return, not only to cover the higher cost of scarce capital but also to allow for the greater risk and uncertainty that existed. Obviously, the higher this rate was, the fewer opportunities there would be that a businessman would find promising at any time.

All this suggests why the general rate of investment in modern factory industry was quite low. In addition, there were factors that account for different responses by different groups. Basically, they rest on the fact that knowledge of the Indian and the international economies was not perfect. Different groups of businessmen had different kinds and amounts of knowledge, based on experience and the sophistication of the institutions at their disposal. This meant that each group would calculate the elements of an apparently identical opportunity--demand, costs, and rates of return--and the reliability of estimates about each quite differently.

Generally speaking, British entrepreneurs tended to invest mainly in activities focused on foreign markets, while Indians generally responded to opportunities that catered primarily to domestic demand because this was the way each group could make use of the institutions and knowledge available to it and select the areas where risks were lowest. This explains why Indians invested so quickly in the cotton textile industry despite their exposure to great economic and political pressure from Manchester and why they were so late to invest in the jute fabric industry even though there was no very great British competition. It also helps explain why the British were so unsuccessful in iron and steel as against the Indian success.

All apparent exceptions to this hypothesis seem to be capable of being explained without doing violence to the facts. The same formulation can be used to explain why some Indian groups entered the modern industrial sector while other did not enter or came into the scene much later. The formulation, based on the nature of risk and uncertainly faced by specific groups, can be extended into other societies. It is not restricted only to South Asian experience.

SOURCES

Material on the problem of entrepreneurial decision-making is fairly extensive. Until recently, it was not very inspiring, being repetitive and uninfluenced by detailed research. One lead into the literature is M. D. Morris, "Values as an Obstacle to Economic Growth in South Asia," *Journal of Economic History*, XXVII, 4, December 1967, pp. 588-607. Evidence to support the argument in this summary will appear in the chapter on Industrialization in the forthcoming "Cambridge Economic History of India." An alternative view which stresses the otherwise neglected influence of British discrimination against Indian businessmen is Amiya Kuman Bagchi, *Private Investment in India, 1900-1939* (Cambridge 1972), particularly Chapter 6. A major survey of current thinking on the subject is the volume edited by Milton Singer, *Entrepreneurship and Modernization of Occupational Cultures in South Asia*, (Duke University Press, 1973).

An interesting and very detailed study of the social character-
istics is G. V. Govind Mudholkar, "The Entrepreneurial and Technical
Cadres of the Bombay Cotton Textile Industry between 1854 and 1914,"
(Unpublished Ph.D. dissertation, The University of North Carolina, 1969)
One should also not miss Thomas Timberg, "A Study of a 'Great' Marwari
Firm: 1860-1914," *Indian Economic and Social History Review*, VIII, 1971.

INDIAN COTTON OPERATIVES.

TOPIC II: DEVELOPMENT AND CHARACTER OF MERCANTILE ELITES (continued)

Session 3

DISCUSSION

122

Session 3

Moderator - Dilip K. Basu

Discussant - Eugene F. Irschick

Susan Lewandowski, *Merchants, Temples, and Power in Madras*

Chris Furedy, *British Tradesmen of Calcutta, 1830-1900: Citizens in Search of a City?*

Robert Eric Frykenberg, *The Morphology of Madras as a City State*

Morris D. Morris, *South Asian Entrepreneurship and the Rashomon Effect*

BASU - This morning we have four papers. The first is by Susan Lewandowski.

LEWANDOWSKI - As the title of my paper indicates, I am dealing with a cultural and social as well as an economic and political analysis. I am attempting a synthesis of different aspects of Madras in its formative years. Moving away from a standard Eurocentric analysis, this paper looks at the indigenous development as an interaction between the colonizers and the colonized, with a stress on the world view of the people involved.

The questions I have raised in this paper are: To what extent were merchants involved in urban development in pre-colonial Asia? What patterns of urban development emerged in terms of their exercise of power? How did their role change after the arrival of the Europeans? And in what way were they responsible for the growth of indigenous institutions and the maintainance of urban settlement patterns which left a mark on port cities in Asia in the past few centuries?

The paper is divided into three sections, the first of which deals with the nature of indigenous urbanization processes, and it is chronologically organized.

123

In this section I look at the period from the thirteenth to the sixteenth century, the period of the Vijayanagar Empire, in order to trade the emerging patterns that became important in the early history of Madras. I have found a model evolving during this period which became important in the colonial port city: Under the early East India Company rule, power over the majority of the urbanites was in the hands of a commercial elite who employed a traditional model of kingship in their exercise of power. The model centered around constant arbitration or the settling of disputes within the domain, many of which were past-oriented.

The second section deals with the intervention of trade and commerce, and the third relates to the preservation of the sacred order which involved the building and the maintenance of temples. This was an important social ritual in south India that I've especially chosen to emphasize in the paper. The fourth is the patronage of art and learning in what I characterize as courtlike environment. The fifth is the use of certain ceremonial elements to delimit status--the use of music, dancing girls, palanquins, and other kinds of ceremonial accoutrements.

The main concern of the paper is the way in which merchants encouraged trade and commerce while attempting to preserve the sacred order. I believe this interaction between the economic and the ritual aspects has been a significant characteristic of Indian Social history.

I deal with the notion of the merchant-broker as king during the period from 1639 to 1800. Although the focus of the paper is the nineteenth century, it has been necessary to provide a historical buildup to this period during which Telegu merchants migrated from the area north of Madras into the Tamil-speaking Madras region. They were the most important merchants who, like many merchant groups in other colonial port cities, were outsiders.

I stress the role of powerful individuals as brokers in the networks that were established. The *dubash*--speaker of two languages--was the broker, and he exercised a great deal of power in this city.

The *dubash* role can be seen in the banking and minting of coins, in urban land investment, in the encouragement of migrants to settle in the city, in a manner that helped maintain his control over left and right hand caste factions and other groups.

Caste issues were most significant in this early period. I argue that, as more groups migrated to the city and rules determining caste hierarchy no longer functioned the way they did in the village, the arbitration power of important individuals increased. Much money and effort went into the building of temples that were redistribution centers for wealth as well as centers for social, cultural, and residential activity. As "ceremonial centers" emerging in the eighteenth century, these were replicas of earlier patterns of urban development in a non-colonial context but were now brought into the colonial city and incorporated as a part of it.

By extension, this meant that the building of temples brought into the city master-builders, carpenters, laborers, etc., affiliated with the construction of temples. This is especially the model that I lay out for the period up to the turn of the nineteenth century. After this period, I see a shift taking place as the British took over political control in South India. They introduced municipal institutions-- hospitals, schools, Western political associations. The nature of trade was also changing. The *dubash* was no longer as important as he had been at an earlier period; agency houses were developing, and it was necessary for merchants to come together in corporate activities within the city. The role of one individual as a powerful force was no longer possible the way it had been at an earlier period.

Along with this, one sees certain Telegu groups responding to new economic opportunities, involving themselves in timber, sugar, cotton, indigo, founding joint stock companies. They were thus participating in a modern sector economically. Yet the temple remained extremely important throughout the nineteenth century where status was affirmed within the city. This has to be seen in the context of the growth of large numbers of powerful and wealthy individuals in the city to a scale that did not exist before. There were people who used their wealth before to develop the ritual sector, but now we see a great deal of competition going on in the city, which was something new. Perhaps the coming together of the ritual and economic aspects in a different way than it happened in traditional India was an important characteristic of the colonial port city.

Pradip Sinha and S. N. Mukherjee point to a similar evolution taking place in nineteenth century Calcutta. They see the powerful individuals in trade also presiding over *dals*, or multi-caste factional groups somewhat analagous to left- and-right-hand factional groups in south India. Also, they point to the emergence of a "raja" model in Calcutta in the same way I have noted its growth in Madras.

The question I ultimately raise from this paper is whether we can find any comparable ceremonial component similar to the function the temple played in the south Indian city, in other cities in India, and Southeast Asia. This is an important component to consider when we deal with the colonial port city: We have to look beyond the economic aspect and deal with the world view and the perception of the people who lived in it.

BASU   -   The next paper is by Chris Furedy.

FUREDY - With this paper we return to a Europe-centered perspective. My main purpose is to draw attention to the
category of retail tradesman--a diverse group of shopkeepers,
craftsmen, and producers, such as watchmakers, bookmakers,
as well as quasi-professionals, such as dentists or journal-
ists--in the economic life of the colonial city.

It is a neglected dimension and not just for the
colonial city. One can find little by way of studies of
retail business in the nineteenth century British cities,
partly because retailing is often regarded as non-productive
and relatively unimportant economically. Naturally, shopkeepers are subordinate in status and significance to industrial entrepreneurs and commercial men. However, I think
that if we are to understand how people lived in a colonial
port city we will have to look at the retailers.

A study of retailing bears upon some major issue areas
in the economy and social life of the port cities, such as
the nature of entrepreneurship. Studies of entrepreneurship
do not usually include shopkeepers and retail traders; they
concentrate on commercial men or industrial initiators. How
do the tradesmen fit into the picture of economic development?
While attempting to answer this question, I wondered how historians of British nineteenth century history have defined
the term "entrepreneur." I came across P. L. Payne's excellent
short study, *The British Entrepreneur in the Nineteenth Century*. Payne
quotes G. H. Evans on the definition of entrepreneur: "The
person or group of persons in a firm whose function it is to
determine the kind of business that is to be conducted, including the kinds of goods and services, the values of them,
and the clientele to be served."

There is nothing in this definition that precludes a
retail firm and its founders. I became aware of different
levels of entrepreneurship as a result of conceiving of the
tradesmen--or some of them at any rate--as entrepreneurs.
Some were, perhaps, only petty entrepreneurs, but some were
not so petty in the end.

Port cities, indeed, cities in general, require different types of entrepreneurship. Looking at a category of people
such as tradesmen, beginning first with British tradesmen then
extending into Indian retail traders, would help us understand
the different qualities of entrepreneurship that were needed
in the port city system. Even within the one category of entrepreneur, the qualities associated with success may have changed
over time. For instance, the person who initiated a new form
of business activity may have needed certain qualities, such
as initiative, the ability to accumulate capital, the ability
to take risks, foresight, etc., that may not have been demanded
a generation or two later by the person who managed the firm.

In looking at the evolution of retail trading in Calcutta,
I find it difficult to disentangle the developments of retailing

126

on a worldwide scale from the particular conditions of the colonial city. Further research is necessary to determine to what extent retailers in Calcutta were being innovative at certain times. I hypothesize in the paper that they were innovative in informational techniques. For instance, in order to reach the upcountry clientele, the large Calcutta retailers developed, in the later nineteenth century, elaborately illustrated catalogues, "Sears Roebuck" style, which impressed British visitors to India. I get the impression that they were ahead of their time in developing such techniques so as to reach out to a distant clientele scattered throughout India and beyond, to Burma, Ceylon, and even, later, Aden.

Retailers used both railways and the postal service to reach their most distant customers. The two are, of course, inter-connected, but the retailers' use of the postal system was especially interesting. An important development for Calcutta retailers was the ability to have a C.O.D. system (or "Value Payable Post" as it was called in India). It was something, in fact, that they pushed for in the 1870s. It was a great fillip to their ability to reach out to more distant customers and to maintain their virtual monopolies in certain lines. They were greatly agitated when the Government of India allowed V.P.P. direct between Britain and India early in this century.

British retailers provided an arena for interaction between the bazaar, or what T. G. McGee calls "the lower circuit" of the urban economy, and the modern or "upper" circuit. First, there was the movement of Indians into modern retailing. The trades they first moved into were publishing, pharmacies, tailoring, and hardware. How did they learn about British retailing techniques? Did they simply observe what the British retailers were doing and copy them? Did Indians become apprentices and learn something of these techniques from the inside? To what extent did the British employ Indian craftsmen in businesses such as tailoring, boots and saddle-making, furniture manufacture, and so on? We know they did all these things, but the extent to which they learned these things and the sorts of interactions that resulted, we know little of at the moment. It is important to emphasize, however, that the Indians were not always at the receiving end in these interactions--European jewelers learned from their Indian craftsmen, too.

We know that Britishers became interested in establishing bazaars in Calcutta in order to control the quality and conditions of sale of food. There were attempts in the 1860s and later to set up bazaars in competition with Bengali-owned bazaars, the Dharamtala Market, for instance. Private enterprise having failed, the Calcutta Corporation was persuaded into the venture, and New Market was opened in 1874. Ostensibly modelled on British municipal markets of the 1840s, especially those established in Birmingham and Manchester, it also had

characteristics of the more traditional Calcutta produce
bazaar. The Calcutta New Market may provide a prime example
of interaction between modern British retailing and the
Indian bazaar economy.

Another area of interest is the relationship between
the retail sector in Calcutta and the commercial sector of
the import-export trade. There was, I feel, a much greater
inter-connection prior to 1850 than we have suspected. Some
of the Calcutta shopkeepers acquired goods for retail from
the agency houses rather than importing directly, although
the larger retail firms did import on their own behalf. (This
explains why the Calcutta Trade Association obtained representation on the Calcutta Port Commission and shows an interest
in the affairs of the Port, especially import duties, custom
duties, currency regulations, and so on.)

The agency houses largely cornered the retail and wholesale market of wines and spirits, though the impression I get
for after 1850 is that the retail and commercial sectors became more separate, more specialized in their institutions and
their operations.

The present paper is divided into two parts. In the
first part I gather together information on the nature of
European and British retailing where the major issue is the
nature of the partnership companies dominating the retail sector.
Very few of these retail companies converted into limited liability companies in the nineteenth century. A great deal of
capital was not required and, therefore, there was no particular reason to start a limited liability company. The Great
Eastern Hotel was one of the few which, after financial trouble,
was converted in the 1860s from a partnership company to a
limited liability company. Most retail businesses were single
proprietary or had two or three partners.

Unfortunately, we do not know much about the operation
of the retail companies. Issues that Morris has raised in his
paper on entrepreneurship about the amount of capital necessary
to operate, the risks taken, profitability, even the nature of
the clientele are obviously critical, but we have at the moment
little data and, as partnership companies were not required to
register in the nineteenth century, we may never know much.

The recruitment into the partnership companies--yet
another question of entrepreneurship--seems to have been predicated on the premise that the partners would naturally draw
upon kinship networks while choosing a successor. But most
had difficulty in enticing sons and nephews into coming out
to Calcutta to take over a bootmaking operation or some such
thing, and so unrelated assistants were often promoted into
partnership. Again, there is a dearth of information about
these men--they were not important enough to be noticed in the
press, in obituaries, for instance. The interesting personal

128

details that one searches for so seldom turn up that one is
forced to conclude that this feature of the colonial city
will perhaps remain incompletely understood.

In the second part of the paper I deal with the
tradesmen's influence in local affairs. From about the 1820s
and the 1830s, the tradesmen emerged as probably the only
group of non-official Britishers who took a consistent interest
in the condition of Calcutta, and who were, in fact, in the
forefront in demanding municipal reform and certain citizen's
rights, first for the Britishers, of course, and then for
substantial Indian ratepayers. They had an influence on legal
institutions as well, being largely responsible for the
foundation of a Small Causes Court in Calcutta.

An interesting dimension of the activity of this group
of "free citizens" in Calcutta was their interaction with
Hindu notables in the 1860s and 1870s within the Calcutta
Corporation. For a time there was a close agreement on the
municipal policies and action among both groups of representatives. It was at this time that a theme of persistent concern
in Calcutta's municipal government emerged--ratepayer representation in the municipal constitution. Many people have the
impression that this concern originated with the Surendranath
Banerjea group who entered the Calcutta Corporation in 1876.
Now it is clear that the themes of how the Calcutta constitution
should be shaped and what powers should be secured to municipal
commissioners had been thrashed out by the interaction between
tradesmen representatives and Hindu property owners in the 1860s
and were taken up by the later "nationalists" who re-echoed
these themes for the remainder of the century.

The history of such interaction (between tradesmen and
Bengali property owners) in municipal affairs is a short one.
It broke down partly because of the introduction of elective
principle in 1876. It was not, however, that tradesmen objected
to Indians entering the municipal system via election. They
believed that the Bengal government had granted election to
Calcutta only by putting much stronger controls on the Corporation, and they largely boycotted the first elections. The
Ilbert Bill agitation further eroded the spirit of cooperation
with the Bengalis at the local level. After 1882, the trades-·
men, instead of representing a liberal force in municipal management, began to side with the more conservative elements among
Calcutta's non-official British population who consistently
objected to the growing Bengali influence in the city's municipal affairs.

The picture one gets by the end of the century of the
British tradesmen group is a rather depressed one. The tradesmen were hard hit by fluctuations in the value of the rupee
which affected them more severely than it affected those in the
import-export trade. And yet they couldn't attract much sym-
pathy for their plight. For instance, there was no trades

representative on the Currency Commission. Concurrently,
they felt resentment that their pioneering role in the city
government had yielded gradually to Bengali domination in
municipal affairs. By the end of the century, one finds
them expressing doubt about their place in Calcutta's society
and politics.

     I haven't made comparative remarks in the paper for
the simple reason that I couldn't find any publications on
retailers in the other colonial port cities. However, there
are several comparative issues I can pose: To what extent
were Calcutta tradesmen as a group unique in India? They
were the largest group of retail traders. They seemed to
have played a much more prominent role in shaping the issues
for urban development. I don't find much mention of the
Bombay Trades Association--there was one, but does one ever
hear anything of it? But the Calcutta Trade Association had
something to say on all the major issues in Calcutta in the
late nineteenth century. So, are they unique in the role they
played and in the concern they showed? And what happened to
the development of British retailers in cities where there
was an indigenous group who entered into modern retailing--
in the Southeast Asian cities, for instance? Perhaps in
Bombay the relative insignificance of the (European) Trades
Association is due to the fact that the Parsis entered into
modern retailing there very early, which must surely have
restricted the opportunities for Europeans. I suggest the
whole area of retail trading and entrepreneurship is ripe for
more research.

BASU - The next paper is by Robert Frykenberg.

FRYKENBERG - The paper I have put before you is the result of
     many years of questioning some of the basic assumptions about
     the Eurocentric way of looking at political systems; the
     connotative freight we carry along with our concepts of "state,"
     "kingship," authority, land "ownerships," and so on.

          What I am trying to do is put together perceptions of
     a social-political system. I also tend to shy away from the
     word, "order." One could well be daring and try to call it a
     "system-of-force-in-a-colloidal-suspension," if I can borrow
     the term from chemistry. It is hard for me to find a single
     writ of law or a single set of political circumstances that
     applied in all places at all times. Because of this, I have
     put together a polycentric, multi-cultural, "multi-polity"
     model--if I may coin a new word--for a city structure in which
     one sees a process by which gradual overlays of metropolitan
     development occurred without disturbing the internal self-
     governing entities that had been there all along.

          With regard to how one arranges space or how one
     arranges power and kinship, an equivalence between the term
     "king" and "raja" poses problems. The way these arrangements

were perceived was so different within the outlook of families
and villages and of little kingdoms and big kingdoms within
the south Indian context that I'm not sure we can take our
nice, neat European and English word, "King," and apply it
easily in India. Depending on the context, it sometimes could
have meant "prince" or "noble"; at other times it could have
meant something else. When one comes across the term "raja"--
which is not a Telegu word nor a Tamil word--and when words
other than *nayak, poligar* are found in the records, their sense
and impact may vary from "kingpins" to "big wheels" or
"important fellows." (Usually, in English records the Tamil
and Telegu or other local concept then in use is our only
concept.) A good Telegu word was "Pedda Dora," or "big lord",
but he could be the "big lord" of anything from a village to
a family or a temple or any large-spread, important operation.
It is a word by which to identify who was the "Boss."

I'm not sure we can easily transfer these concepts
across cultures. What I have tried to do in my paper is to
identify at least three levels of analysis, although there
are perhaps other levels of analysis. These can also be seen
as successive stages of development. What I have perceived
is a series of successive overlays, a process that commenced
but did not end.

First I have attempted to explain the growth of a coastal
and maritime polity out of a highly segmented social and cultural system within a pattern of highly segmented social and
cultural system within a pattern of highly segmented communal
spaces, growing in power and size until it encompassed well
over a hundred villages, to say nothing of the fields and
paddies that lay between them--all under the shadow of a somewhat segmented "Raj."

The Company's role, especially in its earlier stages,
was very much within the traditions of this segmented pattern,
insomuch so that, even when more metropolitan developments were
occurring in the eighteenth century, there were centers in
Madras that were at variance with Fort St. George, a circum-
stance leading to disputes as to where the real or the greater
ritual or cosmic power was actually located. Was it at Fort
St. George, or outside? We need to remember that the Mughal
Nawab of the Carnatic was a permanent resident of Madras from
the middle of the eighteenth century onwards and was drawing
around himself a circle of English, Armenian, Tamil, and Telegu,
as well as Muslim, courtiers and power-brokers. English brokers
were working under him, both in India and in Europe. So one
has a sandwiching effect in which the English were serving
Hindus and Hindus were serving English in a multiple-layered
system in which the Nawab himself did not hesitate to send his
brokers to Calcutta or to London, and so on.

At the second level, I have sought to discover how, out
of all this complexity, a consensual system evolved in which

more than simple force was applied by a superior or "colonial" power over others. The Company's "state" rulers commanded neither the money nor the men to be able to bring this about on their own. Nor could much be expected from London. It was necessary to get a general or ruling consent of all concerned communities to submit to domination by a profitable enterprise that was mutually profitable.

A great deal of indigenous and local material--Indian money and Indian manpower--was involved in this operation. Here I seek to show how a metropolitan system, a governing corporation or sets of interlinking corporations, could be forged so that none of the elite groups--whether martial or mercantile, ritual or sectarian--were irrevocably or violently alienated. The power of one or two of these groups to destroy or undermine the emerging structure was quite significant, and I don't think this angle has been explored enough.

Eventually, in spite of highly unique, insulated, ritually-separated, individually self-sufficient and self-governing sets of communities, each with its own village or its own settlement or its own temple, town, quarter, or hamlet, an overarching metropolitan system emerged. The perception of the outsiders was very important here--a point that both Lewandowski and Neild have made in their papers on Madras. The Portuguese were outsiders, the Telegus were outsiders, the English were outsiders--on the metropolitan scale. All of the rulers were outsiders, and yet this in no way affected the sense of pride or of complete self-sufficiency, I might almost say, a kind of cosmic and eternal arrogance, that continued in Mylapore. With regard to these "scrubby" types that came in to make money, Mylapore people remained unflappable. But, many centuries earlier, had not even the Brahmans of Mylapore themselves come as outsiders?

Thus, whether they maintained their own distinctness and strength ("magic") within an enclosure of a fortress or of another enclosure, such as in the Nawab's case of Chepauk Palace or, for sectarian ritualists, within the enclosure of a temple, each was part of the plurality being put together. There were, therefore, multifarious kinds of "kings," kings that went to the temples, kings that went to the Mosque, and still others, as in the case of the Armenians who found their satisfaction and satisfied their sense of ritual importance as to who was the "big" Armenian of Madras by going to the Armenian church.

The density of churches in Madras surpassed the density of churches (per square mile) elsewhere in India. The density of temples and, curiously, even the density of mosques, was also greater in Madras. There was a Muslim space in Madras long before the Muslims began to perceive of themselves, after the eighteenth century, as being politically out of the picture.

Recently, in connection with my research on Tinnevelly, I have discovered another fascinating feature: It is the fact that roads and streets were "private"--that is, communal--that they were meant for you and your people and your clients, and not for anybody else. Only as a metropolitan system over-laid these private roads did the "public" highroad emerge. This was really a radical event in Madras. Prior to this time only certain special people were allowed on proper roads, and the ritually unclean were not allowed on many roads and streets. This has come as a rather jolting realization, especially as we assume that roads have always been public. Apparently, they were not.

A common municipal authority with a central metropoli-tan government began to provide the minimal essentials for all and overlaid all communal localities. Previously, each community had provided for its own watchmen, guards, police, justice, water, food, and other amenities. Within its com-pound walls it had governed itself. And I would say that each had its own view of what "ownership" or "property rights," in terms of land, was or was not. There wasn't a common view of "ownership" until the Company imposed it and codified it with-in a common body of law. And, even then, this view prevailed only in places or in spheres where the Company imposed it.

What Neild has described in her paper as the re-defining of the boundaries of the city came slowly toward the beginning of the nineteenth century. The strength of the common insti-tutional authority that grew in direct proportion to the number of burdens surrendered to that authority, or taken up by such authority, whether by appropriation or by imposition, constitu-ted a long and gradual and complicated process. This process is still incomplete. That is why the question as to exactly at what time a modern city can be declared to have come into existence in Madras remains problematic. That's why people still jokingly call Madras a village or a collection of villages.

Finally, at the third level of analysis, I have examined "the cosmopolitan element." How is it that Madras was at once Telegu and not Telegu? Madras was and is cosmopolitan in the sense that this was a city of India, not just of south India, and, ultimately, a city of the world. This is a separate sub-ject, and I really haven't examined it very far nor shall I attempt to elaborate upon this theme here.

BASU - Thank you. Our last paper is by Morris D. Morris.

MORRIS - I'm concerned in this paper with the question of why was Indian development so slow during the nineteenth and twentieth centuries. The typical answer has been, of course, government policy or culture, the social structure and values of the system. This provides a framework for a statement, but it doesn't tell us why entrepreneurs made specifici deci-sions and it doesn't tell us why the decisions are distributed in the way they were.

133

When one reads the literature on Indian entrepreneurship, one gets the impression that only the government was
making decisions, and the State was taking all the action.
In reality, however, what we have are private decisions made
by private individuals. The question to ask then is, Why
did individual entrepreneurs make the choices they did?

Here I stress cost and demand, profitability, which
offer some insight into a rather worn-out subject like entrepreneurship, into some of the paradoxes that otherwise remain.
The most obvious paradox is that, if government policy was
so important, why did the Indians organize a cotton textile
industry? If there were one industry that any entrepreneur
wouldn't dare touch because of the government policy, the
textiles would be that, but the Indians still plunged full
steam into it and built the fourth or fifth largest textile
industry in the world against Manchester. They defeated Manchester, not only in India but also in the yarn markets of
China in the late 1890s. This paradox should be viewed in
contrast to the non-entry of Indians into the jute industry.
Manchester was surely far more important in the whole busines
than the trivial jute industry was in Britain. I am proposing
a functionalist approach that may help explain this riddle.

First, I point out the general low level of investment
in the Indian economy. Here I am focusing mainly on the factory system because that is where my research experience lies.
I argue that there were just generalized barriers to extensive
investment, if one defines it as a private decision-making
operation. The structure of demand in the Indian system was
unfavorable. Average per capita incomes were very low, and
this is historically true. It is not only that the average
per capita income was low, but also that even where some incomes, like urban incomes, were reasonably high, those incomes
were high for certain purposes in places where industry and
entrepreneurs were most exposed to competition.

Another factor ought to be taken into account here, something we have neglected too much. It is the climatic instability in the Indian system which affected the structure of
agricultural incomes and produced an area of uncertainty because of capital destruction, which is important.

If the structure of demand in general was unfavorable,
let's look at the structure of supply, especially the costs
that were involved. In general, they were relatively high because of the under-developed character of the system vis-à-vis
all others. The only thing in which India was largely favored
was in its supply of raw labor which was adverse to moving
toward mechanization and encouraged a pattern of using labor
rather than capital. There were, therefore, real cost differences as well as great uncertainties.

This explains why entrepreneurs--European as well as
Indian--were not aggressive. The Indian system was such that
134

it wasn't going to attract enormous amounts of investment. But then the question is that there are barriers that affect different groups differently.

Economists assume that opportunity is hard to come by and that it is the same thing for every group in the system. So we ask ourselves, Why didn't the Indians respond to opportunity if it were the same thing for them as for Europeans? The point that derives out of my scouring of Karl Mannheim is the theme that knowledge and social organizations are not perfect, that groups fit into social settings, that groups have different perceptions of real costs and risks; there are different kinds of uncertainties, different kinds of knowledge by virtue of the position in the social system where one exists. And this leads to different perceptions of costs and rates of return.

I suggest that, in India, one can identify four different groups in terms of behavior. One: foreign participators who really didn't mix with the native environment. This would include a large part of the managing agency system. Second: the foreign participators who _were_ involved in indigenous enterprises, behaving more like Indians in certain circumstances. It was true of some of the foreigners in Bombay who were distributors. Third: the sophisticated, urban Indians, the Bombay Parsi participants, for example, and then most *mofussil* groups.

Now, each of these groups perceived the investment setting quite differently, responded differently, and faced a different range of choices. This may help to explain, I suggest, the puzzle of why Indians didn't invest in railways, although they were not denied access to them. There were two rates of profit to which the groups were responding; the Europeans were making judgments in terms of the prevalent British system, so that anything above the British rate was a good rate of return. Indians were looking at alternative opportunities essentially within the Indian setting, and the guarantee of 5 percent was not lucrative to the ordinary Indian participant, while it represented a much more meaningful thing to the British participant.

In other words, the outsiders operated from different bases, with different perspectives, and made their judgments accordingly. Obviously, they understood the foreign trade activity the best, which explains their widest participation in that sphere. But, as they began to think in terms of operating inside India, they faced a whole series of uncertainties so that the risks became greater for them as they moved up-country. From the point of view of the Indian, the problem was exactly the reverse.

If we look at the entrepreneur's choices this way, the particularities of British investment don't have to get involved in the obfuscations of the imperialism problem. One can still talk about why British capital was shipped abroad, but the particular forms of it didn't depend on exploiting the society in a particular way. It represented the choices that were quite reasonable for participants in the Indian system.

I also deal with the problem of not only European *vs.* Indian but of how different Indian groups made a choice. I suggest that there was no specific virtue to industrialization: It might have been desirable to society to industrialize, but the private entrepreneur was mainly concerned about the maximizing of a rate of return. To the Indian entrepreneur, involvement in social and cultural activities was significant. I have a footnote on how, despite all the changes, Hinduism still looks much the same.

I identify the changes within Hinduism as ritual foreshortening, ritual specialization, ritual neutralization, and ritual rationalization. It seems to me that an enormous amount of change might take place without affecting the formal structure. One can look at the formal characteristics of Hinduism and find them unchanged whereas, in fact, they were and are changing.

Then I raise the question of how caste and social structure bear on the problem. I raise the point about the Marwaris, why they specifically come into the picture. Without making a particular argument, I would use the broad brush. Private decision-making was crucial here as elsewhere, and a close look at this may help explain the Indian absorption of the modern corporation, the limited liability company. Why did Indians use the joint stock company where the British did not? And why did they use the Managing Agency which was created by the British?

One can show here how values entered into the institutional arrangements that were at stake; in the British cotton textile industry, the partnership form was decisive up to World War I, except in spinning in a minor flurry in the late 1880s. There was, in general, either individual proprietorship or partnerships even with fairly large cotton textile enterprises.

On the other hand, in India there was this leap for the joint stock device. Why should the Indians have leapt for this great modern innovation while the British were not using it even though they invented it? The answer lies in the reality that the Indians were unable to and have not used the partnership within families, but links among families are extremely difficult to find. Why? Partnership implies unlimited liability which, in the extended family structures, would raise problems of uncertainty--who would bear the liability? How would one sort it out among participating family groups? But the

136

corporation created an impersonal pattern of capital: A
pool of capital was put out in the middle of the table;
shares were issued and handed out to the families involved.
This, then, didn't get one involved in the structure of
the family. By accident, the joint stock devi e solved a
lot of problems for Indian entrepreneurs who used it as a
mechanism for distributing risk among a wide variety of
people, in fact, making it a more efficient mechanism for
mobilizing capital than it was in Britain or in the United
States for a long period of time.

BASU - The discussant this session is Eugene Irschick.

IRSCHICK - First, let me address myself briefly to the problems
raised by Frykenberg and Lewandowski. The problem that Lewandowski raises is that of the merchant-prince who came to
Madras as an outsider and assumed the role of a lord who not
only exuded political ambiance but cultural and, specifically,
religious ambiance as well.

Frykenberg has some questions about terminology. I'm
not much concerned about terms and am more interested in how
these lords acted in reality. I am convinced that they were
lords. I find Lewandowski's point that these Beri Chettiars,
Komatis, and Balijas were Telegus from Andhra who settled
down in the Madras area meaningful in more ways than one.
One finds their counterparts settling in other Tamil-speaking
rural areas. For instance, there is enough evidence to show,
following Burton Stein--although his is secondary evidence--
that a large number of *zamindars* in the Tamil region were Telegus. These people, however, didn't come like the Beri Chettiars
and Komatis from a trading caste background but were martial
groups. The interesting point is that both groups operated the
same way: they attracted artisans, built temples, and managed
to maintain their authority and control over textiles. I have
no doubt in my mind that the process Lewandowski suggests as
operating is in a large way correct.

My main criticism is that she doesn't address herself,
perhaps by purpose, to the fact that, as the nineteenth century wore on, more and more of these "local princes," or
whatever terms one chooses to use, came from Tamil castes.
Many of these men were *Mirasidars* who either had the area that
the city took over or they were directly from the outside area.
Some among these men, interestingly, formed the group that
ultimately emerged into the basis of the Justice Party in 1916.
It is of interest also that, in 1956, when the Andhra State
was formed, Telegus left Madras city in droves, and the amazing
thing is that almost all came back. The point I'm trying to
make is about continuity; what had taken two, three hundred
years to build up in Madras were things that could not easily
be replicated outside of Tamilnad.

Under the Tamil Nationalist party--the D.M.K.--government,
Telegu and merchant families adopted Tamil names, joined the

137

D.M.K., and some have become important politically. In other words, the development that Lewandowski describes obviously took many years to form and was not something that even a hostile political force could mutilate. The Telegu families now control the High Court of Madras. This is interesting. Because it used to be in the hands entirely of Tamil Brahmins, but now it's entirely in the hands of the successors of these merchant princes from the seventeenth and eighteenth centuries.

Such resiliency and continuity suggests that the transactional relationships the merchant princes had developed were obviously functional. They were outside the purview of the British; when the British stopped giving money to the temples, according to the Act of 1863, the power of the merchant princes became even stronger. Although they were told to pay rates, my argument is that such a measure enhanced their authority, making them lords in their own right.

Finally, a few remarks on Furedy's paper: The tradesmen were definitely entrepreneurs if only because they were taking risks. They didn't do well sometimes when they took risks as there was a basic shift in the balance of their exchange. In the early part of the nineteenth century there were people obviously who offered goods and services essential to the management and continuance of the British in Calcutta. They appeared not to have invested themselves in any great way in land. In the last part of the nineteenth century, they lost this balance of authority, they lost the equipment that was needed, and they didn't have the land and the political control that was essential. What this suggests is that the British tradesmen had lost their importance. My argument, however, is that the British tradesmen kept right on going. Even after Independence, British tradesmen have functioned importantly in Calcutta. So, I am stressing continuity here, too.

I will leave Morris's paper. It is a provocative paper, though I feel that Morris is right in suggesting that the notion of risk-taking is entirely an individual matter. I am impressed most firmly by his railways argument, showing how the British were able to use the advantage and the Indians were not. The point about the Indian family structure being more valuable in terms of their use of Company structure is well taken. But I would like to leave it there.

BASU - Thank you. It's now open to discussion.

NEILD - It is interesting that both Frykenberg and I have come up with pretty much the same analysis of Madras, although working quite separately. I'm not sure if that means we're right or else that the analysis is very obvious.

In my work, I try to delineate the various components of Madras that he refers to as "the segments." I also emphasize

138

the overlay of what I call "colonial space," which he calls
"metropolitan space," over the many ethnic parts of the
city. In both our views this is an example of the way the
ruling power gradually penetrated and brought together, to
some extent, the segments in the town. This also fits in
well with the remark that Professor Das Gupta made yesterday
about the changing role of these cities from port enclaves
to actual colonial cities within a larger system about the
end of the eighteenth century. This overlay of European
influence and power in Madras City, occurring in the late
1700s, reflected the city's new function as a colonial power
center.

MURPHEY - I wish to make some brief comments on Morris's
paper. I find it enormously helpful. People involve themselves in matters that they understand. People who knew the
domestic and regional markets and their problems would obviously involve themselves among them. Outsiders were excluded, not simply by the usual guild rules, although these
operated in certain cases. They was an effort to exclude
outsiders, by which they meant not simply pale-faced Westerners
but other Indians or Asians as well.

On the other hand, the goods for which markets were
external, primarily Western, most of what was flowing out
from all of these Asian countries was monopolized--again, not
principally because foreigners attempted to discriminate
against Asians in keeping them out by guild rules, but because
they, the Asians, didn't seek entrance. They didn't understand
that market. They realized that they were not able to function effectively in it. The only footnote I would offer in
this connection is to say how beautifully this explanation fits
the China Coasts, right down to the last needle.

The curious thing in China--I'm sure you can find
parallels elsewhere--is that there was this split also among
the Chinese merchants who remained in control of their own
system a great deal more effectively than the Indians did.
They had for a long time, traditionally--and it has continued
through the period of foreign domination--made a distinction
between Chinese merchants dealing primarily in overseas trade
to Southeast Asia, who were a different group and were excluded
from (or perhaps did not seek entry into) the domestic market
where a different group of Chinese merchants managed. These
merchants had the same problems or opportunities, serving as
links between an overseas market they knew something about and
where their kindred or representatives were based, on one hand,
and the internal networks from which and to which goods from
Southeast Asia were then being distributed.

The overseas Chinese merchants, in effect, operated
only abroad. They brought goods into the ports and then turned
the whole business over to a different set of Chinese merchants
who managed distribution and assembly. Foreigners were fitted

into the traditional Chinese notion of tributary trade. In this sense they represented nothing new. They were just people who came from a little farther away, who were specialists in overseas markets as Chinese merchants before them had been but who had no place to stand, no way of operating, in involving themselves in matters internal. That was a different set of specialists. That, to me at least, is very helpful.

METCALF - I find the Madras papers fascinating. They fit in better than I thought they would with yesterday's discussion of Karachi and the western Indian port cities. When we talk about segmentation and separation, about migrants like the Telegu merchants in Madras City, we are placing Madras as in the same ballpark as Karachi.

I would be inclined to withdraw the dichotomy about the east and west coasts of South Asia that I proposed yesterday afternoon, although I would still emphasize that they were all very colonial. But I don't want to worry about the term "colonial" now. The term that bothers me today is "kingship." The term has a reductionist ring. Let me quote a sentence from the Lewandowski paper: "These merchants use wealth acquired through their association with the East India Company to legitimize their status in the building of temples and the patronage of religious institutions already in existence in Madras." This does not strike me as being anything more than a standard process of social mobilization and raising of status which was done by everybody from the English wool merchants of the fourteenth century who build churches to William Randolph Hearst's castle on the California coast. This is a general phenomenon; it has little to do with the Hindu kingship.

LEWANDOWSKI - What I see as important here is that it was not until the Vijayanagar period that large numbers of temples were built in South India and that worship became temple-centered. I see a continuation of this process into the colonial period. The analogies with church-building, etc., do not relate this as a way of perceiving what was happening.

FRYKENBERG - A quick comment: Before the great superstructures that were being raised during the Vijayanagar period, there were few, if any, great "temples." But what do we mean when we talk about temples? What were the indigenous words that were once used to refer to "temple"? What is the Tamil word for "temple"? What's the Telegu word for "temple"? The Portuguese gave us the word "pagoda," --a word that then swept across Asia. The Telegu word for "temple" means "big house." Perhaps it was a palace and, hence, it was a private, personal, familial, and communal, not a public institution. It was also a collectivity or cluster of endowments and functions relating to a deity, with various communities (or "persons") struggling over privileges of proximity and *puja*. As such, it served as an avenue (or agency), not just for legitimizing one's own

140

position within the greater and larger spheres of domain, but it also serves as an instrument for the enhancement of one's own status--if you will pardon any mixing of metaphors: for one's being "a big wheel" on the scene, or for one's being a mountain among molehills.

Thus, relationships and transactions with a "personage" of royal-divinity, forming an image dwelling within the innermost recesses of its "palace" or "great house" (i.e. "temple") would tend to be individualistic and polymodular rather than centrally bureaucratic or hierarchically integrated. Without a reigning deity--as a focal point (or linchpin)--separate pieces would have no reason for relating to each other, no structure or status. The "princely" attributes associated with a temple deity were somewhat like those of the head of a multinational corporation or a scattered chain of retail outlets rather than those more purely "political" ones that we tend to associate with great monarchical kingships such as that realm, that integrated State, ruled by the "Sun King" of France. In this sense it is a very different kind of segmented or modular "kingship" that was being legitimized in each temple transaction.

MASSELOS - Lewandowski is obviously relating the theories of kingship to mercantile caste. What I would have like to see in her paper is some information on the ethos of mercantile castes before they migrated. Did they have the same ethos then? Certainly, once they were in the cities she is convincing over the point that merchants did build temples, and that they were usually private. This would also seem to be the case elsewhere--thus, most of the examples I can think of in Bombay were also private.

MILONE - I would like to ask, What was the position of the temple in relationship to the city? One normally thinks of the temple as the central focus of the town. Were the temples in Madras City foci of self-contained districts?

LEWANDOWSKI - This is something I haven't mapped out spatially, but I'm arguing that the temple provided a center for activity and it is the center that I am focusing on rather than the boundaries that defined that center. What I've done is to take a look at those temples that had *vahanas* or cars, vehicles for processions.

In a city like Madurai, which has car streets, the constant processional around the temple defines that space. The streets exist because it is necessary to have a certain width in order to hold the festivals. A large number among the temples that exist in Madras today do have *vahanas*. What this means is that the streets wouldn't have been as wide under other circumstances.

CONLON - I think Masselos's suggestion about looking at the ethos of the merchants is a good one. This should be viewed

141

in conjunction with the fact that the merchants Lewandowski talked about in her paper had very little status in the community. Another important facet worth probing is that these merchants, among other things, resolved disputes. I would argue that this was a "kingly" function.

IRSCHICK - There is a reference in Lewandowski's paper to the involvement of the East India Company in temple affairs. Were the British also in the thrall of this generalized model of kingship?

LEWANDOWSKI - I believe so. In the patterns of interaction, this emerged. For instance, when a merchant completed an economic transaction with a company official, he demanded to be honored with a piece of scarlet cloth. Such compliance was almost taken for granted. And the English responded by having processions with dancing girls and musicians in their honor. Bernard Cohn is working currently on a similar situation in North India on the British use of the function of the *Durbar*.

BASU - One may ask at what point were the merchants mimicking the kingly model, and when perhaps were they simply mimicking the model of rich merchants who had done it before? Was it, in effect, a mercantile rather than an exclusively kingly style emerging?

NEILD - While the merchants' influence was great in the city, it must be balanced against that of older agrarian-based authorities. For one thing, the merchants' temples were built mainly during the eighteenth and early nineteenth centuries, but in Madras Town and the suburbs there also existed many older temples that were still controlled by local landowners.

Moreover, the merchants' role as arbitrators in conflict resolution competed with that of other more traditional arbitrators who still held authority within the city. For example, there was the institution of the Nattar-Desaye which controlled much of the right-hand caste activities within eighteenth and early nineteenth century Madras. The Nattar was a Tamil Vellalar of agriculturist headmen with strong local roots. The Desaye, a Baliga Chettyii, who, since Vijayanagar days, was responsible for adjudicating caste disputes among the lower ranking right-hand Telegu castes. They were jointly recognized by the company as the chief right-hand caste spokesmen and leaders, and were routinely referred to in caste matters.

REED - In Southeast Asia, the temples in periods of early urbanism played a critical role in the actual definition of the city. They marked the nuclear area; they were the catalysts of development and the generators of urban space. Control of the temple implied ownership of the city and, thereby, dominion throughout the kingdom. This condition endured until the coming of the Europeans. But even then the Buddhist pagoda, the Hindu temple,

and the Christian church remained important as symbols iden-
tifying urban communities. The question is, How was this
temple of commercial genesis viewed by the people? Did it
also mark a distinctive community?

LEWANDOWSKI - It depended on who built the temple. One example
is the Kanyaka Parameswari temple built by the Komatis whose
head man happened to be a rich merchant in the city. The
temple is still, in 1976, owned and controlled by the Komati
community. It is an integral part of the community, and its
deity, Kanyaka Parameshwari, is the symbolic head of the
community.

Beginning with the late nineteenth century, there were
changes in the use of space. As Susan Neild has shown, there
were indications of European, or metropole, spaces, and
people were beginning to move out of the Blacktown area where
these temples were located, into the suburbs.

There was a disaggragation of residential space from
the temple. The temple was no longer functioning traditionally
as a cultural center the way it did before. So, my conclusion
is that the temple still remained an important economic institution and a place where power rested but it was no longer a
residential or a cultural focus as it had been previously.

REED - I have two questions: One: A nuclear urban zone demar-
cated by imposing temples of commerce and known as "the central
business district" in America as well as in certain cities of
Western origin elsewhere in the world, began to suffer some
decline in recent generations as outlying commercial areas
developed in expanding metropolitan regions. Can this phenomenon be observed also in the Indian city?

Two: Could you approach the problem by using mental
maps of the people who were formerly affiliated with the
community center? Could these people be identified as they
migrated to other parts of the city? This was important in
the Southeast Asian city in providing a definition of the
community and conditioning the suburban sprawl.

LEWANDOWSKI - The Komatis were building institutions in the
suburbs, outside the area where the central temple was located,
especially for marriage ceremonies. These were networks that
still went back to the central temple, however, Residentially,
a different use of space was emerging.

BROOMFIELD - One comment about the business of Madras not being
the big smoke. Scholars in Bengal studies often assume that
Calcutta was and is the all in all to all Bengalis. In the
Madras case, it is clear that Madras was not to the Tamil region what Calcutta is to Bengal in many ways. But in terms of
sacred places, Calcutta fares badly except for Kalighat and
Dakshineshwar, compared to places like Nabadwip, Brindaban,
and Benares.

143

BASU - In Calcutta, as in Bengal generally, temple-building has been very much a part of social mobility. A recent study by Hitesh Sanyal bears this out.

In my own work on Calcutta I have come across temples that were built by merchants both for public as well as familial purposes. People seeking piety or virtue have gotten names of their loved ones inscribed on the steps of the Kali Temple. The Setts and Bysacks, the founding fathers of the city who came from a weaving caste, arrived with their lares and penates, setting up the family shrine of Govindji. This still survives in Bara Bazaar, and outsiders are admitted during special festivals. The Subarnabanik merchant families, another pioneer community, also have their own domestic gods or deities. What is more interesting is that these merchant communities, especially during their heydays, contributed generously to aid the cause of public pilgrimage. Many built temples in Bararas and Brindaban.

Raja (a "King") Sukhomoy Roy of the late eighteenth and early nineteenth century, built a road to Puri. A simpler or more common form was to build *ghats* on the river that were used both for ritual bathing and commercial purposes. Such acts of piety and public affairs were, at least in part, inspired by the colonial authorities who had started to confer titles such as "Raja" or "Maharaja," often based on the person's record of public contribution. One finds similar trends among merchant communities in Canton and Southeast Asia.

ANDERSON - Let me add a few comments: The Chinese and Indian temples in Southeast Asian cities such as Kuala Lumpur, Singapore, are the foci for merchant association development and sustenance. The institutional form of the associations has changed, but the focus remains the same.

Thus, it clearly relates to a point that was raised earlier in the discussion regarding the low status of merchants and the various opportunities that were available to increase prestige and raise status. One finds such trends in non-colonial set-ups like Osaka's. In early Tokugawa we knew that swords were bought, Samurai titles were purchased by merchants, and it will be worth probing whether efforts focusing on religious edifices also occurred there.

Switching a bit, I wish to draw our attention back to some of yesterday's discussion on the importance of economic personalism in linking not only the development of entrepreneurship to the city, but the operation of the city and the hinterland as well.

Economic personalism has remained important in Asia in the maintenance of trade, in extraction, in marketing activities. Although I find much to ponder in Professor Morris's presentation, I believe what we need is a level of analysis in which we could look beyond economic rationality in terms of the structure of incentives that was available to those who entered entrepreneurial activities. Because of imperfect knowledge of relevant variables, unpredictability in market places, there is an important limit to the rationality of the choice available to someone wishing to create an enterprise with the resources he could muster.

I would insist again on indigenous meanings we discussed yesterday and that surfaced again this morning. We must try to grind our analysis down to where we can see the indigenous structure of incentives, the perceived opportunities embedded within something broader than a purely economic framework. Embeddedness, cultural and social variables, were just as relevant to certain entrepreneurs because these could be resources by which they could mobilize labor and, even, capital. Perceived opportunities and resources are also imperfect. I am impressed by the fact that entrepreneurs, as retailers, pressed on in the face of really staggering odds from a point of pure economic rationality, as Furedy's analysis suggests.

This is still an untapped research area among anthropologists and sociologists working on India. Fred Bailey, Ralph Nicholas, and others following them have focused on the political arena, but a focus on the economic arena may be equally rewarding. In fact, the political and the economic arenas are not that much separated and segregated, as we will soon know.

FUREDY - I have a brief point on the issue of market and commercial information from the point of view of the retailers. We've talked about certain groups having access to information that enabled them to operate. But groups do not always have solidarity. Within any one group there could have been barriers and concerns that inhibited certain firms or operations from having information.

One of the functions of the Calcutta Trades Association was an information-sharing function for British retailers in Calcutta. But problems arose over the perception of that function. They wanted to share a certain amount of information to help each other, but really not too much. For instance, there was an attempt to establish a trade register that would give information about retail firms that immediately met with resistence, and it never got off the ground. The retail firms did not want to reveal too much of their access to market information or connections back in England with suppliers.

BROOMFIELD - The Anderson comment is a little tangential to Morris's argument. As I understand it, Morris is not suggesting that we leave out cultural factors but that there may be good economic arguments alone to explain economic questions. Too often scholars have viewed the Indian response as different by attributing the difference to Hindu culture. What is interest-

145

ing about Morris's paper is that he says there were economic reasons or economic constraints on all participants, although for some the knowledge was different, the capital supply and the opportunities were different. This makes sense to my current interest. The entrepreneurs I'm looking at were embedded in Bengal peasant society, but their greatest interest was in making a profit whenever they perceived a profit possibility.

I would like to make some specific comments on the joint stock company. The experience of the Sahana family I'm studying fits Morris's theory. That family was decimated, as were many families in rural Burdwan and the neighboring districts of West Bengal, by something known as the Burdwan fever, which was probably malaria. In the expansive family with portable inheritance things were getting difficult. Suddenly, thanks to the fever, everything for two generations was consolidated on one man. Because Satya Kinkar Sahana was the only surviving member of his branch of the family, and the surviving members of the nearest branch were much younger, he had for almost forty years everything consolidated in his hands. During that period he ran the family businesses as partnerships. When the cousins became ornery, as when they grew up, and particularly when his own eldest son--who was older than all the cousins--became difficult, Sahana went into the joint stock model. It provided the best handle on the family disputes. This is not just conjecture on my part. I have clear information that fits Morris's argument perfectly.

Morris's point on the expansion of existing operations in the context of the constraints of market insecurities, "the incalculability of demand, uncertainties of the cost of production," is also well taken. Under these conditions, one way to cover your bases was to simply build onto an existing enterprise rather than moving on to something new. With labor in abundant supply, an entrepreneur in eastern India could contract for strip-mining, lumber cutting, road transportation, building, whether for a bungalow for the British or for a food supply station for the local military. If times got difficult, one could pull back from some of these operations or simply pay the labor less.

In Bengal I found another characteristic that is fascinating. It is a sort of subinfeudation of business along the lines of what happened to land in Bengal. This can be documented from the history of the family I am studying. The family was in rice milling and, when profits had reached a plateau, they wanted some capital free to put into coking coal mines. They did this by renting out part of the operation of their rice mill--the par-boiling--to someone else. The latter could rent it out to another person, and so on, so that at one point the rice mill was run by five different levels. This form of "subinfeudation" applied to almost all family operations. When the coal business started to decline, they just kept the

146

most profitable part of it, the haulage from the pit head
to the railroad, and rented out the rest. Then, when the
coal business boomed again, they went back into it as the
written contract provided for this on six months' notice.
This was indeed a remarkable way of spreading and changing
the risk around.

I would like to make one more point on entrepreneurship by returning to a point that Bayly made yesterday, to
the effect that, around 1900, the lines of trade centered
on the Delhi-Agra-Kanpur access, shifted from Calcutta to
Bombay and western India. This is fascinating in the sense
that it might have been an indicator to the shift of the
strength of the Nationalist movement away from Calcutta as
well. I've looked to an economic explanation for the movement of the strength of Nationalism into the countryside,
which Gandhi relied on from about 1920. But no one as yet
has thrown up a suggestion that perhaps the economic focus
in India was shifting to another access, namely, the Delhi-
Agra-Kanpur access linked to Bombay and western India.
Allowing for a *Behari* or two, it is from here that the great
leaders emerge from the 1920s on.

BAYLY - Let me make a brief comment on social values. These
are not as tangential as John Broomfield was saying, in the
sense that one has to define what the entrepreneurs were
maximizing. I'm not sure that the highest level of profit
was always what they went for. They probably went for a combination of both security and profit, which puts us back into
the familial context. People were often concerned to remain
with an existing source of income, say from a base in land-
holding, rather than moving into something that was immediately
more profitable but involved risks.

About Chris Furedy's paper: I wonder if the entrepreneurship of the retailers was limited by race--to what extent
did they try to penetrate the Indian market? Was there a
social boundary to the extent of their entrepreneurship?

FUREDY - I don't have much information about what was being sold
and who was buying. But there is evidence that the British
retailers were importing British and European goods, and that
they were not handling, in any sizable amount in the nineteenth
century, Indian-produced commodities. They were interested in
expanding the market among Westernized Indians. For example,
they tried to interest Indians into patent leather shoes and
European-styled clothing and mattresses! They had, indeed, an
expanding market among Westernized Indians and the princes
who began to buy all manner of British goods. In this sense,
they were trying to penetrate quite aggressively.

REED - Certain parallels and an interesting contrast might be
discerned at some future date if one had time to look into
the work of the entrepreneur in the cities of Southeast Asia.

Some interesting work has been done on entrepreneurship in
the Philippines, Malaysia, Thailand, and Indonesia. Striking
contrasts and parallels are evident in these various countries.
But a comparative study of South and Southeast Asian entrepreneurship is yet to come.

MURPHEY - There are a few odds and ends that deserve to be
put together, *en passant*. The Anderson point about temple
building and merchant roles in traditional Japan--I don't
know about Osaka, but the temple complex in Tokyo was a merchant accomplishment a good deal before there was much in the
way of Western imprint.

Next, regarding Bayly's comment on the Morris thesis
as to continued molding of merchant behavior toward traditional
outlets for capital, whether or not they were necessarily the
most profitable in terms of their rate of return. Land-holding
in Bengal is an obvious case. There is some evidence to suggest that it was not an uneconomic, certainly not a non- or
anti-economic decision on the part of Bengal *zamindars*. In
China it is difficult to get a clear picture of what the different rates of return were to a holder or possessor of capital in
the late nineteenth or twentieth century. But a variety of
things--salt, for example, which had been a profitable invest-
ment--the rate of return was declining. Land-holding was
steadily losing its profitability during these years, and yet
newly-earned mercantile capital still tended to go into land.

A final note on the Morris thesis as to why foreigners
were able to make it in the indigenous systems: Invariably,
it was because they were able to move into them on the basis
of their knowledge of external markets. For example, foreigners ran the show in Ceylon because its primary economy
was in rubber and tea, and their markets were in Europe and
America. The American Tobacco Company and Standard Oil alone
were able to make it into the interior of China, again for
obvious reasons.

TOPIC II: DEVELOPMENT AND CHARACTER OF MERCANTILE ELITES (continued)

Session 4

Engraved by J. Tingle.

The European Factories, Canton.

150

THE IMPACT OF WESTERN TRADE ON THE HONG MERCHANTS

1793-1842

by

Dilip K. Basu

The origin and development of the Hong system or the Cohong
still remains murky. Its early internal structure has been described
in terms of certain myth-rituals indicative of a corporate, guild-like
character; it has also been described as a firm of "brokers" rather
than merchants. But, by the early nineteenth century when we come
across the Hongists dealing with Western traders, the collective bargaining power and guild-dictated price-fixing mechanisms seemed to have
altogether disappeared. Instead, one or two senior merchants virtually
lorded over the Cohong.

The majority of the Hongists, additionally, had become dependent
on foreign merchants in the course of their ordinary business transactions.
Many of them were in constant need of cash credits. The outside shopmen
of Canton, technically without the official permission to trade directly
with foreigners, often seemed more secure and solvent than some Hongists.
The wealth of the senior merchant families of Puankhequa and Houqua was
proverbial. Yet they, too, became characteristically dependent on their
Western compeers: They invested their fortunes in contemporary international trade through personal "combines" with American, British, Parsee/
Indian, and Swedish private traders.

Exactly when the Cohong's internal autonomy broke down, leading
to the emergence of the above trends, is difficult to pinpoint. There
is little doubt, however, that its intertwinement with foreign commercial
interests was a critical factor. If, in the Canton system, Chinese merchants covertly tilted toward the foreign traders, helping them circumvent
the system's multiplex restrictions, aiding and abetting opium smuggling,
providing secret communications and intelligence reports or Chinese language instructors, there must have been some solid reason. And it was
not necessarily because they were minions of the much-maligned red-headed
"barbarians" (hung-mao kuei), although there was enough fraternizing and
junketing between senior Hongists and their Western collaborators.

The break with its collective and corporate structure probably
occurred during 1760-1771. This brief interlude experienced an abortive
Ch'ing attempt to ordain a group of inexperienced and indigent merchants
into the Cohong (Kung-hang), giving them monopoly control and price-fixing
privileges. The Ch'ing design in this seemed to have derived from a policy

151

decision to seek a better handle on both Chinese and foreign merchants.
Canton was made the sole port of trade open to Western commerce. Though
the Hongists were anointed with corporate powers, they had no right to
communicate on their own with foreigners or borrow money from them.
(chiao-chieh wai-kuo k'uang-p'ien ts'ai-wu li)

The Ch'ing attempt failed principally due to the lack of adequate
funds and a credit base among the Hongists. Puankhequa (P'an Chen'ch'eng,
1714-1798), the most solvent Hongist, appealed to the E.I.C. for help,
and the latter ultimately bailed out most of the indigent merchants. The
cash advances made by the E.I.C. constituted the first "Hong Debts" sometime around 1777. From this year onwards, Hong dependence on the Western
traders deepened in proportion to the galloping increase rate of the debts.
The Chinese authorities made an effort to rectify the situation, guaranteeing debt recovery services to the foreigners. They also often threatened
to revive the *Kung-hang* in apparent bids to stem the slippage of their
control over the Hong merchants.

In describing the structural changes occurring within the Cohong
since 1777, I have chosen to employ the term "pidginization." In structural terms, pidginization refers to the dependent relationship that
emerged between the Hongists and Western traders. As the Ch'ing government continued to frown on debt incurrence, often banishing defaulters
to Ili, the result was to draw the Hong merchants inevitably toward the
foreign traders. This gave the latter an upper hand in the relationship.
Structural elements of the relationship also extended to other aspects of
Hong organization and function. For instance, the Hongists attempted to
face their debt problem by relying on the traditional guild institutions,
Kung-so and *hui-kuan*. Such attempts invested the senior merchants with
new authority and power.

The role of Puankhequa in the creation of the original debt provided the leadership model. But even the internal debt settlement processes were not immune from external influence: The foreign traders were
vitally interested in their outcome. Finally, the senior merchants who
built up vast private fortunes also became dependent on the foreign traders
in a special way. Without adequate opportunities for domestic investment,
they put part of their accumulated wealth in international commerce. Such
investments were illegal in the eyes of Chinese law. Most of them, therefore, followed a clandestine route where personal connections and friendship with foreigners were vital.

Instead of going into a detailed history of the Cohong, this paper
emphasizes the above structural aspects of pidginization on its (1)
origins, early growth, and the rise of Hong leadership, (II) creation of
Hong debts and its impact on the merchants vis-à-vis foreign traders,
the role of the traditional guild factor in debt settlement, and (III)
the propensity of wealthy merchants to invest in international commerce.

There are differences among scholars as to when precisely the Hong
merchants or their corporate organization, the Cohong, came into existence.
It should suffice to say that, at the time of the opening of Canton by
the Ch'ing to foreign trade, (1684) the Hongists were already there.
Chinese Communist historians characterize the early Hongists as vestiges

of the "feudal-bureaucratic commercial" elements of the murky world
of traders and smugglers who were engaged in illicit business relationships with the European, the Dutch in particular, at the time of the
Ch'ing conquest of Canton (1660-1684). Such characterization probably
represents an attempt to trade back the despised role that is usually
attributed to the early nineteenth century Hongists for their alleged
collusion with Western traders during the shameful days of the opium
traffic.

Nevertheless, it helps clarify the important distinction between
the ubiquitous traditional *hang* system of South China and the foreign
trade specialists, the Hong merchants. There were, no doubt, traditional
aspects to the latter's function, especially in their frequent efforts at
organizing themselves as a "guild," dictating prices to the early eighteenth century European traders. However, these attempts failed in the
long run for two basic reasons: The lack of capital solvency among the
majority of the Hongists that could help them overcome the vagaries of
the trade from season to season--from accepting orders for goods to delivering them and, correspondingly, the strong presence maintained by a
minority of Hongists who had the capital and the collateral that others
lacked.

The result was the assured dominance of the latter, usually two
or three top merchants, called the "Senior Hong Merchants" in the British
records. While this gave the seniors unusual leverage over the juniors,
the dependence of both on Europeans and, later, on Americans, deepened.
In 1771, the great Hongist, Puankhequa, reportedly accepted from the
British 100,000 *taels* in bribe monies to go into the pockets of local
officials in return for "abolishing" the Cohong. Abolition is not the
correct word, for the Hong system continued but without the monopoly
prices as part of an administered trade. This, of course, meant the loss
of their superior bargaining power in relation to Western traders.

Not surprisingly, this significant, structured change in the
organization of the Cohong coincided with the phenomenal increase in the
demand for tea in the Western markets. By 1760, tea had ceased to be a
"preciosity" and had become a vital item in world trade. The East India
Company's authorities became forthright in their demands for better terms
of trade. The arrogant and pugnacious behavior of James Flint, who was
sent to Peking with a satchel full of complaints in 1759, was indicative
of the importance the English had begun to attach to the China trade.

If petitioning the Ch'ing government was largely unsuccessful,
the clincher that tightened the Western grip on the Hong merchants and
and the China trade came with the Hong Debts--first created in sizable
amounts in 1777--which spiraled at an astonishing speed until the coming
of the Opium War. The debts were mostly incurred by the junior merchants
to Western traders in the normal course of trade and were directly or
indirectly underwritten by the senior merchants. The high rate of interest
and the annual returns on the debt satisfied the European creditors; controversies and frictions were settled *sotto voce* because of the strict
Ch'ing injunction against debt incurrence with foreigners.

A distinction ought to be made, however, between the debts incurred during the period of the East India Company China monopoly (until

153

1834) and those incurred thereafter when the Free Traders had swarmed
the China coasts in great numbers. During the early period, debts
were, from the Ch'ing standpoint, illegal and were therefore arranged
and paid for through mutual understanding among the Chinese and Western
merchants and traders. During the post-1834 period, the Ch'ing implicitly accepted the existence of the debt, a legal nicety that was quickly
interpreted by the creditors as that the Chinese government would assume
the ultimate responsibility for the unpaid debts.

The notorious Hingtae debts of 1836, owing to only one family
firm in the staggering sum of $2,261,439 can be attributed to such an
assumption. The foreign creditors of Hingtae charge the Tao-kuang emperor
"to respect and enforce the rules he has himself laid down." Consequently,
a debt settlement mechanism was established: three senior Hongists and
three foreigners would constitute a committee to examine the claims and
agree on a final settlement. Sitting in the Hong merchants' guild-hall,
the Consoo *(Kung-so)* House, the six trustees worked out the detail of a
nine-year schedule of payment on the Hingtae debt.

If the language barrier had caused considerable difficulty in
the past Sino-Western relations, the availability of a handful of Sinolo-
gists at Canton helped to overcome the problem in the 1830s. The Consoo
account books were no longer mysterious. On the contrary, the Consoo
books now became subject to Western methods of bookkeeping. The availability of one such book at the Public Record Office in London helps us
document this trend. Instead of recording the debts in the traditional
cash book *(liu-shui)* style which often left room for "jumping"*(fei-chang)*
the account by keeping a secret book *(ch'ing'p'u)*, the new practice
spelled out in corresponding English and Chinese column the names of
creditors, the amount of claims admitted, etc. This kind of innovation
was a long way from the usual commercial transactions in pidgin, often
based on *parole*. If the Hong accounting system underwent pidginization
as a result of the incursion of the Western element into it, the controlling hand of the foreign trustees that accompanied it cannot be lost
sight of.

Despite skyrocketed debts, bankruptcies, and constant pressures
for *douceurs* and public contributions from the Chinese authorities, a
few senior Hongists succeeded in building up vast private fortunes.
Western sources describe the incredible wealth of at least two Hong families, Pa'n and Wu: Puankhequa and Houqua were probably two of the
wealthiest merchants of the world in their times. These two merchant
families remained invulnerable to the growing dominance of the Western
traders that resulted in the Hong debts. This should have given them
considerable edge in the dealings with the Western traders. But we find
them developing an indirect dependence on the latter.

With little scope for investment in inland enterprises due to
institutional constraints, part of the senior Hongists' wealth flowed
outward in investments in contemporary international trade, dominated by
the emergence of the world-capitalist system. Close contact with their
European and American peers provided these merchants with an intimate
knowledge of the workings of world trade networks. They were alerted to
the possibilities of quick returns of handsome profits on modest invest-

154

ments. The risks were often great as the Hongists had no institutional contacts with the metropolitan world trading centers in Asia, Europe, and the Americas. The investments, therefore, assumed a personalist form based on longstanding friendship with trusted Western traders in Canton.

The classic example is the investment that Houqua made in the amount of a half million dollars in the American economy in 1836 through John M. Forbes of Boston. Forbes set up the J. M. Forbes and Company with this capital outlay and funneled it to a number of major railroad building projects that he had undertaken on his return to Boston from Canton.

SOURCES

Among the major primary sources consulted mention may be made of (1) Public Record Office, London: F.O. 233/189, F.O. 682/841, Chinese language series; (2) India Office Library, London: Chin Factory Records, II Series; Museum of American China Trade, Milton, Massachusetts: Archives of Capt. R. B. Forbes; (3) John M. Forbes Co., Boston Papers; (4) Baker Library, Harvard Business School: Heard Papers.

Among the major secondary works, (1) Louis Dermigny, *Les Memoires de Charles de Constant sur le commerce a la Chine*, Paris: S.E.V.P.E.N., 1964; (2) H. B. Morse, *The Chronicles of the East India Company trading to China*, 5 Vols., Taipei: Ch'eng-wen Publishing Company (reprints), 1966; (3) Anne B. White, *The Hong Merchants of Canton* (Unpublished doctoral dissertation, University of Pennsylvania, 1968) may be mentioned.

China Street, with part of the European Factories, Canton.

A TALE OF TWO CITIES: CANTON AND HONG KONG

by

Ming K. Chan

The purpose of this paper is to examine aspects of the economic
relations between Canton and Hong Kong from 1840 to the 1920s within
the context of rivalry and interdependence. Part I sketches Canton's
commercial decline and the birth of Hong Kong. Part II looks at some
of the geographic, political, and institutional factors behind Hong
Kong's growth and their effects on Canton. Part III is a case study
of the economic consequences of the 1925-26 General Strike-Boycott
as a historic confrontation between the two port cities. Part IV, the
epilogue, offers a glimpse of more recent developments reflecting past
trends.

The Opium War was settled by the Treaty of Nanking in 1842 which
ceded Hong Kong to the British and opened four other ports in addition
to Canton along the China coast to foreign trade. The subsequent economic
decline of Canton, however, was not due to the early development of Hong
Kong. It was, rather, a combined result of the end of Canton's monopoly
in foreign trade and the rapid rise of Shanghai. With its superior geographic location--at the mid-point along the China coast and at the mouth
of the Yangtze River--as well as cheaper and better transportation links
with the major production areas of tea and silk, the two most important
items in the Chinese export trade, Shanghai soon displaced Canton as the
preeminent port of China.

Beginning in the 1840s, a drastic yet natural geographic shift in
the silk and tea trade routes occurred and led to a general economic depression in the Canton area. Dislocation and unemployment ruined the businessmen and workers, while coastal piracy and local uprisings rose sharply.
Amidst urban disorder and rural unrest, anti-British sentiments ran high
as the Cantonese understandably blamed the British for the Opium War and
subsequent misfortunes.

Hong Kong, as the new British stronghold in south China, was caught
in the crossfire of Anglo-Chinese hostilities and, at the same time, often
became the attack target of Chinese nationalistic outbursts as evidenced
in the strike-boycott of 1857, during the Arrow War. The 1860 Treaty ended
the war but did not save Canton. The Treaty awarded Hong Kong the peninsula of Kowloon, a provision which secured British control over the whole
harbor. Shanghai's commercial ascendancy over Canton was reassured with
the opening of new treaty ports along the Yangtze. Despite all these,
Canton's doom was not inevitable. In fact, it achieved partial recovery
by the 1870s. The secrets lay in Canton's own residual strength and, paradoxically, Hong Kong's growth.

157

Many factors were responsible for Hong Kong's rise as the fore-most port in south China. Although Canton is located at the center of the Pearl River delta, a highly productive and fertile area interlaced by an endless web of waterways, its harbor is too narrow and shallow. Some ninety miles downstream, Hong Kong has the finest natural deep-water harbor on the China coast. As the British dominated shipping in the Far East, Hong Kong easily became a key stop in the coastal and ocean routes.

Institutional factors were also important. Hong Kong's political status as a British colony guaranteed stability and security; in times of upheaval in China, such as the Taiping Rebellion and the civil wars during the Republican era, the colony became a haven for the Chinese. The massive migrations from China provided the colony with much needed capital inflow and an abundant supply of inexpensive but intelligent manpower--two vital elements for any successful economic development. Hong Kong's treaty-sanctioned status as a duty-free port and the *laissez faire* economic policy of the colonial government made the colony even more attractive as a trade center and international entrepôt. The establishment of an efficient, modern financial system with a sound currency issued by the giant British banks further facilitated the colony's growth.

Hong Kong's prosperity, however, depended on the China trade. Although wars and disturbances in China drove capital and labor into Hong Kong, the colony preferred peace and stability in China in order to maintain normal trade conditions. Indeed, Hong Kong by itself was not and should not be responsible for the misfortunes of Canton or China. In fact, Hong Kong and Canton gradually developed a close working relationship in foreign trade and overseas migration. With its superior harbor, modern commercial institutions, and international shipping network, Hong Kong served as the "foreign trade department" for south China, while Canton, the political and economic hub of the Liang-Kuang region, became its department of purchase and collection of Chinese exports as well as the distribution center on the mainland for foreign imports.

In other words, Hong Kong dealt with the foreign markets on Canton's behalf, but Canton was the real supplier of exports and buyer of imports which passed through Hong Kong, the entrepôt and the middleman. A similar pattern also existed in the Cantonese migration traffic in which the workers from the delta region would first come to Canton where a few might get a job and settle down while many others would proceed to Hong Kong. The colony would then absorb a number of them in its business and industries, but the rest would migrate overseas from its harbor. Of course, Hong Kong bene-fitted not only from this very heavy passenger traffic but also from its role as the center of supply catering to the needs of overseas Chinese communities and from their substantial remittances. In a sense, these two port cities can be considered as a functionally integrated commercial entity with Hong Kong as the internationally more prominent component unit.

So it seems in such an economically interdependent relationship Hong Kong was able to dominate and gain greater profit than Canton, its largest and closest trading partner. Yet, even though Canton was commer-cially overshadowed by the colonial upstart, the growth and prosperity of Hong Kong also helped, through their close partnership, Canton's commercial recovery. As the total shipping tonnage through Hong Kong increased over the years, so did Canton's shipping. Furthermore, as long as the China trade remained indispensable to Hong Kong, Canton was not without bargaining power. Thus, Hong Kong's economic influence over the south China hinterland might be dominant, but it was never complete and absolute.

The sixteen-month long Canton-Hong Kong General Strike-Boycott of 1925-26 demonstrated very clearly the helplessness of Hong Kong in a confrontation with the determined Cantonese on the mainland. While life became difficult and business bankrupted in the colony, Canton enjoyed unprecedented prosperity. For example, the Cantonese currency circulated at its face value as the Hong Kong notes were boycotted as the medium of trade, and new routes of shipping were established, linking Canton directly with its markets and suppliers, bypassing Hong Kong. Even the British had to concede that the colony's past prosperity was won partially at Canton's expense and that Hong Kong could hardly survive without Canton and the China trade, but Canton could carry on without Hong Kong indefinitely. In other words, Hong Kong might have dominated the foreign trade of south China, but it did not and could not control the whole economy of the Canton Delta hinterland.

As events in the early stage (1927-38) of the Sino-Japanese War and in the post-1949 period have shown, both cities can benefit from a close economic working relationship. Despite its imperialistic overtone, colonial image, and past affronts to Chinese national pride, Hong Kong still prospers on the China coast today. This underlines the fact that, as long as Hong Kong does not dominate the Chinese hinterland but serves functions useful to Chinese interests, it can perhaps be considered a "clear gain" to China and thus can be tolerated as a British colony. The semi-annual international trade fairs held in Canton undoubtedly reflect the possibilities of mutually beneficial arrangements between the two port cities.

SOURCES

Various original sources in both Chinese and English were consulted in the research of this paper, such as the Colonial and Foreign Office archives at the Public Record Office in London and the official yearbooks of the governments of Canton and Hong Kong. A number of secondary works also provide useful information and important references. Among others, the following were particularly helpful:

Endacott, G. B., *A History of Hong Kong* (1958)
Hao, Yen-ping, *The Comprador in Nineteenth Century China,* (1970)
Hughes, Richard, *Hong Kong: Borrowed Place, Borrowed Time,* 1968
Murphey, Rhoads, *Shanghai: Key to Modern China,* (1953)
Rabushka, Alvin, *The Changing Face of Hong Kong,* (1973)
Szczepanik, Edward, *The Economic Growth of Hong Kong,* (1958)
Wakeman, Frederic, *Strangers at the Gate,* (1965)

I have also relied heavily on my own dissertation, "Labor and Empire: The Chinese Labor Movement in the Canton Delta, 1895-1929," (Stanford, 1975), especially for the section on the 1925-26 strike-boycott.

160

SILK-REELING ENTERPRISES IN CANTON AND SHANGHAI

by

Robert Y. Eng

In the treaty ports of China that were opened to commerce after the Opium War of 1839-42, the Western powers and Japan set up concessions under their direct administration where their nationals could freely trade invest in banking, industry, and construction, and engage in missionary and cultural activities. Thus, these ports were fucntionally similar to other Asian colonial port cities as linkages to the metropolitan countries. By examining the history of one important extractive industry in two of the most important treaty ports of China, this paper will hope to provide some insights into the relationship of Chinese entrepreneurs to the foreign sector and into the broader question of whether port cities serve as beachheads of foreign exploitation or as centers of modernization.

The upsurge of world demand for East Asiatic raw silk in the last half of the nineteenth century was due to two external developments: the spread of silkworm disease in Europe between 1854 and 1858 and the rise of the American and French silk-weaving industries. The preference of American and European weavers for the more regular and elastic steam filature silk over hand-reeled silk prompted the establishment of fila- tures in China. Silk was to remain China's topmost export commodity until the 1930s when the Chinese silk industry suffered a disastrous contraction because of the deepening world depression, the increasing competition from such artificial fibers as rayon, and dumping by the Japanese silk industry.

Shanghai would seem to enjoy more favorable preconditions for the expansion of its silk-reeling industry than Canton. Not only had Shanghai quickly supplanted Canton as the center of Sino-Western trade after its opening in 1843, it was also located within Kiangsu-Chekiang, the leading silk-producing region of China in both quantitative and qualitative terms. Moreover, after the looting of Western merchant houses during the Arrow War, foreign enterprises stayed away from Canton. Indeed, Cantonese fila- tures, the first of which was founded in 1872 by Ch'en Ch'i-yuan, were an exclusively Chinese affair. In contrast, the Shanghai silk-reeling indus- try was initiated by Western entrepreneurs, including the British import- export firm of Jardine, Matheson & Co., and enjoyed the availability of Western technical personnel and machinery.

Yet progress at Canton was more rapid. By 1891 there were fifty or sixty steam filatures in the province of Kwangtung, while only three filatures were in operation at Shanghai. By 1896 there were twenty-seven filatures at Shanghai, but capacity remained little changed until about 1907, after which the number of filatures and the number of reels rose

161

slowly until after the onset of World War I. The 1920s was the next and last period of expansion of Shanghai filatures, which numbered over one hundred by the end of the decade. In 1918 there were close to three hundred in Kwangtung Province, mostly concentrated at the Shun-te and Nan-hai districts, near Canton. In the 1920s the number of filatures seems to have declined but, even as late as 1929, there were still 146 filatures in the Canton region.

Not only did Canton surpass Shanghai in total production capacity, but average plant size was larger there: A typical Cantonese filature had from 400 to 500 reels, whereas the scale of production in Shanghai declined over time from over 300 reels per filature before 1910 to 227 in 1929. In addition, Cantonese filatures seem to have been more stable. The average number of years in business for Shanghai filatures was 4.4 years in 1897, 4.5 in 1926, 5.0 in 1928, 5.2 in 1929, and 2.5 in 1931. On the other hand, the mean number of years in business for 299 Cantonese filatures in 1918 was no lower than 12.8, and at least 14 percent had been in business for twenty years or more. Although many filatures did go out of business soon after getting started, those that continued operations did so over a long period of time. Nevertheless, this stability disappeared in the 1920s. Only eleven of the 299 filatures operating in 1918 survived until 1929.

The temporal and quantitative gap in production scale and capacity and in industrial stability between the two regions was reflected in the quantity of exports. Filature silk began to displace hand-reel silk at Canton at an earlier date. Starting with 13 percent of all exports in 1882-83, filature silk corners more than three-quarters of the market by 1891. In Shanghai, as late as 1894, only 9 percent of white silk exported was filature silk, and it was not until 1911 that exports of white filature silk surpassed exports of white hand-reeled silk. Cantonese white filature silk exports were about three times the level of Shanghai exports before 1908; thereafter, the faster expansion of Shanghai exports closed the gap but, except for 1915, Canton always exported more annually than Shanghai before 1929.

Did the earlier and faster growth of the Cantonese silk-reeling industry suggest that the advantage of the availability of Western capital, entrepreneurship, and technical personnel at Shanghai was outweighed by the disadvantage of Western competition which inhibited Chinese enterprise? Direct foreign competition did not retard the development of Chinese filatures in Shanghai, for the foreign share of the industry soon faded into insignificance. Already, by 1897, only three of thirty-one filatures were owned outright by foreigners and, by 1911, the Ewo Filature, operated by the Jardine, Matheson & Co., was the only filature under foreign ownership and management. In fact, many Chinese filatures were registered under foreign ownership since foreign licenses entitled them to lower export taxes. Even the capital for the few foreign filatures probably came in large part from the Chinese: 60 percent of the stocks of the Ewo Filature, for instance, was sold to Chinese.

Many Westerners who went to seek their fortune in China in the late nineteenth century were adventurers with limited financial resources who depended largely on Chinese capital and thus diverted it from native use.

Moreover, the foreign banks also siphoned off much Chinese capital since China was forced by treaty stipulations to deposit her customs and salt revenues with the foreign banks in order to contract foreign loans to pay off indemnities. Thus, the advantage of Shanghai in the availability of foreign capital might be illusory.

Shanghai filatures were also handicapped by their weaker business and management organization. At some stage proprietors began leasing out their filatures instead of operating them themselves or through hired managers. In 1922, some 40 percent of filatures were managed by entrepreneurs who leased the physical plant; in 1928, the proportion had risen to 90 percent. This separation of ownership and management not only accentuated the lack of horizontal integration in the industry but also encouraged speculation and discouraged renovation and expansion of the plants.

Canton might have enjoyed certain advantages in the supply of raw materials, labor, and capital. Cantonese filatures were located mainly in the market towns and villages near or at the silk-producing areas rather than in the port of Canton itself. This minimized the problem of securing cocoons as input. Shanghai filatures were separated by much greater distances from the silk districts. Moreover, they depended for their annual supply of cocoons mostly on the spring crops in Kiangsu and Chekiang. Cantonese filatures could spread out their purchases since the mild climate of Kwangtung allowed for an annual harvest of seven or more crops of silkworms which, at the same time, permitted the full-time employment of women in all phases of sericulture and silk industry.

One important source of Cantonese filature workers were the *tzu-shu-nu* ("women who dress their own hair"), sisterhoods of women whose independence and collective decision to remain single made for a stable labor force. In addition to the possibility of employment in the silk industry, the male emigration from the overpopulated silk districts--by removing male control over income earned by women in some instances--also contributed to the existence of the *tzu-shu-nu.*

Overseas remittances from these emigrants also formed an important source of capital for these filatures, either directly or through the native banks. The expansion of the Cantonese silk-reeling industry demonstrates that, given the proper stimulus, Chinese could start a modern enterprise on their own, without the benefit of Western example, and that Chinese-generated capital might be a more stable and reliable source of investment funds.

Nonetheless, differences between Canton and Shanghai filatures were quantitative rather than qualitative. The winter cocoon crops in Canton yielded far less in quantity. The low wages paid in Shanghai filatures suggest the availability of a pool of female labor through the push of rural poverty, and the Shanghai foreign banks did funnel back some Chinese capital indirectly through choploans to the native banks which, in turn, supplied the Chinese filature operators with working capital. Cantonese filatures remained just as dispersed in ownership and just as much lacking in horizontal integration as Shanghai filatures and, while the majority were managed by the owners or their agents, some were built and rented out by the clans.

Most importantly, filatures in both regions were subjected to the foreign domination of shipping and the import-export business, the natural corollary of which was the prominence of compradors and export merchants in silk-reeling. Not until the 1920s did the Chinese in Shanghai succeed in gaining a precarious foothold in foreign trade in general and the silk export trade in particular. As late as 1934, foreign firms still controlled all of the raw silk export trade at Canton.

One major reason for the inability of the Chinese to capture a share of foreign trade was undoubtedly related to their inability to develop transoceanic shipping. After 1900, the Chinese share of total shipping in China stayed at around 20 percent and was confined to mostly inland navigation. This was partly the result of foreign competition and partly official oppression. To protect the monopolistic privileges of the China Merchants' Steam Navigation Company, a joint official-merchant venture, Li Hung-chang repeatedly rejected numerous petitions by Cantonese and Shanghai merchants to establish steamship companies during the early 1880s. The economic consequences of foreign domination of trade and shipping were, from the micro-economic point of view, the inability of a filature to integrate trade or shipping into its operations and thus increase its profits and potential for expansion and, from the macro-economic point of view, the leakages abroad of profits to foreign middle-men and shippers and the resultant diminution of the potential benefits of silk export growth to the domestic economy.

Dependence on foreign shipping and exporting facilities placed Chinese silk producers in an inferior bargaining position versus the foreign trade companies, which increased their share of the profits at the expense of the producers through various means: They reserved the right to conduct their own silk tests and stand on their results, which could not be disputed by Chinese sellers and, during periods of business depression, they would use every pretext to reject the consignment of silk bought on forward contract.

Chinese filaturists not only faced a price squeeze at the distribution end but also a cost squeeze at the production end. The diffusion of silkworm disease as sericulture spread and breeding practices deteriorated not only limited the expansion of cocoon production and kept up the price of cocoons, it also increased the amount of dried cocoons needed to produce a given quantity of raw silk because of increased breakage and wastage. For Shanghai filaturists, the quantity of cocoons was further restricted and prices kept high by the monopolistic control over distribution by government-licensed cocoon guilds in Chekiang and Kiangsu, which received their monopoly privileges in return for acting as government agents in the collection of likin, a surtax on goods in transit. As late as 1928, likin per picul of cocoons amounted to about 8 percent of the purchase price. Similarly, a Cantonese filature in the 1920s had to pay a whopping $417.50 likin and other taxes per picul of raw silk transported from the filature to Canton for export, as compared to the freight cost of $1.20. Likin, then, remained an onerous addition to silk producers and a serious impediment to trade in general.

Governmental efforts to reform sericulture remained localized and temporary in character and seldom involved the introduction of modern scientific techniques of seed selection and silkworm breeding which were vital to check and eliminate the spread of silkworm disease and to improve the quality of cocoons. More extensive and concentrated efforts to reform Chinese sericulture did not materialize until the American Silk Association, wary of becoming overly dependent on the Japanese who had developed a monopsonistic position on the American raw silk market, turned to the possibility of greatly expanding the Chinese supply.

In the 1920s, the American Silk Association and the International Committee for the Improvement of Sericulture, formed in 1917 in Shanghai by French, British, and American silk interests, set up or financed experimental stations and sericulture departments at Chinese universities in both the Shanghai and Canton regions. However, these efforts came too late to enable China to challenge Japan's preeminent position as the world's leading supplier of raw silk which owed much to extensive government financial support and promotion, including the establishment of silk inspection stations and sericultural colleges.

Although the Chinese government hampered the Chinese silk industry by its lack of leadership in the reform of sericulture, imposition of likin and export duties and the failure to develop banking and infrastructure its options were severely limited by imperialist aggression, while the Japanese government operated under much lower intensity of foreign pressure as Westerners looked to China rather than to Japan as the market with rich potentialities. Nor were Chinese governmental branches under foreign management necessarily more effective agents of constructive reform: the Maritime Customs was set up to facilitate and provide order in the China trade and for the efficient collection of customs revenues hypothecated for foreign loans rather than to develop China's export potential.

Similarly, foreign firms were not necessarily agents of technical innovation either as they were principally motivated by possibilities of profit-making. The Chinese silk-reeling industry, while benefitting in some respects from the foreign presence, also suffered from the unequal relationship between Westerners and Chinese. The foreign presence in China was Janus-faced, setting in motion the forces of modernization on the one hand and hindering them on the other.

SOURCES

This paper has relied heavily on the documentary collections of materials on the history of agriculture, industry, and handicrafts in modern China made by Communist Chinese historians in the 1950s; on the Decennial Reports of the Maritime Customs; on contemporary periodicals such as *Nung-hsueh pao* (Agronomy Journal), *Chinese Economic Bulletin*, *Chinese Economic Months*, *Trans-Pacific*, and *Millard's Review* (later the *China Weekly Review*) and some secondary literature in English and Chinese.

TOPIC II: DEVELOPMENT AND CHARACTER OF MERCANTILE ELITES (continued)

Session 4

DISCUSSION

Moderator - George von der Muhl

Discussant - Christopher A. Bayly

Dilip K. Basu, *Impact of Western Trade on the Hong Merchants of Canton, 1793-1842*

Ming Chan, *A Tale of Two Cities: Canton and Hong Kong*

Robert Eng, *Silk-Reeling Enterprises in Shanghai and Canton*

VON DER MUHL - The first paper is by Dilip Basu.

BASU - I find some of the general questions that surfaced during the discussions of the last two days' panels germane to my paper. Yesterday and this morning we talked about the definition of colonialism, we talked about continuities among mercantile elites from the pre-modern to the colonial period with special reference to entrepreneurship, the role of religion, temple building, etc. Anderson's and Vorster's paper has raised the important question of royal influence. All these issues directly bear upon the subject matter of my paper. I don't raise the issue of religion, although it was, as I said during the discussion of this morning's panel, important and significant. The issue of colonialism poses a problem for Canton as it was, until 1842, a Ch'ing government controlled port. The Ch'ing had limited China's foreign trade to Canton and had given the Hong merchants the exclusive right--a monopoly, in fact--to manage foreign commerce. Two critical works are relevant to this question of "administered" trade. One is Karl Polanyi's concept of "Ports of Trade," and the other is Immanuel Wallerstein's more recent world-system approach to pre-capitalist trade as trade between "external arenas."

Any definition of colonial port city must take into account Polanyi's definition of "Port of Trade." This is Polanyi's name for a settlement that acted as a control point between a market and a non-market economy when commercial intercourse between them became inevitable. Trade of this kind was normally treaty-based, administered by officially appointed authorities; competition was excluded and prices set over long terms. Polanyi makes a distinction between "embedded"--non-market--and "disembedded" market economies. Trade and market were only marginally important in a non-market economy. When they occurred, there were fixed prices and official supervision.

Political authority in these situations was usually located inland. It shunned the coasts and vagaries of external trade. If coastal or foreign trade still developed, there was an attempt to neutralize the effects with enforced control. Even a cursory view of the Ch'ing commercial policy and what was known as the "Canton Commercial System" will suggest enough similarities between Polanyi's theoretical projection (some of his students empirically worked it out in case studies of Eastern Mediterranean and African ports) and the situation that existed on the South China coast. But was Canton really a "port of trade" during the 1793-1842 period?

In attempting to answer this question, I find Wallerstein's work more germane. Wallerstein focuses on the origins of what he calls the World-Capitalist System with its core, semi-periphery, and peripheral areas. Colonial port cities will fall in the latter category where the ensuing trade with the "core" might result in their "peripheralization." "External arenas," on the other hand, belonged to world-systems--Polanyi's embedded economy--outside the world economy. Trade in these two, when it occurred, was in "preciosities," or luxury items. But once these luxury items started to become vital to the world economy, like slavery had become, the external arenas fell under the threat of peripheralization. The rise of tea trade from China and its great importance in the late eighteenth century in the commerce of the world economy can be viewed as a transition from a preciosity to a vital item of trade. Was Ch'ing commerce and Canton System then inevitably, if subtly, being peripheralized? The answer to this question will help us decide to what extent Canton, during the pre-1842 period, falls within our rubric of a colonial port city.

I attempt to provide an answer in this paper, not with the aid of either Polanyi's or Wallerstein's theories--although both have been extremely helpful--but by turning to an internal model suggested in my empirical materials. Looking at the advent and impact of Western trade, especially in its later, "vital" form, I find Asian merchant classes in the port-cities in terms of my empirical knowledge of Canton and Calcutta, facing two entrepreneurial choices: First, one could work within and/or for the superimposed Western commercial institutions such as the Agency Houses, Managing Agencies, commercial banks, and joint stock companies. Many who worked <u>for</u> such institutions were no more than *factotums*, but then there were a few brilliant entrepreneurs who, while working <u>within</u> these institutions, attempted to relate and engraft them onto the existing Asian institutions. The result could be something viable that was both Asian and non-Asian, perhaps syncretized is the word.

I think Dwarkanath Tagore's remarkable entrepreneurial innovations in the 1830s and 1840s in Calcutta would come close to this condition. One may hasten to add that this was possibly more of an exception than a prevailing trend. The second choice was a frank acceptance of the status quo of the existing constraints imposed by both Asian and non-Asian institutions and making the best of a bad bargain, as it were.

If the first were syncretic, the latter was perhaps eclectic. If joint stock companies and commercial banks were the preferred form in the first, "loose" partnerships and business relationships based on trust among Asian and Western traders was the practice in the second. The common element was the dominant impact of Western trade. The Western traders held the trump cards by maintaining their control over commercial intelligence and the flow of information--a vital factor in overseas commerce.

The term I use to describe the impact of Western trade on the Hong merchants and their institutions is "pidginization." It is an insular term in the sense that it represents a local phenomenon and derives its name from the local business dialect, Pidgin, but the process it describes is structural and is of value in analyzing the second situation from a comparative standpoint.

I'm not, however, the first person to use it. Louis Dermigny, in his magisterial three tomes on Canton trade, has used it, although in a much more general way. Anthropologists and linguists recently have been looking at pidginization from cultural and linguistic standpoints. Dell Hymes, the noted anthropologist, has edited a volume a few years back that shows that pidginization has fascinating social and cultural ramifications and may, in fact, represent a new science of communication.

My purpose in employing the term in Canton's context is modest. Pidgin was, as you know, the medium through which the Europeans, Americans, Chinese, and other Asians communicated with each other. Chinese, English, Portuguese, Hindustani, and Malay words were freely intermixed, though the basic Chinese syntax and structure remained unchanged. I am suggesting that in day to day commercial intercourse Chinese and non-Chinese traders in Canton related to each other essentially at the level of the language they used to communicate with each other. This communication level extended to their mutual business relationships; it profoundly affected their credit operations and, to some extent, their social life and perception of each other.

171

Unlike pidgin, the language where the Chinese syntax
and structure pretty much remained in tact, the process of
pidginization, I argue, resulted in some structural erosion
due to the operation of the "colonial" element or due to
the exposure of the "external arena to the world economy.
The traditional Chinese merchant institutions, like the
Kung-so and Hui-kuan, were no longer (did they ever?) serving
the mutual aid interests and deliberations of the merchant
guilds but were instruments of the entrepreneurial few who,
in turn, were dependent on and conditioned by the interests
of foreign trade and Western traders.

Let me just summarize what I have attempted to present
in the paper along these lines. First, we face the Hong
merchants in the early eighteenth century as an Imperially-
annointed group. They were appointed specifically to deal
with Western trade when Canton was re-opened for intercourse
with the outside world in 1685. A Western trade Hong was
created. We know from available sources that this Hong essentially attempted to deal with Western traders in a traditional
guild-like fashion. In 1720 they formalized their guild operations, but the Europeans didn't like it as the guild always
dictated prices. In their search for competitive prices,
European traders in Canton went outside the Hong monopoly
system and attempted to deal with "outside shopmen"--the
non-monopoly Chinese merchants who were willing to oblige.
The result was that the "administered" trade of Canton didn't
really work.

A second attempt was made during 1772 to administer
the trade again from above, with dictated prices and tight-
fisted guild control of the Hong, but the result was again
disastrous. Many Hongists who had entered the trade without
adequate credit or collateral were bankrupted completely,
and even the official "monopoly" in its formal sense could
survive only after a large infusion of foreign credit con-
tracted by the chief Hongist, Puankhequa.

With this began the structural erosion or the entry of
the colonial element into the picture. The huge "Hong Debts"
that were created in 1772 and were owed by the majority of
the Hongists to Europeans snowballing in the 1790s were not
liquidated until after the Nanking Settlement of 1842. I
argue that the debts introduced a control mechanism that gave
Western traders considerable leverage, reducing the Hongists
to a position of dependence.

H. B. Morse, one of the early writers on the Canton
trade, characterized the Hong merchants' predicament as one
between "the devil and the deep blue sea." There is no doubt
that the merchants had trouble from both ends, but in this
analysis the "deep sea" elements were certainly more difficult.
One of my best sources on the Hong debts is a *Kung-so* account
book that I found in the Chinese documentary piles at the

Public Record Office in London which spells out in vivid
detail the bonds that the debts imposed on most Hongists.

The officially appointed Hong merchants were never
a large body--the number varied from eight to sixteen at any
given time. Only three or four among them were solvent and
commanded the fabled wealth that is attributed to them. They
were called the "senior merchants" in the English records.
Although the recognition of Hong leadership goes back to tradition, I argue that the "seniority factor" was critically important to the pidginization process. If, in the past, seniors
were responsible to the Chinese authorities for the solvency
and proper mercantile behavior of the juniors, they now were
guarantors to Western traders on their behalf who otherwise
would probably not have advanced the loans in the first place.

There was a good reason why senior merchants would be
willing to do that. The Hong merchants, according to Chinese
law, were not allowed to invest in internal enterprises.
Those with idle capital, therefore, turned to external possibilities. Houqua, the wealthiest among the Hongists and, in
the estimation of some Westerners the wealthiest merchant
in the world, looked for opportunities for investment in contemporary international trade. He established close personal
business relationships on what can be called "fraternal partnerships" with American traders, John P. Cushing, John M.
Forbes, and others. In 1836 he provided the seed money for
the establishment of John M. Forbes and Company in Boston to
the tune of half a million dollars. In the Forbes Company's
account books, the Houqua money was entered into as the American Investment Fund and American Stock Investment.

John Forbes, as some of you may know, was a pioneer
railroad builder in the mid-nineteenth century. He funneled
Houqua's capital to Iowa Land Association, Burlington Railroad, and Michigan Central Railroad, and other corporations.
The business relationship was continued until 1880 with Houqua's
descendants. Houqua's case was not an isolated one. His
predecessor in the eighteenth century had similar relationships
with the Swedes; one can find evidences of such relationships
among other Hongists who were Houqua's contemporaries. I cite
him as a case study because I have the best documentation on
him.

Finally, I would like to make two points. Merchants
like Houqua, despite their wealth, were also peculiarly "dependent" on Western traders if, for no other reason, for the vent
the latter provided for their excess capital, for the flow of
information and commercial intelligence that was needed to
sustain their investment. Secondly, if one were looking for
evidence of integration between Wallerstein's "external arena"
and the world-economy, what can be better than this nugget
of information on Chinese capital being invested in American
development during the nineteenth century?

VON DER MUHL - The next paper is by Ming Chan.

CHAN - Let me summarize some of the highlights and tentative
conclusions of my paper: The first section deals with the
decline of Canton as the result of the two Opium Wars, the
Treaties of Nanking in 1842, and the Peking Convention of
1860 which deprived Canton of its monopoly in the foreign
trade and opened up Shanghai and other coastal ports.

I demonstrate that Canton's initial decline was not
due to the rise of Hong Kong but resulted from the spectacular growth and development of Shanghai. If you consider
Shanghai as the Rotterdam of China and the Yangtse River its
Rhine--and that is not too far-out an analogy--you have the
essential picture. So, it is unfair to blame Hong Kong for
Canton's misfortune in not having the monopoly any longer.
Since Hong Kong was a British creation, a "part of the package"
of the two cities that ended Canton's prosperity and domination of the foreign trade from the Cantonese point of view,
the blame could be attributed to the British in particular,
to Hong Kong as a Crown Colony, for all their misfortunes
since the Opium Wars. This explains the stormy relations that
ensued between the two cities from the very beginning.

Here we should be very careful about the actual economic
and material impact of foreign imperialism which was often
quite different from the political and psychological effects
of foreign intrusion as perceived by the Chinese themselves.

The second section of the paper deals with some of the
natural as well as institutional factors that contributed to
the spectacular growth of Hong Kong. For one thing, Hong Kong
enjoyed the best natural harbor along the China Coast--on this
I quote Professor Murphey. But even if Hong Kong didn't have
the finest harbor, it could still overwhelm and overtake Canton
due to its sheer geographic and locational advantages.

To the Cantonese, what was most irritating was the fact
that Hong Kong was under British control. Yet Hong Kong's
development served a useful economic function to Canton. It
absorbed the surplus labor of the over-populated Canton Delta
which had perhaps an even higher density than in the Low
Countries in Europe.

The development of Hong Kong opened new opportunity of
employment for Cantonese workers. Hong Kong's connection with
the British Empire and the rest of the world served as a
useful entry point for Chinese coolies to the Americas, to
Southeast Asia, and to Africa. On the other hand, the stability
and security offered by the Hong Kong government, its *laissez
faire* attitude and its institution of limited liability company,
its modern banking facilities attracted Chinese entrepreneurs
and investors.

The instability of the political situation with China, the fragility of the government, threats of rebellion and disorder, warfare and invasion, persuaded the enterprising few to get out of Canton and come down to Hong Kong with their money, skill, and business. In this sense, Hong Kong replaced Canton and Hong Kong seemed to prosper at the expense of China's misfortunes. A common argument is that Hong Kong did not create, at least directly, most of China's suffering and misfortune, but that it just happened to be there to take advantage of the inflow of refugees and their capital. A former governor of Hong Kong had this in mind when he remarked that Hong Kong was so useful that, had it not been there, either the Chinese or God would have had to invent it.

As it finally worked out, Hong Kong's international, cosmopolitan commercial networks evolved into a partnership with Canton. Hong Kong could be considered South China's foreign trade department. It was taking foreign orders, was in charge of shipping, insurance, banking, and accounting, while Canton became the domestic collecting station, a centralized marketplace for the South China export as well as domestic trade. There was a resultant division of labor between the Inland River Port and the Outer Harbor on the oceanfront, somewhat parallel to the relation in Germany between Bremerhaven and Bremen. In functional terms, Canton and Hong Kong could, in the pre-1949 period, almost be considered as two parts of a single port city.

As the civil war and political disorder in China continued unabated, Hong Kong's economic domination (which, in translation, was British domination) increased. The 1925-26 General Strike and Boycott illustrates the extent of British domination. The Hong Kong currency had, *ipso facto*, become the standard currency in South China. For instance, the stock exchange price in Shanghai was not quoted in Chinese currency but in the Hong Kong currency rate. China's foreign exchange rate had long been based, not in the Peking or Shanghai quotation, but in the Hong Kong and Shanghai Bank's quotation in Hong Kong.

As the civil war worsened, even the Chinese political bosses and warlords started to deposit money in the foreign banks, with the Hong Kong currency as the basic unit for transaction.

In the post-1949 period, Hong Kong is still useful as the Chinese window and the outside world. China now earns 20-25 percent of foreign currency exchange through Hong Kong or directly in the Hong Kong market. It is not an accident that today the semi-annual Canton Trade Fair is hosted in Canton. Its geographic proximity and institutional links with Hong Kong have something to do with the decision to hold it there. From Hong Kong's point of view, Canton is the gate to the South China hinterland but, from Canton's point of view,

Hong Kong's hinterland is not China; it is the international market, the whole world. As the 1925-26 General Strike and Boycott has shown, Hong Kong exerted very great influence but did not really control the Cantonese hinterland economically.

There is something in Hong Kong's experience that is relevant to this morning's discussion of Indian entrepreneurship. Some Indian entrepreneurs from Calcutta and Bombay had established their banking houses in Hong Kong, one of them with the dubious title of "Bank of China," and another with "Bank of the Orient." But they all failed. The only two banks that really mattered were the Charter Bank of London and the Hong Kong and Shanghai Bank. The Charter Bank was based in London with its East Asian headquarters in Hong Kong, while the Hong Kong and Shanghai Bank was chartered in Hong Kong and also headquartered in Hong Kong. From their Hong Kong base, both banks dominated the Indian trade in the Orient. This partly explains why the British still, even after Independence, dominate Indian banking and trade in these parts of Asia. The Indian banks simply failed to penetrate East and Southeast Asia effectively.

VON DER MUHL - Thank you. The next paper is by Robert Eng.

ENG - Although my paper specifically focuses on the silk industry, I also address the general historiographical question--some may even call it a cliché--of Modern East Asian history. The question relates to the lack of economic development in the nineteenth century China in contrast to Japan's remarkable progress in that area. One of the major features of Japan's achievement was her ability to capture the export market in raw silk in Europe and the United States.

Students of Japanese economic development have come up with the hypothesis that the silk industry played a leading role in Japanese economic development up to around 1930, providing around 40 percent of the exchange receipts. This, in turn, helped pay for the import of capital equipment and thus financed the development of the Japanese infra-structure. The interesting fact is that China was a bigger producer than Japan before this period. The question naturally emerges then, Why couldn't the Chinese silk industry develop the way its Japanese counterpart did? It is with this broad question in mind that I started my investigation of the silk industry in Canton and Shanghai during this crucial period.

We have learned from Ming Chan how, after the opening of Shanghai and after the Opium Wars, Canton went into a decline as the center of Sino-Western trade. Before the opening of Shanghai, teas and silks were transported overland into Canton but, after its opening, it made better sense for silks and teas to be transported over the water routes, giving Canton another setback.

As Ming Chan also points out, there was a recovery
of Canton's position in the late nineteenth century. I believe the reason behind this was due primarily to the surprising development of the silk industry in the Canton region.
It was surprising because Shanghai enjoyed the obvious
advantage of being located in a region where silk culture
was much more developed. Canton was a distant second in
terms of both quantity and quality.

In addition, the development of filatures in Shanghai,
which produced exclusively for the foreign markets, started
much earlier and was exclusively in the hands of the Western
trading companies like the Jardine, Matheson and Company, and
the Russell and Company. So, it is rather paradoxical to discover among a mass of statistical figures that the Canton exports expanded faster, maintaining a leading position off and
on until about 1930, despite the fact that there were no foreign
silk enterprises in Canton.

It has been suggested, as an explanation of this paradox, that the advantages of the availability of foreign capital
and entrepreneurship in Shanghai were neutralized by foreign
competition. This explanation, however, doesn't go far since
all the foreign companies that were engaged in silk production
eventually dropped out of the picture with the exception of
Jardine, Matheson and Company.

Much of the capital that financed the Canton industries
came from overseas Chinese sources, facilitated, to be sure,
by the development of post and telegraph lines and the modernization of communication between East and West. The role of
Chinese capital--and by this I don't mean Overseas Chinese capital only--is noteworthy here. For even the Western banks obtained much of their capital from Chinese mercantile sources.
Also, the reparations and indemnities that China was forced to
pay during the nineteenth century were deposited with Western
banks which were mostly in Shanghai. But capital availability
alone is not sufficient. I therefore look into the local conditions which I believe favored Canton.

Availability of female labor, overseas Chinese mercantile
capital, as well as climatic conditions that made possible the
harvesting of cocoons on a more continuous basis throughout the
year were decisive advantages that Shanghai didn't enjoy to the
extent Canton did. If this explains the regional growth of the
silk industry in Canton, it doesn't answer the developmental
question that I posed earlier. Here, perhaps, Basu's "pidginization" has some relevance for we find that, both in Canton and
Shanghai, the silk entrepreneurs had to form foreign connections.
The simple reason for this was the fact that the foreign trade
sector was entirely controlled by foreign firms. From this I
suggested the reason why the Chinese were unable to capture the
foreign market in silks was because they were unable to develop
trans-oceanic shipping. And this lack of development in trans-

177

oceanic shipping was a critical difference from the Japanese situation.

The economic consequence of foreign domination of trade and shipping was that silk firms were not able to integrate phases of production with distribution and thus increase their profits. This is not just an abstract point. I have the empirical data on a certain filature that engaged in direct shipping and which was able to increase its profits considerably. The implication is that there were constraints in the export sector that minimized the potential benefits of the growth of silks for the domestic economy as a whole.

In the last part of the paper there is some descriptive material on how the pidginization process worked in the Chinese silk industry. I describe ways whereby the foreign export firms were able to increase their profits at the expense of the Chinese producers. One can, of course, ask why didn't the Chinese come to shipping and export directly and, conversely, why didn't the foreign companies continue their work in direct production? Professor Morris has supplied us a paradigm that explains the individual choices of different lines of economic enterprise, both native and foreign. But I believe we should go beyond the economic rationale and look at the political forces that insured the continuation of the advantages of the foreign import-export firm and the foreign domination of the export industry.

VON DER MUHLL - Christopher A. Bayly is the discussant at this panel.

BAYLY - These three very interesting China papers provide us with comparative material for the rest of the seminar. I'll pull out some of the general themes, and I hope that others with more knowledge than myself in the China field will take up the particular themes.

Basu's paper addresses itself to Canton in the period 1793-1842. It is essentially a study in an Asian port city in which Europeans were becoming the dominant external trading group and developing relationships with power within the city and, crucially, with the outside political powers, that is, the officials of the Chinese government. So, Canton in these years is analytically similar to, for instance, Surat in the 1730s or 1740s or other cities where Europeans were moving from a position of being a partner trading group to being a dominant trading group.

What seems to me to be crucially different in the case of Canton from these earlier and more fragile periods of European dominance in a largely indigenous trade is that the working out of these relationships, the subordination of the Co-Hong to the East India Company and the private traders was done against the background of a changing structure of external trade. That is to say, the British by the 1780s and 90s had worked out a system of trade in which political power re-inforced an existing, substantial European advantage in the control of international shipping lanes and of local capital circulating in Asian trade. This system, this changing structure, was then tied into a rapidly expanding demand in Europe.

Now, what defined British trade to Canton as a specifically colonial or extractive trade rather than simply a trade of European expansion was the rise of the political power of the East India Company in India that made it possible from the 1770s to finance its trade with Canton by the use of land revenue and political power wielded in Bengal. At the same time, political power gave the European private trader a great advantage in building up capital in this newly developed Asian trading system. The undermining of the independence of the indigenous Co-Hong merchants in Canton, the galloping advance of the Hong debts--the main agency of European dominance over the indigenous Cantonese merchants--was closely related to external inputs from the trading system as a whole.

"Pidginization," then, was connected with the growth of political power in Bengal. The result was, as Basu puts it, the Co-Hong's collective personality could not simply work under the new conditions: the presence of abundant private capital pumped out of Indian sources--the lack of capital among most Hongists--the resultant incidence of heavy debts, etc.

So, we have two aspects of the situation. One is the great external advantage which the development of political power was giving the colonial trading system. The other was the problem of the mobilization of internal resources. In the context of the latter, the Hong merchants were in a difficult and somewhat fragile position in Canton. The institutional pressures from the Chinese government--that is, the possibility of forced loans and the fact that merchants who collapsed into debt could be exiled as a punishment--were certainly detrimental to capital accumulation on a long-term basis. They also lacked access to the Inland Chinese investment arenas. Basu doesn't explain this fully which, I hope, will be brought out in discussion.

These themes relate not only to aspects of transition to European dominance in a particular port city but to the problems faced by indigenous port city traders and industrialists in a high colonial period also. The problems of the Hongists in the 1780s or 1790s were not dissimilar in some respects to the problems of Shanghai's indigenous entrepreneurs raised in Eng's paper. In a broad sense, the modernizing *Bhadrolok* of Calcutta, entrepreneurs like Dwarkanath Tagore, faced a similar situation. It was partly a question of the institutional base, the problem of capital and access to inland resources, as well as the dominance of the external system by the Europeans.

Eng provides a valuable discussion of the benefits and disadvantages of the proximity to the colonial port city for the local entrepreneur and relates substantially to the argument whether colonial cities acted as channels of technical innovation or, in fact, dampened activity in their surroundings. The answer seems to be that Canton entrepreneurs got off to a better start than those of Shanghai because of the dependence of the latter on European capital facilities that led to a greater pidgination, to use Basu's phrase.

The Chinese-generated capital was, he says, a more stable and reliable source of investment funds. The paper also addresses itself to the important question of the entrepreneur, and Morris's "Rashomon principle" seems to be working effectively here. That is to say, the exact social context of the entrepreneur in regard to local labor, capital, and a perception of his room for manoeuver, local demand, and local political circumstances were more important than any general characteristics of the entrepreneurial mentality, and so on.

One of the things that surprised me in this discussion of the entrepreneur in these papers is the absence of any discussion of values in the bland sense that they are sometimes still used in the Indian context. Confucius seemed to have bitten the dust, and I'm not quite sure why that should be. Two aspects, particularly interesting to us in regard to port cities, come out of Robert Eng's paper: first, the importance of European control of shipping, insurance, and freight charges. He points out clearly that one of the main reasons for the inability of the Chinese to capture a share of foreign trade was undoubtedly related to their inability to develop trans-oceanic shipping in Shanghai in the 1890s. As in Calcutta of the 1830s and 40s, the great value markup was going to the external shipping, insurance, and banking facilities.

In much of South Asia, since about 1750, the growing dominance of all external sources of information, credit, and facilities by the Europeans has been the case. But the advantages of the Europeans seemed to increase during the period 1840-47 by certain structural changes in external trade related to the telegraph, steamship, to the rapid information that aided these European coastal-based export firms to an even greater extent. It seems, however, that a simple control of the international facilities was not enough to guarantee total European dominance. It is certainly not a sufficient explanation either of colonialism or of the colonial port city.

Eng provides a key explanation with his emphasis on political power. As he puts it, "One must not forget, however, that the Chinese government's options were limited by Imperialist aggression; for example, indemnities due the foreign powers helped drain the Ch'ing Dynasty of its financial resources and forced it to turn to such taxes as the *likin*. Without denying the energetic reform efforts of the Japanese government, it may be observed that it operated under much lower intensity of

180

foreign pressure: the Westerners in the second half of the 19th century looked to China rather than to Japan as the market with rich potentialities. This, therefore, echoes the concern expressed yesterday that, within any definition of colonialism and colonial port city or imperialism, a political factor is crucially important.

Chan's paper gives us an interesting account of the rise of Hong Kong as a colonial port city-state at the expense of Canton. His analysis shows how political action and dominance of import-export facilities directed much of the South China overseas and even local trade through Hong Kong. We get the picture of the drift of population, of mercantile communities, of facilities, to Hong Kong in a similar way as the rise of Melaka, Batavia, and Goa affected other cities in the earlier period. It can also be, in some ways, compared to the declining inland towns of central India with the rise of the new type of extractive colonial towns that I described in my paper.

But the crucial point I get out of Chan's paper is the continuing strength of Canton as an inland entrepôt and controller of supplies, of labor, of produce. This would seem to reinforce Murphey's general point about the great strength of the inland Chinese market as opposed to the port city systems. Chan's discussion of the 1926 boycott also reinforces the other point--about the importance of political and institutional control as a fundamental element in a definition of colonialism and colonial port cities. He shows that the boycott by Cantonese brought Hong Kong to its knees very rapidly. Hong Kong didn't have sufficient control over its hinterland. This brings us back to the question of the nature of colonialism which I think must be defined, not merely in terms of the control of a particular type of high-density overseas trade and facilities, but also in terms of political control of the inland resources of a particular area.

DAS GUPTA - My question relates to an earlier period. The Chinese had an important maritime merchant class around 1500. Whatever happened to them? Between 1500 and the time Basu begins, something went dreadfully wrong. The Hong merchants were first government-appointed, and then they became dependent on the British. But the early sixteenth century Portuguese sources speak of steady Chinese traffic, sometimes in spite of government prohibition, which kept the Southeast Asian trade going.

Incidentally, the Chinese fleet was the only fleet that definitely defeated the Portuguese twice, in 1521 and in 1522. Nothing else like it happened in Asian waters. Has this story been told, touched upon, by anyone?

BASU - I don't have any specialized knowledge of the sixteenth century period. I am familiar only with the general literature.

181

A number of scholars, Jung-pang Lo and Gung-wu Wang among
others, addressed the question some time ago. The late
Professor Joseph Levenson posed the question succinctly in
a little book he edited before his untimely death: *European
Expansion and the Counter-Example of Asia.* If there could be an
Age of Vasco da Gama, why wasn't there the Age of Cheng Ho?
Cheng Ho was, of course, the great "Ming" navigator who
sailed probably the world's then-largest fleet as far as
Africa.

        Mark Elvin, in his stimulating book, *Patterns of the
Chinese Past,* has also attempted to deal with this subject.
We know that soon after Cheng Ho's expeditions, the Ming government deliberately decided on a policy of closure. Each scholar
I mentioned has his theory on the anti-maritime policy of the
Ming. I can make only some general observations. I believe
the reasons for Ming withdrawal were, in the main, geo-political
and strategic. If we compare and contrast the Chinese world
empire with the Mediterranean world that Pirenne and Braudel
have described, we are struck by the absence of a basic seaward
push: The center of political forces was inland, with constant
military threat coming from the Inner Asian frontiers rather
than from overseas. This led to a continentalized attitude
that considered maritime adventures as wasteful and unnecessary.
One thing to bear in mind is that only the state had the resources to undertake a massive program of naval development:
We must remember that Cheng Ho's expeditions were sponsored
by the state. The withdrawal of state sponsorship had the
obvious deleterious effects.

        This doesn't mean that maritime activity ceased alto-
gether. The hard-honed Fukien sailor continued to go to Southeast Asian countries. There were often some remarkable spurts
in their activities. There is evidence to suggest that local
authorities, the imperial prohibitions notwithstanding, often
invested in such enterprises, causing the occasional spurts.

MURPHEY - I agree. It is important to note that only the huge
war junk type expeditions ceased, but commercial navigation
continued on and even increased. Chinese overseas trade, in
Chinese carriers, in Chinese hands, went to Java, Malaya, and
perhaps beyond. It was not a case of mysterious disappearance.

BASU - Yes. During the sixteenth century this kind of commercial
navigation did indeed suffer a setback due to the increased
activities of the Japanese Wako pirates. The Wakos established
along the coasts of Southeast Asia substantial fortified settlements that were thorns to the Chinese as well as European shipping that plied the seas. The interesting point is that this
kind of Chinese shipping eventually survived such setbacks and
even the advent of European shipping. Traditional junk shipping
was cheaper, especially for heavy haulage, and there is little
evidence to suggest that it declined. What probably happened
was specialization and a division of labor with European shipping
catering to new markets and trade.

MURPHEY   -   If we could now turn to the issues raised in these
papers, I would like to ask Basu whether Houqua was pleased
with his investments in the United States through Forbes?

BASU   -   Houqua died in 1843, and the Forbes Company was established in 1936. I have come across some nice, affectionate
letters that transpired between John and Houqua that suggest
Houqua had complete confidence in Forbes and that he considered the investment to be safe.

In 1839, Houqua was publicly humiliated by Commissioner
Lin's forces, and when Forbes heard about it, he proposed to
Houqua that he could perhaps immigrate to the United States
and settle in Florida! He had enough money invested in the
United States to give him a comfortable income, but Houqua pol-
itely turned down the invitation. I have appended, at the end
of my paper, the figures from the Forbes account books that
give us a picture of returns until 1880. They were modest.
One suspects that they should have been higher.

MORRIS   -   All the three papers on this panel commonly emphasize
foreign trade. Eng and Chan, especially, leave the implication that somehow, if China had had her foreign trade and
shipping companies in her hands, there would have been more
development. Indian historiography also has followed a similar
focus which I think is now being redirected. The problem with
this focus is that it turns away from the whole array of basic
preconditions which don't exist within the system at all.

The question of setting limitations on foreign trade
opportunities is only relevant to a small proportion of the
total market, whereas we are essentially dealing with the
general problem of capital accumulation, widening markets, increasing agricultural productivity, and the like. The issue
is, therefore, not why didn't China follow the Japanese model
but the structure of Chinese society which, like the structure
of the Indian society, was not prepared for rapid industrial
growth for a long period of time.

ENG   -   Back in the '50s, economists emphasized trade. I think
it was Robertson who coined the phrase that "trade was the
engine of growth." Now we are getting away from that idea.
The new faith is that "trade is the handmaiden of growth."
Foreign export growth can lead to industrialization only in
a framework that already has the necessary prerequisites for
economic growth. In other words, the foreign export sector
cannot, by itself, be the dynamic that will transform the
economy. I agree, but I don't think it is by all means clear
that there wasn't any potential for growth within the Chinese
domestic economy.

The "sprouts of capitalism" is a well-known argument in
Chinese history. According to this argument, certain areas and
regions had reached a high state of development before the in-

trusion of Western Imperialism which interrupted this process
and thereby aborted the potential for growth. There is little
doubt that certain regions in China, as in India and Southeast
Asia, had a very high concentration of mercantile capital.
Why this capital couldn't be channeled into industrial uses
is a matter that historians would continue to ponder, but I
don't think it's a closed matter that the domestic economy
was too impoverished to have any dynamic possibilities of
its own.

ANDERSON - I am interested in a few factors that I would like
to ask the panelists to try to tie together for me. The first
one relates to the lineage system as it developed in South
China, providing for a mobilization of resources within the
lineage for certain kinds in a way that wasn't common in other
regions of China.

As Eng points out, filatures were built and rented out
by the clans, a primary and ubiquitous form of organization,
and the province's largest landowners were unique to South China.
I'm not surprised at that because I am impressed by the development of the clan system as represented in Friedman's works.

A second point is that South China was, in the nineteenth
and twentieth centuries as well as in earlier eras, the center
for the recruitment of overseas migrants to the Nanyang. I am
thinking of the Philippinos--who came from a few towns in Fukien
and Kwangtung provinces. I would like to know how the Nanyang
trade stimulated the development of the lineage system and,
perhaps, provided also a mechanism for the internal mobilization of capital.

ENG - I have attempted to outline the mechanism in the paper.
Usually, people who migrated overseas sent remittances back to
their families which either directly or indirectly found a way
into the native banks of Canton.

ANDERSON - My question is, How early did this get started?
I'm asking whether this is something just seen as an artifact
in your paper or had an older, earlier origin?

ENG - I suspect that the overseas remittances started to come
in soon after large numbers of Chinese migrated overseas.

CHAN - I believe this could be traced back probably to the mid-
nineteenth century, by which time both Singapore and Hong Kong
had a substantial number of Southern Chinese immigrants. In
addition, there were many in Thailand and the Dutch East Indies.
We do not have good records on the remittance until 1865 when
the Hong Kong and Shanghai Bank in Hong Kong was founded. The
Chinese characters for "the Hong Kong and Shanghai Bank, *Hui
Feng* (way foong), means "an abundance of remittance," which is
self-explanatory.

BASU - I don't have much to add to this question. I would like to, if I may, pursue some of the points that Bayly raised earlier while discussing our papers.

First, there was upward social mobility among the Hong merchants who expressed it, as did the Indian merchants in Calcutta and Madras, in certain cultural forms, including the assumption of gentry lifestyle: one can throw in a bit of pidgin influence here and there. Some of them liked to collect books, including books on the West, and maps; others built temples or contributed to local academies. What is most striking is their general preference for gentry status, the counterpart of Lewandowski's "kingly" status or model. The Confucian social ethos was, no doubt, important here. Even the British recognized this. Houqua III was respectfully addressed as Mr. Houqua, Esquire! It is important to note that none, if any, among the Hong merchants continued as *compradors* after the abolition of the Co-Hong in 1842. At least, none among the leading merchants.

The question about inland investment: Technically, according to law, they couldn't invest internally as the Hongists represented a government monopoly and even had a bureaucratic rank. There were digressions from the legal position, of course. Houqua, for instance, had tea estates in the Fukien hills. Yet he was not certainly a great inland merchant. I believe the Hongists, being essentially port city merchant-brokers, found it hard to dent the quarry of internal markets and networks.

Another point is that the Hong merchants were essentially "new men." Although the *hang* itself was an ancient institution, those who became prominent Hong merchants in my period came from pedestrian backgrounds. Some started as menials in the Canton system, acquiring the tricks of the trade on the spot; others started as apprentices in a larger Hong. Houqua's father was a "purser" in the establishment of the eighteenth century Hongist, Puankhequa. This made sense, for the Hong system, as it evolved in Canton, required specialized skills such as a knowledge of pidgin, foreigners, and foreign trade that only the locals experiences in the Canton commercial system possessed. This is corroborated by the fact that, whenever an attempt was made to induct an outsider, the classic case being that of the "Emperor's merchant" in the early eighteenth century, into Hongship, it met with unmitigated disaster.

My point is that the Hong merchants were foreign trade "experts" who couldn't be expected to do well in internal trade. This is analogous to the position of Banians in Calcutta who also failed to dent the inland networks. Whether this was true of other Asian port cities' merchant classes, I don't know. But it seems to be a good comparative question, deserving of further study.

185

BAYLY - Two questions: While looking at the tea trade in the early period, one gets references to the heads of the Co-Hong in every individual city involved in this brokerage function. Was there no institutional connection between the Co-Hong of the individual cities? Secondly, why didn't the Shansi bankers, internal trading groups, develop the same kind of lien on coastal skills and facilities that the Marwaris did in India, thus linking together the internal and the coastal networks?

VON DER MUHLL - Professor Murphey, do you wish to get in on this?

MURPHEY - Foreigners often referred to the Co-Hong when they attempted to trade along the China coast in the early period. They would run into a supervisor of trade or the local intendant in charge of the official policy regarding foreign trade who might say, "You cannot trade here except with official permission." The foreign response was that the specter of the Co-Hong haunted them everywhere, its tentacles reaching from Canton throughout the country. Foreign trade policy in China was more centrally controlled as a matter of imperial policy than was the case in India. It is not, therefore, surprising that foreigners got the same kind of response wherever they tried to knock throughout the country.

The case of the Shansi bankers is puzzling. They were the principal agency for the transmission of funds from one part of the country to another. But they didn't emerge as a controlling factor, even before the Treaty Port period, either in Canton or in the other coastal areas. Obviously, there was a division of function between movement and financing of trade internally, and its movement out into export channels was handled by different groups.

BASU - There was a Co-Hong system in Amoy, but after 1760 all other coastal ports were closed to foreign trade except Canton. A few Amoy merchants did migrate to Canton where the action was. The Shansi bankers served as depositories of government funds and acted as agents of transmittal of funds from one region to another. They continued in this role through the nineteenth century. They were "world empire" type bankers, attached to the imperial government. They declined completely after the 1911 Revolution. In this they are somewhat comparable to the Jagatseths of Bengal who were also government bankers and who declined after Plassey. The Marwaris who made it in Calcutta's trade came later.

MILONE - One last question: In the papers presented earlier this morning, we found that the Calcutta merchants had some impact on the drive for an independent municipality government; in the case of Madras, the merchants had some impact on the morphology of the town by building temples. What impact did the Hong merchants have on Canton? Did they have any influence on the way the city looked, or on any of the institutions that

186

were founded? Were any of the funds that had been extracted
from the Hong merchants used for construction in Canton?

BASU - The Hong role in Canton was similar, but there was a
difference of scale. In the 1660s, the conquering Ch'ing
had pretty much demolished Canton city. One reason why the
Ming injunction against foreign trade was ended and Canton
officially opened for trade was that the trade revenues
could go into reconstruction. Canton was substantially rebuilt during the late seventeenth century. How much direct
Hong contribution went into this is difficult to tell. But,
during their heyday, they built garden villas in Canton suburbs, temples, and academies. Morphologically, their impact
on that part of Canton where foreign trade was conducted was
considerable. They ran and maintained the "Thirteen Factories"
where foreigners lived; their guild hall was an important land-
mark in the city. In addition, they maintained downtown offices and quarters which had considerable morphological impact
as centers of activity. But there was another part of Canton,
the administrative and governmental part, where their impact
was minimal if not non-existent. The government exacted from
the Hongists periodic contributions to public works in cases
of floods and famines which, of course, fall into a different
category than voluntary contributions.

VON DER MUHLL - During the break, an urban sociologist who
knows even less about Asia than I do observed that he thought
Basu had invented a new subject: Colonial Port Cities! To
an outsider who is a social scientist and whose interests ram-
ble around the globe, it is interesting how much one can learn
from historical detail. I found the panel papers and the subsequent discussion a singularly sensitive perspective from
which to examine the contact of the East and West. Thank you.

Golden Island.

137

TOPIC III: RISE, GROWTH, AND MORPHOLOGY OF
               THE COLONIAL PORT CITY

Session 5

ARCHITECTURAL PLANNING AND OTHER BUILDING ACTIVITIES

OF THE BRITISH IN MADRAS, BOMBAY, AND CALCUTTA

(c. 1630 - c. 1757)

by

Partha Mitter

This paper proposes to investigate the principal architectural
considerations that governed the evolution of Madras, Bombay, and Calcutta, the three major colonial port cities in India during their formative periods (c. 1630 - c. 1757). In this connection I also wish to
consider the important issue of town planning raised by Sten Nilsson in
his fine work on *European Architecture in India: 1750 - 1850*, published
in 1968. Although his work deals primarily with neoclassical architecture introduced in India after the establishment of British hegemony,
he has much to say about town planning and general building activities
of the preceding period, the late seventeenth and early eighteenth centuries when Madras, Bombay, and Calcutta were founded.

Nilsson describes the European cities in India as representing
a "uniform lay-out of the houses within the walls, the uniform blocks
and streets which intersect at right angles," and he contrasts this with
the haphazard and "organic" growth of Indian towns. His argument that
colonial towns were uniform and regular in plan is further developed to
suggest that they were centrally planned along the lines of an ideal
Renaissance city. Central plan, first applied to Renaissance churches,
is taken to mean that, in a city, there is a fixed center towards which
streets, laid out at right angles to each other, converge. Taking Madras
as an example, he comes to the conclusion that it was a uniformly laid
out town with streets intersecting at right angles on the evidence of the
1688 map reproduced by the French Orientalist, Langlès (1821). This map,
however, bears a closer relation to an ideal, notional diagram than an
actual survey map, and the great authority on Madras, H. D. Love, had
been rightly suspicious of it.

In fact, by far the most reliable map of the period must be the
one produced in 1710 under Thomas Pitt's orders. This map, which Nilsson
fails to take into account, was the outcome of a very careful survey of
the town. This particular map shows that the streets were fairly regular
and wide. In fact, contemporary accounts frequently praise the handsome
streets of Madras. But the same map also makes it clear that there was
hardly anything like comprehensive planning. The absence of regular planning is also evident in the two other cities, Bombay and Calcutta, which
arose a little later than Madras.

Professor Robert Reed's mention at the Conference of the appli-
cation of a grid plan in the sixteenth century city of Manila brought
home to me an important lesson. When the Spaniards created an ideal
central-plan city in Manila, the influence of the Renaissance was paramount in Spain, and the *tabula rasa* of the new colony provided the ideal
ground to test out Renaissance theory. Similarly, in India, the centrally-
planned sixteenth century Portuguese town of Daman belongs to this period
of Humanist influence in the Iberian peninsula. On the other hand, when
Madras was founded in the seventeenth century, Britain was far removed
both in space and time from the Italian Renaissance. In this period,
architectural planning simply concentrated on individual buildings. It
therefore seems unlikely that a central-plan system would be imposed by
the British on Madras.

Moreover, Nilsson's assumption that central-planning was unknown
in India is open to question. Even he recognizes that the traditional
eighteenth century city of Jaipur follows a perfect central-plan where
the streets intersect at strict right angles. Apart from the fact that
Harappa and Mahenjodaro, two of the earliest cities in India (c. 2500 –
1500 B.C.) were laid out on a strict grid plan, traditional Indian architectural manuals prescribed perfect central-plan towns much in the manner
in which Renaissance theorists wrote. But to realize such a plan as in
Jaipur, one required an absolute ruler like Jai Singh II with unlimited
funds. This sort of ideal situation did not exist for the three colonial
settlements whose early histories were marked by incessant conflicts between the Company officials and the Home government over funds for essential constructions such as fortifications, let alone the sheer luxury of
city planning.

Therefore, even assuming that they had such an intention, the
East India Company officials were constantly frustrated in their attempts
to undertake large-scale building projects. Even in cases such as fortifications or hospitals, whenever financial assistance was requested it
was either turned down or partially granted after great delays. In this
situation, Aungier's plans for the development of Bombay and similar projects naturally failed to get off the ground.

Madras was founded in 1639, Bombay ceded to the British in 1663,
and Calcutta was established in 1689. If they were not the outcome of
conscious planning by their founding fathers, what different social, economic, and political factors affected their respective developments? For
the early form of colonial structures in India we must turn to the general
form of the colonial port city in Asia. This will help us to understand
why they were so unlike traditional Indian towns. In the seventeenth
century the English factory, the nucleus of a port city, drew inspiration
from Dutch colonial architecture of Batavia. A typical example is the
factory building at Surat, leased from a Mughal official, whose structural
modifications show Dutch influence.

From early records it appears that defense against external
enemies was uppermost in the minds of the founders of the three cities.
In the period under consideration, Madras was the most developed settlement and much information has been left us about its early history. Within fourteen years of the founding of Madras, the first phase of its forti-

fications was completed when it became the best defended British town in the subcontinent. On the other hand, some thirty-five defense works were undertaken piecemeal in Bombay during the first hundred years of its history. The first Fort William at Calcutta was completed in 1712, but its defensive walls were too low to withstand sustained assault. Its illusion of security was cruelly shattered when it was easily reduced in 1756. Therefore, one of the first tasks of Clive was to build an impregnable fort further down the river in 1773. To repeat, the three settlements suffered from a chronic lack of funds which generally stood in the way of successfully completing defense projects.

Not only fortifications as such but the very spread and layout of these three cities reveal defense considerations. In all three instances the fort, situated near the water's edge, formed the pivot of the port city. The subsequent expansions that took place were lateral, namely to the left and right of the fort along the water's edge, with less thrust into the interior. The typical shape of the port city as a narrow strip along the coast suggests the need to have easy access to the sea since, in this period, the English had very little control over inland politics. Even in the case of Madras where the British had less to fear from the local powers the initial expansion was along the coast. In accordance with the concept of centralized planning it would have been more aesthetically pleasing to have built the governor's mansion in the center of town, but in India defense considerations shifted the focus to the fort near the water's edge. In short, the chief danger was from land while open seas were regarded as the safest refuge. This significant point is not fully appreciated by Nilsson when he states that Madras had the strongest defense facing the sea.

Apart from defense, public buildings included, first and foremost, the governor's (or the president's) residence which stood out as the most imposing private building. However, in contrast to the imperial period, there was little attempt to apply a particular European architectural style with any consistency, although contemporary sources use the term "Tuscan" in a loose sense when speaking of English buildings in India. Contemporary prints give us some idea about the appearance of these buildings. In 1683 the Fort House in Madras underwent extensive alterations. In this period it was described as of noble appearance. The governor's house in Bombay was never very conspicuous, partly because the former Jesuit seminary in the suburb of Parel, set amidst luxurious groves, generally served as his residence. From contemporary prints one forms a clear impression of the handsome house in Calcutta, built for the President in 1702-6 and burnt down by Shiraj-ud Daulah in 1756.

As early as 1687, Madras received its Charter for a representative corporation. Although this body did not have as much say in building matters as the governor it was, at least, able to build for itself a sumptuous town hall with an elaborate vaulted roof and an ornate cupola. Unlike Madras, Calcutta had its town hall much later in the nineteenth century.

In the period under review most of the building activities were concentrated in two areas: the hospital, which catered to the physical needs of the population, and the church, which ministered to the spiritual

193

ones. There are few pictorial records of hospitals of the early period. The earliest hospital in Madras was set up in 1664 which was subsequently moved in 1692 to a house in the "Tuscan style." Pitt's map mentions a hospital and, for a while, even the Capuchin church served as one. The Directors at home criticized the colony for extravagantly introducing "various ornaments which now appear in the elevations of the ...hospital, though the orders of the Board were that those buildings should be as plain as they could consistently be made."

Bombay periodically suffered from such ill health that a hospital became a dire necessity, particularly during the outbreak of the plague of 1690-1708. In 1677 the old court was converted into a hospital which was replaced by a proper building in 1733 at the site of the Marine yard. Hamilton's description suggests the existence of a hospital in Calcutta in the 1690s. The Presidency hospital, however, followed in 1709, three years after the building of the President's house. Contemporary records mention another hospital, dating from 1750.

Churches were the most conspicuous early structures in the three port cities, as attested to by contemporary prints. Here, in marked contrast to the situation at home, colonial policy was liberal with regard to all denominations as well as other faiths. The Capuchin church, which preceded the Anglican Church by several years in Madras, was given its permanent site in 1675, but an even larger edifice of some architectural importance was constructed in 1721, imposing with its campanile. Partly with subscription raised for the purpose, the Anglican Church of St. Mary's was opened in Madras in 1680, the first masonry structure in the town. At the time of the Portuguese cessation, Bombay contained a number of major Catholic churches, but the Anglican Church of St. Thomas was not built until 1718 even though the need to impress the natives had been felt for a long time. In Calcutta, St. Anne's was consecrated in 1709, but the damage caused by the 1737 earthquake led to its rebuilding. St. Anne's handsome spire dominated the waterfront until its final demolition by Nawab Shiraj-ud Daulah.

In one area the port cities represent an important innovation; this was the great popularity of garden houses, parks, and gardens, a concept neither wholly European nor wholly Indian. There already existed in India both Mughal formal gardens and informal groves. The English settlers chose to develop by preference the informal groves in their cities which were closer to the "jardin anglais," increasingly favored in Britain in the eighteenth century. Pitt's map is a testimony to the extensive gardens owned by the Company servants. Pitt himself was responsible for laying out gardens and parks and for various horticultural developments in Madras. In Calcutta, great gardens which formed major landmarks in the early maps were owned by both the English and the Indians. One of the reasons why Surat failed to develop as a colonial port city may be attributed to the lack of space for gardens inside the town.

A particularly interesting aspect of studying the evolution of the colonial port cities is the confluence of two traditions, European and Asian, and the problems this raises. When the British settled in the three cities they naturally brought over European architectural tradition with them to serve their needs. Thus, the most obvious aspect of these cities is the development of European architecture in them. And yet these were not pure European cities for they sprang up on an alien soil and in an alien climate. Moreover, from the outset the East India Company encouraged the settlement of Indians and other ethnic groups. A significant development in the port city was the early segregation of the population in its different parts. In the eighteenth century the European part was clearly marked as the White Town while Indians lived in the Black Town, although this division was not so evident in Bombay. We know a lot more about the building activities of the European parts of Madras, Bombay, and Calcutta than the Indian sections, and much more work is needed in this last area.

My conclusion about the European parts, based on contemporary accounts as well as on pictorial records, is that the three colonial port cities evolved organically during the period under consideration, although occasional efforts were made to impose an architectural style on buildings or to introduce some amount of town-planning. This was, however, a far cry from total, centralized planning. It was only after Plassey that the victors began to think consciously of creating architectural grandeur in India, a period so ably documented by Sten Nilsson.

SOURCES:

Baldaeus, P.	*Beschreibung der Ostindischen Kusten Malabar und Coromandel*, 1672.
Burnell, J.	*Bombay in the Days of Queen Anne*, 1710.
Busteed, H. E.	*Echoes of Old Calcutta*, 1882.
Carre, Abbe	*The Travels of Abbe Carre*, 1947.
Factory Records	(Fort St. George, also Misc.) India Office Library
Foster, W.	*Founding of Fort St. George*, 1902.
Fryer, J.	*A New Account of East Indies and Persia*, 1698.
Grose, J.	*A Voyage to the East Indies*, 1772.
Hamilton, A.	*A New Account of Voyages*, 1727.
Hill, S. D.	*Bengal in 1756-57* (Indian Record Series), 1905.
Ives, E.	*A Voyage from England to India*, 1773.
Langles, L.	*Monuments anciens et modernes de l'Hindoustan*, 1821.
Love, H. D.	*Vestiges of Old Madras*, 1913.
Manucci, N.	*Storia do Mogor* (Tr. W. Irvine), 1906-08.
Original Correspondence Series. India Office Library
Ovington, J.	*A Voyage to Suratt in the Year 1689*, 1695.
Sheppard, S. T.	*Bombay*, 1932.
	The Gazeteer of Bombay City & Island, 1909-10.
Wheeler, J. T.	*Early Records of British India*, 1878.

196

THE FOUNDATION AND MORPHOLOGY OF HISPANIC MANILA:
COLONIAL IMAGES AND PHILIPPINE REALITIES

by

Robert R. Reed

On the eve of Spanish *conquista* the patterns of settlement and society in the Philippines differed markedly from those prevailing in nearby regions. While indigenous urbanism and the territorial state had flourished elsewhere in Southeast Asia for more than a millennium, the Filipinos continued to occupy thousands of small and widely scattered villages. When Miguel López de Legazpi and his forces overran the Visayas and Luzon, most coastal and lowland peoples shared in common a form of socio-political organization based on kinship, specific to the local community, and known as the *barangay*. These living groups, which consisted of from one hundred to five hundred people whose mode of ecological adaptation combined in greater or lesser degrees hunting, fishing, gathering, and *swidden* (shifting cultivation), were usually expressed on the landscape as small, comparatively isolated and frequently impermanent villages of from thirty to one hundred houses. Although some *barangay* in the nascent *sawah* (wet rice) region of Central Luzon had become quite fixed in place and occasionally clustered together for protection in times of conflict, even these communities continued to function as independent social and political entities.

In each autonomous *barangay* the foremost of several ranked descent groups consisted of the *datu*, while free-born *maharlika*, commoners termed *timagua*, and servile *alipin* held subordinate positions. Nevertheless, all members of the local community were firmly bound by traditional systems of social, religious, and economic obligations. Although several supra*barangay* confederations had begun to crystallize at Cebu and Manila during the decades immediately before the advent of the Spaniards, they remained unstable creations sustained only through the ultimate sanction of force. Even Rajah Sulayman, the able, ambitious, and comparatively powerful Muslim leader of precolonial Manila, experienced serious difficulties in forging a durable association of communities within the immediate environs of his large port settlement. Because Islam, which was spreading to various parts of Central Luzon and Mindoro during the second half of the sixteenth century, carried the heavy burdens of external authority in religious matters and frequent interference by outsiders in social and political affairs, many *datu* and their followers firmly resisted the overtures of the aggressive Muslims. Accordingly, regional confederations of *barangay* proved ephemeral in time and place for their leaders had few methods of legitimation other than superior military might. It cannot be denied that Islam helped make the notion of supra*barangay* affiliation more acceptable to many Filipinos, but it did not foster the generation of towns and cities or even of truly stable chiefdoms in pre-Hispanic times. The development of urbanism and the state in the Philippines depended, ultimately, upon the introduction of the combined instruments of superior political organization, an integrative religion, and overpowering military force. These were provided by Spain.

From the onset of colonization in the Philippines, the Spaniards were repelled by the socio-political decentralization of the *barangay* and frustrated by the dispersion of villages. As citizens of the greatest colonial empire in the world, proselytizing Catholics and heirs to Mediterranean urbanism, they deeply cherished traditions of national and international association. To the Spanish colonists the Filipinos were a simple people who lived without polity. Not only did the extreme independence of communities clash with fundamental values of the Spaniards, but it also posed a formidable obstacle to the efficient collection of tribute, to the conversion of native peoples, and to their effective administration. The invaders well realized that these three fundamental colonial goals could be met only through a sustained program of resettlement.

Although the extreme particularism of settlement and society clearly presented a formidable physical obstacle to the spiritual and cultural conquest of the Philippines, the Spaniards in the closing decades of the sixteenth century welcomed the challenge and proved ready to show their skills as the most experienced founders and developers of towns and cities in the world. The Americas, of course, had served as their training ground. In an ongoing effort to consolidate widespread territorial gains in the New World, Spanish authorities in Church and State worked together to establish thousands of Hispanicized settlements which embraced both Europeans and Indians. The developing urban system featured a small number of major colonial capitals, each of which functioned as the governmental, religious, and commercial nerve center in a politically discrete dependency and many strategically located provincial towns and cities that served as hubs of regional administration.

The broad base of the resultant hierarchy of colonial settlements consisted of specialized ports, mining camps, fortified frontier outposts, and countless Indian *cabeceras* (mission communities). While the colonial capitals and most other large urban places were considered *ciudades de españoles* (Spanish cities), fashioned essentially for White colonists and *mestizos*, the Crown designed the missions as contact points between European politico-religious authorities and dependent native peoples. Through the unflagging efforts of Spanish missionaries who were the only Europeans allowed to reside permanently in Indian communities, these small provincial centers became the key foci of Hispanization and Christianization throughout the empire. Almost from the beginning of Spanish intervention along the shores of the Caribbean and the Gulf of Mexico, therefore, the ranking metropolitan authorities envisaged colonial towns and cities as essential instruments of territorial occupance, economic exploitation, regional administration, and religious conversion. Indeed, it is no exaggeration to say that Spain's sprawling empire in the New World was secured by an urban keystone.

Predictably Spanish strategies for the colonization and urbanization of Filipinos derived directly from experience gained in the Americas.
Moreover, the procedures for the *reducción* (resettlement) of conquered
peoples were codified in the famed royal Ordinances of 1573 which Philip II
promulgated in order to provide Spanish colonial officials with a master-
plan for the systematic foundation of towns and cities. These planning
prescriptions reflected both practical experience acquired during the
establishment of numerous urban centers in Hispanic America and idealized
designs of proper city form as outlined in the writings of Vitruvius and
Alberti. The Ordinances offered considerable advice concerning the most
desirable physical characteristics of favorable sites and situations for
Spanish settlements as well as detailed instructions regarding the proper
internal layout of colonial towns and cities.

Although exact reproductions of the Hispanic model failed to materialize in the Philippines, clearly recognizable urban images did begin to
appear in Luzon and the Visayas early in the twentieth century and, through
the untiring efforts of Catholic missionaries, continued to proliferate in
the lowlands during the remaining three centuries of Spanish rule. By the
end of their imperial tenure the Spaniards had, in fact, left an indelible
imprint on the Philippine landscape through the formation of more than a
thousand relatively stable communities fashioned according to the Ordinances proclaimed by Philip II. While the great majority of these colonial
settlements were merely provincial *poblaciones* (towns) of from five hundred
to two thousand people when the Americans expelled the Spanish forces in
1898, many did evolve into substantial urban centers. By the turn of the
twentieth century, two hundred places in the Philippines embraced populations of more than two thousand persons; twenty contained between five
thousand and ten thousand inhabitants; several regional capitals exceeded
twenty thousand individuals, and the primate city of Manila, with its
suburbs, embraced over two hundred thousand residents. Through these Hispanicized towns and cities, which functioned individually and collectively
as effective instruments of political, religious, and cultural change,
the Spaniards thus maintained their suzerainty in the Philippines.

Almost from the beginning of a sustained Western presence in the
Visayas and Luzon, Manila ranked as the foremost colonial city. In accordance with orders from viceregal authorities in Nueva Espana (Mexico),
Legazpi's first major objective after arriving in the Philippines was to
establish a secure headquarters from which a systematic program of conquest
and colonization could be orchestrated. Metropolitan officials not only
directed their *Adelantado* (frontier governor) to carefully assess a number
of sites before making a final choice but also offered advice regarding
the proper layout of the proposed Spanish capital. Though Legazpi made
every effort to select a location meeting the criteria set forth by his
colonial superiors, the first choice of settlement at Cebu failed to prosper because of insufficient food supplies, inadequate material support
from Mexico, and Portuguese harassment. Accordingly, in 1569, he removed
the Spaniards' base of operations northwestwards to Panay. But even on
this fertile island the supply situation did not improve in the least,
forcing the *Adelantado* to carry out a third geographic adjustment of the
colonial headquarters. His final choice of Manila was rewarded with success,
for the developing *sawah* lands of Central Luzon insured a growing supply of
food. Furthermore, Manila Bay proved to be one of the finest harbors in

the world and, consequently, provided a secure anchorage for domestic and international trade.

The rise of colonial Manila as a primate city of the Philippines occurred within a matter of several decades. From this strategic stronghold, Spanish soldiers and missionaries embarked on the rapid military and spiritual conquest of Luzon and other major islands. During the first three decades of effective Hispanic dominion, moreover, Manila became firmly established as the civil and religious nerve center of the emergent colony. Through the integrated institutions of Church and State, the Spaniards quickly transformed Christianized sectors of the Philippines into a clearly defined hinterland subject to the economic exploitation and political administration of an alien officialdom resident in the new colonial capital. Manila remained the supereminent city in the archipelago throughout the ensuing centuries of foreign rule and is so even today.

While Spanish authorities were developing the religious and political functions of their colonial headquarters, its diverse European, Filipino, Japanese, and Chinese residents had also begun to convert Manila into a commercial center of considerable international renown. By exploiting traditional Sino-Filipino trade relationships and by forging a tenuous maritime linkage between Acapulco and the Philippines, they soon changed the Hispanicized capital into a flourishing entrepôt which effectively linked the markets of China, Southeast Asia, and Mexico. Late in the sixteenth century, as the volume of trans-Pacific trade in Chinese silk, porcelain, spices, and other luxury goods increased steadily and before metropolitan officials began to issue laws designed to closely regulate the galleon exchange, the emergent primate city enjoyed a tremendous expansion in population and a great economic boom. From a small Muslim community of only two thousand Malays and a handful of Chinese sojourners, Manila in several generations became a multi-racial city of more than forty thousand inhabitants.

During this period of commercial florescence and rapid growth in population throughout the decades immediately before and after the turn of the seventeenth century, Manila was also transformed from a mere cluster of bamboo and thatch huts into a carefully-planned and walled city of substantial stone, brick, and tile structures that reflected many of the planning principles prescribed in the Ordinances of 1573. Perhaps the most distinctive morphological elements of the Hispanic colonial capital were its grid form, a towering Catholic cathedral, many stately public buildings, a nuclear *plaza major* (main square), several sprawling monastic establishments, and hundreds of handsome two-storey houses. Additionally, the Spaniards converted the flimsy wooden palisades of precolonial Manila into massive fortifications of stone and brick which encircled the entire Spanish city of Intramuros. These were further supplemented by a deep moat and a strong fort located strategically at the point where the Pasig River entered Manila Bay (Maps 1 and 2). Before the end of the sixteenth century Manila's core area of Intramuros had been effectively transformed from a mean assemblage of small and highly flammable structures into an imposing colonial metropolis and symbol of Spanish authority which revealed in its very morphology the key institutions of Church and State.

200

Throughout the early period of unrestricted galleon trade Manila was visited by a myriad of foreign merchants and seamen, most of whom moved on to other Asian ports after a sojourn of several months in the Philippines. But three groups—the Spanish, Japanese, and Chinese—remained in sufficient numbers during the year to warrant separate residential districts amidst the growing population of urbanized Filipinos. The Spanish colonists, of course, clustered in the heavily fortified and racially restricted quarter of Intramuros. A sizable group of Japanese, whose numbers had reached three thousand by the 1620s, lived beyond Manila's walls and moats in the suburb of Dilao. By far the largest alien community consisted of Chinese who, through their labors as traders, sailors, and craftsmen, made possible the galleon trade. From a tiny band of forty persons who lived in pre-Hispanic Manila, the Chinese population had grown to more than twenty thousand individuals by 1600 and, despite continuing racial conflict and periodic massacres, fluctuated between five thousand and thirty thousand people throughout the seventeenth century.

Not only was Chinese labor and organizational skill essential to the efficient operation of the galleon trade, but they also dominated almost all crafts and commerce within the Spanish colonial capital. Because of their great numbers, the Spaniards as early as 1581 inaugurated a policy of residential segregation by assigning them to a large urban quarter—the Parian. In addition to this district, which was carefully situated beneath the guns of Intramuros, a substantial Chinese area later developed north of the Pasig River in Binondo (Map 2).

The Filipinos, whose role in colonial Manila during the formative period is often ignored or treated superficially in published and documentary materials, were scattered in a number of outlying communities which had begun to acquire distinctive characters, even in the early year of Spanish domination. The overwhelming presence of indigenous people and *mestizos* in Quiapo, San Antón, Tondo, Bagumbayan, Ermita, and other suburban centers testified to the increasingly important role of Filipinos who originally lived as farmers and fishermen along the bayshore or came to Manila as draft laborers from nearby provinces and were gradually transformed into specialized wage earners.

By the dawn of the seventeenth century and only three decades after its Hispanic foundation, Manila had become the administrative hub of an expanding colony, a renowned international emporium, a center of considerable ethnic and cultural diversity, and a planned city graced by magnificent public and private buildings. While the various residential quarters testified to the presence and contribution of Filipinos, Chinese, Japanese, and other alien Asians, the morphology of Intramuros clearly reflected Spanish ideas of proper urban form. As a durable symbol of external authority, Manila was to remain for centuries the unchallenged and multifunctional colonial metropolis of the Philippines.

SOURCES

The most comprehensive works on settlement and society in the Philippines during pre-Hispanic and colonial times are John L. Phelan's

The Hispanization of the Philippines: Spanish Aims and Filipino Responses, 1565-1700 (Madison: The University of Wisconsin Press, 1959); Daniel F. Doepper's, "The Development of Philippine Cities Before 1900," *The Journal of Asian Studies,* Vol 31 (1972), pp. 769-792.

Robert R. Reed, "Hispanic Urbanism in the Philippines: A Study of the Impact of Church and State," *University of Manila Journal of East Asiastic Studies,* Vol. II (1967), pp. 1-222.

There are many books and articles on colonial urbanism in the Spanish empire. For references and general commentary, consult Richard M. Morse, "Recent Research on Latin American Urbanization: A Selective Survey with Commentary," *Latin American Research Review,* Vol. 1 (1965), pp. 35-74, and J. M. Houston, "The Foundation of Colonial Towns in Hispanic America," in R. P. Beckinsale and J. M. Houston (eds.) *Urbanization and Its Problems: Essays in Honor of E. W. Gilbert* (Oxford: Basil Blackwell, 1968), pp. 352-390.

The Ordinances of 1573 were translated into English and printed more than fifty years ago in Zelia Nuttall, "Royal Ordinances Concerning the Laying Out of Towns," *The Hispanic American Historical Review,* Vol 4 (1921), pp. 743-753.

Among the numberous histories of varying quality concerning Manila are the useful works by Conrad Myricks, "The History of Manila from the Spanish Conquest to 1700," *Historical Bulletin,* Vol. 15 (1971), pp. 1-253, and Pedro Ortiz Armengol, *Intramuros de Manila de 1571 hasta su destruccion en 1945,* (Madrid: Ediciones de Cultura Hispanica, 1958).

Most of my primary sources have derived from the magnificent collection of documents printed in Emma H. Blair and James A. Robertson (eds.) *The Philippine Islands, 1493-1898* (Cleveland: The Arthur H. Clark Company, 1903-1909), 55 volumes.

MAP 1

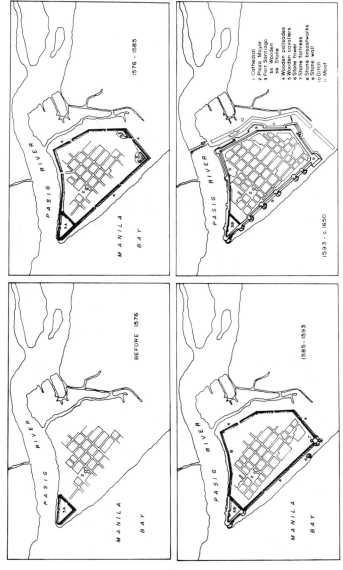

1 Cathedral
2 Plaza Mayor
3 Fort Santiago
3A Wooden
3B Stone
4 Wooden palisades
5 Wooden cavaliers
6 Stone tower
7 Stone fortress
8 Stone breastworks
9 Stone wall
10 Ditch
11 Moat

BEFORE 1576

1576 - 1585

1585 - 1593

1593 - c. 1650

Map 1. Early Development of Intramuros.

203

MAP 2

Map 2. Manila, c. 1670. (After the "Muñoz Map of 1671" as reprinted in Carlos Quirino, Maps and Views of Old Manila (Manila: Bustamante Press, Inc., 1971), (opposite p. 26).

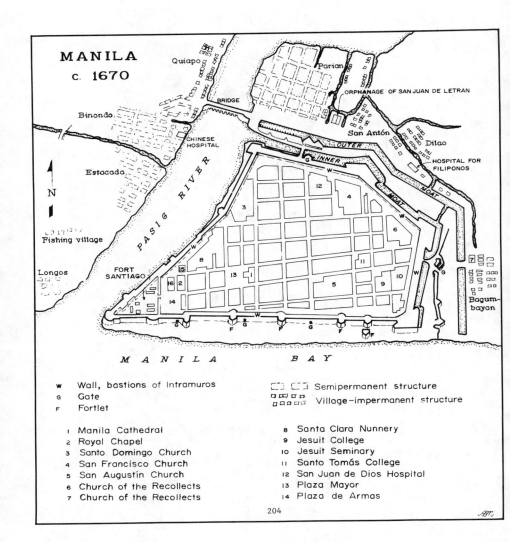

MANILA
c. 1670

w   Wall, bastions of Intramuros
G   Gate
F   Fortlet

⊏⊐ ⊏⊐ Semipermanent structure
▫▫▫▫ Village–impermanent structure

1   Manila Cathedral
2   Royal Chapel
3   Santo Domingo Church
4   San Francisco Church
5   San Augustín Church
6   Church of the Recollects
7   Church of the Recollects

8   Santa Clara Nunnery
9   Jesuit College
10 Jesuit Seminary
11 Santo Tomás College
12 San Juan de Dios Hospital
13 Plaza Mayor
14 Plaza de Armas

PLATE V. Manila in the seventeenth century

PROBLEMS OF A PRE-COLONIAL CITY: SURAT, 1740-1750

by

Ashin Das Gupta

    In the fifth decade of the eighteenth century Surat had, by
and large, ceased to be the Mughal coastal city she had once been, but
she was yet to become a British colonial town. This transformation had
two aspects. For one thing, Surat was losing her prosperity as she
lost her hinterland and her markets. For another, the pressures which
this decline produced were changing her as a city. Concerned as we are
with the changing character of Surat as a city, it is important to notice that the transformation which the surviving and accessible documents
indicate is polycentric, a delicately balanced system of power changing
into something simpler. Mughal Surat did not have the simple dichotomy
of a despot and his subjects. This dichotomy was emerging by the middle
of the eighteenth century when the Mughal system was in ruins.

    The Mughals had, throughout, maintained two governors for Surat,
one for the city, another for its castle. Imperial new writers had
always reported directly to the court, restraining local tyranny. Merchants had maintained agents in the imperial capitals, representing
grievances and pulling strings. Sidi Yakut Khan, the Mughal admiral
and a substantial merchant, had provided a balancing factor in the local
structure of power. The *nagarsheths* of the city were useful rallying
points in emergencies. Surat did not develop a civic consciousness, but
men who lived in the city knew the dangers of despotic power and had
learned how, in their makeshift, *ad hoc* manner, to guard against it. It
was this useful but rickety system that was breaking down in the 1740s.

    At the turn of the eighteenth century, Surat imitated the imperial
cities of the interior and was built around an urban focus provided by
its castle, its mint, the custom house, and the market where the money
merchants had their offices. The world of the Indian Ocean and the world
of interior India stretching to central Asia met in this small compass,
within the four hundred acres of the inner city. Within its generally
defined living areas, there was sub-division according to social and professional affiliations, especially in Saudagarpura. But Surat did not have
the strict residential segregation one would find in a Middle Eastern
city of the times. Men hailing from the same ancestral villages and belonging to the same faith and profession naturally tended to live together,
but there were areas of co-habitation where one would find a Bohra from
Patan within a stone's throw of a Turk originally from Syra. Europeans
had no separate quarters and lived in Saudagarpura as they were able to
find accommodation. The Dutch Company had its lodge at the point where
the two areas of the merchants and the adminstrators merged.

Around these two sectors of habitation there were other clusters of living which can only be called settlements. Men gathered to live in these settlements; occasionally a settlement came into existence because men had already gathered. There were, additionally, a large number of small villages around the quarters of the merchants and administrators. The work force of the city lived, for the most part, in these settlements, somewhat away from the center of the city. The point to grasp clearly is that, with all its fragmentation, Surat was in a sense a homogenous living area. There was no distinction within its walls as between ethnic groups, which was the hallmark of the black-and-white colonial towns. This does not, of course, mean that Surat was in any sense an egalitarian society. But the human situation was such that no one social group could dominate over the others.

Men were born, they lived and worked, and they died within the confines of their social-religious fraternities. To begin with, men were divided according to their religions. They were then divided according to their sects. They were further divided according to their ancestral villages. Thus, a basic functioning unit of Mughal Surat would be, say, the Hindu Banias of the village of Srimal, followers of the Vaishnava sect of Pushtimarg. They would have an organization, usually called the *gnati*, sometimes the *mahajan*, if they were Hindus or Jains. If they were Muslims, these would be called *jamats*. Basically, these were social organizations, but they could take on the color of professional guilds if a particular profession were dominated by a particular social group. There was some cohesion as between the different *gnatis* of the Hindus and the Jains for this purpose, especially as the profession of brokerage was almost monopolized by them.

Professions as such, however, never threw up their guilds. The best example would be the absence of any formal organization of merchants and shippers. Men of different religions were in these professions, and there was a limit of toleration in forming groups. There was admittedly a person called the *nagarsheth*, reminding one of the mayor in a European context. But the *nagarsheth* was no more than the head of the Hindus and the Jains, with undefined and vague authority. The essential function of the *nagarsheth* was to give leadership to the city in emergencies. As the maximum number of men in the city acknowledged his leadership, he was a useful figurehead around whom the citizens could rally. But there were *ad hoc* arrangements; there was no continuing function of the *nagarsheth* for the city as such because, fundamentally, the city was a physical unit of habitation and function, not a social and psychological reality.

Admitting all this, I shall argue that the decline of this precolonial city really lay in the break up of its homogeneity and the further fragmentation within its civic body. Gradually, the European element became more prominent and powerful. The checks and balances that had characterized Mughal Surat were undermined as the powerful Mughal administration gave way. Surat lost its access to the wide hinterland north and west of India, and her major market in the Red Sea was in disarray. The *mofussil* town that was eventually to emerge out of the catastrophe was, of course, not yet in sight in the middle eighteenth century, but the fact that Mughal Surat was lost was clear enough by this time.

208

The basic problem with which the city was unable to cope in the first half of the eighteenth century was created by the decline of the Mughal Empire. It was the breakdown of security in the interior that gradually denied merchants access to centers of production near Agra or at Lucknow and deprived Surat of markets in the cities of the Deccan and Hindustan. Besides, the cities within Gujarat came to be isolated as the Maratha cavalry took over the countryside.

Surat lived an essentially beleaguered existence, and factions within the city fought for power under these abnormal circumstances. There was no hope that the city would save itself by an energetic exploitation of its markets abroad because exports were not available and because the Red Sea trade was moribund. To add to her miseries Bombay, for the first time in the history of the two cities, was drawing away her means of sustenance.

The process of decline had begun by the second decade of the eighteenth century, but by the 1740s the city was profoundly shaken. Two of her major props were already shot away. The Mughal administration of the capital cities, which had been Surat's unfailing court of appeal, was no longer in effective touch with the town, although it still retained a certain nuisance value. The family that controlled Surat in the beginning of the 1740s was a local family, and the one thought of the governor, Tegh Beg Khan, and his two brothers was to head off other competitors from capturing power by obtaining superior authority from Delhi. The authority of the governor was much reduced, but he had enough power to plunder the merchants. The great mercantile families that had previously possessed the means of standing up to this kind of assault had been undermined.

The family of the *nagarsheths* was in eclipse and, given the general situation, there was little this Jain Bania family could do for the city. Under the circumstances, men who controlled the sea lanes were having more and more authority in Surat. Let us, however, notice three facts of some importance which helped Surat in her extremities. Gujarati cities other than Surat were in a worse plight, and men were migrating, especially from Ahmedabad, to try their fortunes in the city on the Tapti, which seemed immune to the worst misfortunes. The trade in raw cotton to Bengal and to China was being energetically expanded by the English private traders. And the merchants of Surat were obtaining, in a curious manner, a greater control over the production in the immediate hinterland. The fact that Surat was never carried by assault during these years gave the city a certain edge over her rivals in Gujarat.

The misfortunes of Ahmedabad, the capital of the province and the largest city of Gujarat, were sensational, and Surat drew away the famous weaving population of the Mughal metropolis in the 1740s. This was partly the result of the Mughal-Maratha struggle for the exploitation of Ahmedabad and, in part, the achievement of the senior officials of Surat and some of the leading merchants of the coastal city. The immigration of the large Muslim weaving population into Surat created vexing, but interesting, problems. Local weavers, mainly Hindus, had been used to paying a tax called the *tour*, which the immigrants refused to pay. Hindu weavers struck work in 1742. The dispute was difficult to settle and, for over a week, the looms of Surat remained idle.

This kind of addition to the city's population, whatever initial problems it created, was welcome to Surat at a time when production centers elsewhere were out of reach. English private traders acted energetically in the 1740s to shore up the morale of the city further. The great boost to the trade in raw cotton was one manifestation of a broader effort of the English merchants to develop the trade to the eastward, mainly to Bengal and China. Very little of it was allowed to appear in the official records of the English Company, but the assiduous, worried Dutchmen of the city recorded their misgivings about the phenomenon almost every year.

The expansion in the trade in cotton was matched by the decline in the trade of indigo. But both with cotton and indigo a new phenomenon appeared in the 1740s. Merchants of Surat began to buy up harvests in advance. Cultivators were so hard pressed by numerous claimants for revenue that they often sold what they expected to produce of their cash crops before they knew what the harvests were going to be. Needless to say, the merchants were not to be cheated, especially in view of the fact that they had the task of physically protecting the crop they bought. The farmers were thus losing to the merchants of the city, but the merchants had little to congratulate themselves on. The wide hinterland of Surat was almost completely lost.

The city of Agra itself was in a bad way. Men were deserting the splendid Mughal capital. Houses were falling to ruin; there was no one even to buy the bricks of the lodges the Dutch had abandoned.

Living in the backwash of the collapse of the Mughal dynasty, the major concern for the merchants was the local government and how to cope with it. Tegh Beg Khan, who had become the ruler of Surat in 1732, proved himself more tyrannical than any ruler before him. The reason was, apart from any personal failing, he faced a worse situation. He had no income to speak of since the countryside was controlled by the Marathas. On top of that he had to agree to the Marathas sharing the incomes of the city of Surat. He had to spend a great deal of money at the imperial court to ward off competitors for his office. In spite of all this there were many alarms of armed attack; necessarily a great deal had to be spent on defence.

Tegh Beg passed on the burden to the citizens. He was, however, careful not to offend the Europeans. There was little in Tegh Beg's way posed by the merchants; he had managed to have two of the richest and most powerful merchants in the city murdered in the course of the 1730s. The *nagarsheth* family was in eclipse. The Europeans were content, and the Marathas bought off. This dangerous situation gave rise to the phenomenon of "protection." Merchants of Surat now began to look for protectors and buy protection from whoever offered. The Europeans naturally offered more than the others. And the documents of the English and the Dutch are replete with instances of eminent men seeking shelter by establishing some kind of working relations with their factories. The careers of the Nagar Bania Lakshmidas, a leading merchant of Surat in the 1740s, and that of Muncrurji Cursetji, a Parsi who acted as the agent of Manakji Nowroji, then a resident of Bombay, clearly indicate that it was the protection of the English Company at Surat in the later 1730s that induced these merchants

210

to do business with the English. The stormy career of another merchant, Mulla Fakaruddin, son of the famed Muhammad Ali, also demonstrate how the trend, especially after the brief civil war phase in the late 1740s, was going in favor of the English. Muhammad Ali had never got on with the English but, in 1748-49, Mulla Fakaruddin was almost a camp follower. William Wake, governor of Bombay, was his patron, and *nagarsheth* Jagannathdas Laldas, broker of the English Company, was described as his "bosom friend."

The Dutch ran into fierce English protests when they attempted to interfere with Fakaruddin's ships. More importantly, it was English support that saved him in his civil conflict with Sayyid Achhan, the commander of the city. The increase in English trade and the expansion of English influence had thus been phenomenal in the first half of the eighteenth century. In the nineties of the seventeenth century, the English factors had been harassed and persecuted by the Mughal administration because they were supposed to be linked with pirates who were taking heavy toll of Surat's shipping.

English trade had dwindled to insignificance at a time when the total annual turnover of the port was probably in the neighborhood of 16 million rupees. By the 1730s the English were dictating terms to the city administration which was no longer Mughal-Imperial.

In conclusion, I should point out that, although Surat was declining because of anarchy, that which survived the decline was still remarkable. In the 1800s, Surat continued to be a city of over a hundred thousand, and much trade still remained in the Indian Ocean and in the north and west of the country. What did change in the interim was her importance relative to Bombay. In the later seventeenth century, Surat was the principal Indian port and, even in the 1720s, Bombay was no more than a trading village aspiring to be a city. The genesis of the situation was that Bombay was a kind of outreach of Surat, a forward position which relied entirely on the mother-city for sustenance. In the early nineteenth century, Bombay was the center of intercontinental trade and the trade of the Indian Ocean. Surat was a staging point where exports destined to be shipped from Bombay were assembled. Soon enough, Surat was to become that well-known phenomenon of British India: the *mofussil* town, headquarters of a district, with its civil line and its bazaar replicating in miniature the neighboring colonial port city.

SOURCES

The primary sources on which this essay is based derive mainly from the Hooghe Regeering series at the Algemeen Rijksarchief, Koloniaal Archief at the Hague, and the Surat Factory Records at the India Office Library, London. For a broader and more general discussion of the issues raised here, see my essay in D. S. Richards, Ed., *Islam and the Trade of Asia*, (Oxford, 1971) entitled, "Trade and Politics in 18th Century India" and "The Maritime Mercahnt, 1500-1800," my Presidential Address to the Medieval Section at the Indian History Congress, Jadarpur, *Proceedings*, 1974.

ALLOCATED OR ENTITLED HOUSING: INSTITUTIONAL PATERNALISM
AND THE GROWTH OF THE COLONIAL PORT CITY

by

Pauline D. Milone

A paradox is observable in the former colonial port cities of
Asia: the poor and traditional attach a low priority to housing of permanent materials; the upwardly mobile actively seek it, and such housing
has high prestige.

Entitled housing means the housing provided by an employers as
one part of compensation for work performed. It is a form of housing,
built of permanent materials, which is highly characteristic of the
colonial port cities. Its antecedents are imprecise. It may have arisen
because accommodation had to be provided for newly-arrived Europeans, unfamiliar with the local language and local system of acquiring necessities.
It appears also to be derived from patterns of royal largesse and of patron-
client relationships in both the East and West, of offering shelter and
hospitality to strangers, travelers, and relatives. It was common in
Europe as well, in the army, navy, church organizations, charitable institutions, staffs of public (boarding) schools, prisons, and hospitals.
In nineteenth century Europe and America, towns, planned by Utopians and
industrialists, offered this type of housing related to work, as well.
However, housing does not appear ever to have been allocated to civil
servants within any European country that became a colonial power.

Almost all housing in European countries that became colonial
powers was of permanent materials. In the whole of Asia almost all housing, whether for commoners or royalty, originally was constructed of impermanent materials, using principally wood or bamboo, and pole and lintel
construction. The exception was India which has an indigenous masonry
tradition. However, even in India, as well as the rest of Asia, masonry
generally was reserved for public architecture or accessories, like
balustrades.

Housing of impermanent materials generally was the same for rich
and poor in Asia, structurally speaking. There was little room differentiation. Only merchants, who lived in shop-houses, had a reinforced inner
room for merchandise. Housing of permanent materials was not an essential
status attribute as it was for the aristocracy of Europe. Ostentation had
other outlets: feasts, jewelry, clothing, acquiring religious merit, and
keeping an impressive entourage which could serve and transport one in
style. However, there were five characteristics that generally distinguished the residences of an aristocrat from that of a commoner: 1. spaciousness
and height, 2. decoration, 3. the use of color, 4. roof shape, and 5. an

213

accompanying garden or park.

In traditional Asian society, there does not appear to have been any formal system of housing entitlement. In royal capitals, housing was not allocated so much as land, plus the labor of assigned appanage villagers to build and sustain service for a structure. Only immediate relatives and essential royal servants had housing within the royal *enceinte*.

Wealthy merchants provided accommodation for clients, relatives, and employees. Caravansaries in India and China provided temporary lodging for travelers, and there were lodgings and space set aside for religious pilgrims. South China had residential compounds for traveling members of the Fang lineages. Ports often had visitor's lodges, and foreigners staying for long periods were segregated in their own districts or camps. Foreign specialists may have been offered housing or land as an inducement to settle and perform services for the ruler and, thereby, invigorate the port.

The first British and Dutch in Asia fitted themselves into existing arrangements. The first Dutch who arrived in Jakarta lived in the Chinese camp, and the first British factories in India looked like Indian caravansaries. In fact, the first European factories combined the characteristics of Asian visitor accommodation with that of Asian shop-houses since the Europeans lived with their merchandise.

The factories established by the Europeans in Asia from the sixteenth to the nineteenth centuries were the first entitled housing. They provided free room and board under collegiate conditions for their all-male staff. The first factories were small, but the last factories established by the Europeans in Asia, the *hongs* of Canton and Shanghai and of Japan, were relatively spacious. Entitled collegiate living continued into the twentieth century for bachelor employees of such institutions as the Malay civil service, the Chinese Maritime Customs, and for private Shanghai firms.

Work and residence had remained combined until Europeans were permitted to build forts in South and Southeast Asia. Forts were miniature towns within towns, and housing and go-downs now were in separate structures. Operating from the secure base that housing entitlement afforded, the first separate dwellings outside the fort were built in walled towns. Then, starting in the mid-seventeenth century, Europeans sought relief from constricted quarters further afield.

Generally, first the Governor-General acquired land for a garden and then, influenced by the image of the European aristocrat as sportsman, they started stud farms and raised horses for riding back and forth and for hunting and recreation. They also indulged in the fashionable enthusiasm for gardening, stimulated by the great landscape architect, Le Notre, and engaged in botanical experiments. Then they began building two-storey mansions in European Neo-classical style. This became a hobby, and they often built several houses and gardens. The move outside of the fort and walled town also was undertaken for health and climatic considerations.

214

The suburban development of impressive mansions took place in several places in Asia; in the Presidency towns of India as well as in Batavia. Usually, first the governor built a country mansion, and then other wealthy officials--army officers and private merchants--followed his example.

The first free housing or entitlement for a separate dwelling was accorded to Governor-Generals in East India Companies in India as well as in Southeast Asia. They argued they needed mansions to impress the local people. Next the Governors-General convinced the East India Companies that they needed entitlement for houses to relax in, to escape the heat. In both Southeast Asia and India, the colonial port cities began to extend to the sites of these retreats and, as mansions were abandoned for residences, they became the public buildings of the town.

Extension of housing entitlement to a larger group related to administrative reform and development of a civil service. It was started in Java by Daendals between 1808-1811, after the bankruptcy of the Dutch East India Company and the defeat of Holland by France. He converted company officials into a civil service, forbade private trade, offering as a *quid pro quo* not land but higher salaries and military rank. He also brought the Javanese rulers within the system. Gradually, emoluments were increased by subsequent administrations to include free housing or rent compensation as well as pensions and subsidized schooling for the children.

The housing allocated was of the type of villa plus extensive garden that had evolved from the original European-style mansions or "garden houses." This type of housing also became characteristic for the Europeans who elected to settle in places like Batavia and Bencoolen and of the Foreign Asian officers, Asian Christians, and aristocratic and wealthy Asians.

In India housing entitlement on a wider scale occurred for similar reasons about a decade earlier, with the promulgation of the 1793 Regulations. During the administration of Cornwallis, private trade was forbidden to the political branch of the civil service, salaries were increased, and free housing gradually was guaranteed.

In India and, later, in Burma, Malaya, Singapore, and the Netherlands Indies, the technical and educational services also made use of housing entitlement. It became policy to provide attractive emoluments in both the British and Dutch colonies to inhibit rapid turnover, which was costly.

Military engineers designed and supervised construction of the first spacious residences in new residential areas in a dispersed fashion, leaving open space for parks, and connecting housing by a planned system of streets and roads to squares and *maidans*, to cantonments, and the rural retreats of the Governors-General and other high officials and fortunates. In line with the nineteenth century European preoccupation with modernizing circulation or ventilating the remnants of the pedestrian-oriented medieval city, they planned broad streets, adapted to horse and carriage traffic.

Military engineers also built the cantonments, another large
source of housing entitlement which contributed to the growth of the
colonial port city. The cantonments in both India and Indonesia became town social centers because of their concentration of amenities.

The Public Works Department built entitled housing for their
own employees, for the railroads, the harbors, government steamship
employees, communications, and other modern services. State-operated
enterprises and large-scale private enterprises also provided housing.
Whole sections of Batavia became identified as housing the employees
of one service or another. Off-duty public works engineers designed
many of the buildings for church organizations and the residences for
private businessmen. Most of Singapore's old mansions are, in fact,
the design of one engineer in the Public Works Department. In India
and in British colonial areas in Southeast Asia and enclaves in the
Far East, even more than in Indonesia, major areas of housing entitlement became expected components of the colonial port city: the civil
lines, the cantonments, the railway lines.

The housing of Europeans stimulated rural-urban migration on
both a revolving and permanent basis: people were brought in to work
on land reclamation, building material collection, or fabrication, construction of roads and canals for transport, house construction, and to
serve as house servants. They often came from far-off areas. In Batavia
the first slaves and workers were Mardijker Indians and Arakanese, then
Javanese and Balinese and Chinese. In British Bencoolen, Penang, and
Singapore; at first Bengali convicts and free men were used, then Chinese
from Kwangtung.

High civil servants in British and Dutch colonial port capitals
had more servants than others; staff of over one hundred were not uncommon up to the beginning of the nineteenth century; they were for
reasons of prestige as well as functionality. By the later nineteenth
and twentieth century staffs of nearly a dozen were not uncommon.

Large country mansions, which were a model for entitlement, brought
in a new concept of housing interiors to Asia: differentiated special-
purpose rooms and specialized furniture, however minimal. Also, space
was provided for leisure and entertaining activities within the housing
compound, a radical new living style.

Housing entitlement contributed essentially to the creation of a
dispersed garden city of residences of people for the most part solely of
one class who relied extensively on transport for all their real and status
needs. In contrast, in Europe, the development of one class residential
districts was strongly related to industrialization.

The development of suburbs in Asia meant reliance on conveyance,
and this dovetailed with the traditional prestige system whereby those of
high status should be carried. Suburbs developed in all the major colonial
ports. This process created a central business district through extracting
housing from trade, government activities, and such services as banking
and publishing.

216

In all accounts of colonial Batavia two things are mentioned: the garden city atmosphere and the tremendous volume of traffic. First, it was a stream of carriages and palanquins carrying civil servants and merchants from suburban residences to work and, later, it was an uninterrupted procession of automobiles, taxis, trams, and buses.

Suburbanization took place in the port cities of Asia several decades before it took place on the same scale in the mother countries for people of the same social status and salary level as colonial civil servants, army officers, and employees of large-scale business enterprises. It created an unbalanced city: one part dispersed with adequate circulation and open space; another, the indigenous sector, densely populated, with poor circulation. Thereby were created the twin problems that characterized the colonial city: the need for intensification (of the garden city) and the need for deconcentration (of the indigenous sector).

How did indigenous people view this new type of housing? For Indonesians, who regarded color and decoration as the hallmarks of aristocratic housing, the startling characteristic was the residences' "whiteness." This might have been influenced by the use of *chunam* on colonial mansions in the Indian Presidency towns. Also, from India, a new style of European tropical residence began to become popular in the nineteenth century, displacing the two-storey, Neo-classical mansion: the one-storey bungalow with its verandahs, sloping broad roof surfaces, and open-plan spacious interior. In Indonesia the one-storey *Indische* house with similar architectural elements modified by Javanese influence, began to displace the Dutch-style two-storey mansions about the same time.

By the twentieth century, committed and romantic anti-urban nationalists advocated a return to identity, equated with a rural indigenous lifestyle. This entailed an active rejection of Western materialism, including European-style housing and furnishings. But this call proved to be too spartan for indigenous civil servants, and entitled housing continued to be popular on the same relatively lavish standard.

Asian civil servants wanted the equivalent of what their European counterparts had enjoyed, and they also wanted the increased income. By the twentieth century, housing entitlement--apart from other benefits-- could result in a man's salary being increased by from 25 percent to 35 percent annually.

Entitled housing has endured in spite of a paradox: a significant part of the early colonial port city's governing population, the Europeans, only resided in towns for short periods, and in rotation. The fact that housing constructed of permanent materials remained, even though the personnel constantly changed, presumedly contributed and continues to contribute to the stability of Asian port capital cities with a colonial background.

For the poor in Asia who retain traditional evaluations, housing of permanent materials still is non-essential. However, for the well-educated, housing entitlement has provided the means of assured material

217

comfort and, ultimately, of financial security.

SOURCES

Primary sources are the Netherlands East Indies Government's Regulations concerning housing and emoluments for various classes of employees as found in the Government Almanacs for the Netherlands East Indies; travelers' accounts of voyages to India and Southeast Asia from the sixteenth to the nineteenth centuries and their observations concerning housing; and from Dutch and Indonesian civil servants' memoirs.

Secondary sources were made up of analyses of administration and colonial policy; commemorative volumes containing information on Indonesian colonial port cities and, for comparative purposes, volumes concerned with British and other European colonial society in India, Southeast Asia, and the Far East.

Less secondary source material will be utilized in the final draft than was utilized in the hastily written conference paper. For theoretical purposes works on planning and architecture were consulted and cited.

Topic III: RISE, GROWTH, AND MORPHOLOGY OF THE COLONIAL
PORT CITY

Session 5

Moderator - Eric Gustafson

Discussant - Rhoads Murphey

Partha Mitter, *Architectural Planning and Other
Building Activities of the British in Madras, Bombay,
and Calcutta (c. 1630 - c. 1757)* *

Robert Reed, *The Foundation and Morphology of Hispanic
Manila: Colonial Images and Philippine Realities*

Ashin Das Gupta, *The Problems of a Pre-Colonial City:
Surat: 1740 - 1750*

Pauline Milone, *Allocated or Entitled Housing: Institutional Paternalism and the Growth of the Colonial
Port City*

---

* Given in conjunction with an after-dinner slide presentation.

GUSTAFSON - The first paper this morning is by Robert Reed.

REED - I started out by working on the colonial morphogenesis of Manila, but then realized that it was impossible to deal with that theme without also considering the Hispanic foundation of Manila. Some general information concerning the strategies of colonialization and of urbanization introduced by the Spaniards seemed especially pertinent to both topics.

My investigation has been divided into three parts. First, I am concerned with the colonial development of urbanism in an extensive insular realm comprised of about seven thousand one hundred islands, islets, and rocks. None of the several dozen major islands in the archipelago had ever accommodated urban communities before the coming of the Spaniards. The Philippines was, in fact, the only major sector of Southeast Asia devoid of indigenous towns and cities.

Secondly, I am interested in the morphogenesis of Manila, in its origin as a colonial capital, in its Hispanic heritage, and in the morphological and cultural impact of the Filipinos and other Asian sojourners in residential quarters within the environs of the city.

Thirdly, I focus on the effectiveness of Spanish planning models in fostering the creation of a properly designed colonial primate city in the Philippines. As conceived by the Spanish officialdom, Manila was to be supereminent among all settlements throughout the archipelago in terms of size and functions. I remain especially interested in the provenance of Hispanic urban paradigms and in the material crystallization of Manila as a morphological replica of the idealized Spanish colonial city. Let me now elaborate upon these three themes.

Since there were no towns and cities in the Philippines at the time of Western contact, I have dealt in the introductory section of my paper with the social and ecological milieus into which the Spaniards projected their particular version of urbanism. Precolonial Filipino society was marked by two basic types of adaptation. In highland areas, small groups of hunters and gatherers had roamed free in search of food for millenia. They seldom remained in the same place for more than a few weeks, and so dwelt in impermanent encampments. There were villages and not cities.

In the lowlands and foothill regions, the Filipinos lived as shifting cultivators who occasionally supplemented harvests

221

by hunting, gathering, and fishing. Their settlements generally displayed greater permanence of place but had not evolved
into substantial centroids of population. The largest village
agglomerations--Manila and Cebu--had only two thousand people.
Socio-political organization was based on the *barangay* , a small
community integrated through ties of kinship and embracing between one and five hundred inhabitants. Each *barangay* was dominated by a *datu* (chieftain) and a sizable class of *maharlika*
noblemen.   The members of adjacent communities were often
at loggerheads and apparently cooperated only when seriously
threatened by external invaders. Before the advent of the
Spaniards, the Filipinos clearly identified with the local
community and had little sense of loyalty beyond the precincts
of the village.

Although the territorial state with its corollary institutions of kingship, codified law, taxation, military draft,
bureaucracy, and craft specialization had not emerged in the
pre-Hispanic Philippines, several supra*barangay* confederations
were beginning to develop in the environs of Manila and Cebu.

Islam seems to have acted as the catalyst of change.
The Muslims, who at the time of colonial contact were functioning as traders and missionaries in many parts of the archipelago,
had stimulated among certain Filipinos a nascent sense of religious and political community on an expanded regional basis.
But, before these conditions could lead to generation of the
territorial state and of urbanism, the Spaniards intervened.

Early documents derived from authorities in Church and
State give the impression that the Spaniards were greatly
offended by the sociocultural fragmentation and village decentralization of the traditional peoples of the Philippines. As
the inheritors of ancient religious and urban traditions of
the Mediterranean, they greatly valued systems of national and
international association. Consequently, the Spaniards, who
were strongly committed to the thoroughgoing Christianization
and Hispanization of Filipinos, considered it absolutely necessary to bring all peoples in the archipelago under the political
and social umbrella of Western colonialism. In accordance with
imperial strategies tested in the Americas, towns and cities
were to be utilized as instruments of control and integration.

The Spaniards faced two major obstacles in introducing
their program of colonization in the Philippines. In the first
place, there were no major indigenous cities that could be
readily transformed into the primary nodes of a balanced system
of urban settlements. The *conquistadores* thus found it necessary
to implement immediately a far-reaching program of resettlement
that was pursued by Catholic missionaries in frontier regions
even until the twilight years of Hispanic rule late in the nineteenth century.

In the second place, at the time of colonial contact
the Philippines remained a realm where food surpluses did not

exist. Instead, the Spaniards encountered between seven
hundred fifty thousand and a million Filipinos who maintained
subsistence economies in a myriad of villages scattered
throughout the archipelago. Accordingly, the arrival during
the three decades after 1565 of approximately five thousand
Spanish colonists as well as nearly fifty thousand alien
Chinese, other Asians, and assorted European sojourners,
placed great stress on farmers, hunters, and fishermen who
had never before provided food for persons outside their own
barangay. Ultimate success of the *conquista* clearly depended
on the reorganization of the Philippine economy in order to
guarantee adequate supplies of food for dependent urban populations. The keystone in this process of transformation was
to be a substantial colonial capital that would serve as a
base of operations, a warehousing center, and a place of refuge
during crises.

Miguel Lopez de Legazpi, the *Adelantago* (frontier governor)
and conqueror of the Philippines, like earlier Spanish explorers
who had ventured across the Pacific from Mexico to Southeast
Asia, landed in the Visayas. This island group, with its seemingly endless coastlines, was marked by an especially dispersed
pattern of settlement and, in many places, a comparatively long
dry season. Legazpi soon selected its embryonic nerve center--
the small port of Cebu--as his colonial headquarters. But the
new Spanish outpost did not prosper. During their first six
years of involvement in the Philippines, the Spaniards were, not
surprisingly, often on the verge of starvation while attempting
to establish a secure Visayan stronghold from which to extend
the *conquista* northward to Luzon and southward to Mindanao.

Yet, initially, they proved unable to force the Filipinos
to produce adequate surpluses of staples for an alien community
of nearly a thousand Westerners whose number grew substantially
with the arrival of each supply vessel from Mexico. Furthermore, when the Spaniards applied force to secure food and other
provisions, the Filipinos frequently abandoned their lowland
villages and fled to more secure environments in the heavily
forested mountain interiors of major islands.

From the Spanish point of view, the problem was clear.
If they were to succeed in organizing a stable colony, it was
absolutely necessary to establish their permanent capital in a
potentially productive lowland agricultural realm where seden-
tary populations could be easily controlled and effectively
manipulated in order to generate regularized supplies of food.

Late in 1570, following two reconnaissance expeditions
by trusted lieutenants, Legazpi began to gather the bulk of his
forces in a temporary headquarters on Panay in preparation for
the conquest of Manila and its hinterland of Central Luzon.
Manila was founded as the colonial capital in 1571 and, within
several years, began to flourish. Its keys to prosperity were
sawah (wet rice cultivation) and the *encomienda*, a Spanish institu-

223

tion widespread in Latin America through which individual
Spaniards were assigned tributary villages in the provinces.
Ownership of land, then, was not critical to the generation
of surpluses. Instead, Spanish *encomenderos* guaranteed the
adequate supply of staples by compelling their Filipino wards,
through words and force, to intensify *sawah* farming and to
give a portion of the increased harvests to the Spaniards.
Accordingly, native peoples were apportioned among colonists
who had rights to their labor and produce in one form or another. Each Spaniard usually enjoyed the services of between
five hundred and two thousands Filipinos who served him and
his family. But Spanish law required that the *encomenderos*
maintain permanent residences in cities.

Manila grew rapidly. In 1571 it had two thousand people
and, by 1600, totalled twenty-seven thousand. The city continued to grow steadily throughout the seventeenth century,
reflecting the fact that Manila had two hinterlands to sustain
its development. The Philippines, which provided growing
supplies of food for the colonial capital and other urban centers, was the first hinterland. Traditional trading linkages
between China and the Philippines allowed creation of a second
hinterland in South China, which provided great supplies of
luxury items for the renowned galleon trade between Acapulco
and Manila.

Predictably, the morphogenesis of Manila was closely
tied to the galleon trade. Wealth acquired through participation in the Sino-Mexican commerce made possible the physical
transformation of Manila according to principles set forth in
the famed Ordinances of 1573. Proclaimed by Philip II, this
integral urban scheme called for careful planning of cities,
a grid street plan, large plazas, monumentality of architecture,
and the construction of buildings in stone, brick, and tile.
In the Philippines, the Hispanic ordinances first found material
expression in Manila's key urban quarter-- *Intramuros*. This
nuclear district not only functioned as the fortified headquarters of Church and State but also became the main residential area of the Spanish elite.

Intramuros soon became the institutional and morphological
model for new colonial settlements throughout the provinces.
During the 333 years of Spanish tenure in the archipelago, more
than a thousand towns and cities of various sizes were fashioned
in the image of the capital. Some centers were comparatively
accurate replicas built according to Hispanic design and constructed of permanent materials, but many seemed little more
than clusters of flimsy native houses focused upon a plaza and
a church. Still, the impact of the Ordinances of 1573, with
time, became increasingly evident in towns and cities everywhere
in the Philippines.

Before the dawn of the sixteenth century, Manila emerged
as a truly shining symbol of Hispanic power and authority in an

archipelagic realm of village peoples who never before had known urbanism. This seems to contrast markedly with colonial experience in nearby Asian realms where indigenous cities had long endured and where native peoples did not quickly succumb to foreign rule. In the Philippines, the rise of colonial Manila indeed heralded the advent of a new political order and the successful introduction of standard urban morphology.

GUSTAFSON - Our second paper is by Ashin Das Gupta.

DAS GUPTA - This paper is about ten years. It addresses the problem of how Surat governed itself while it was changing from the Mughal dispensation to the British dispensation. The answer is that Surat <u>didn't</u> govern itself. The first thing to notice is that the Mughal system of governing, which was polycentric in the sense that there was a delicate balance within the administration and in the relationship between those governing and those governed, had broken down.

In the 1740s, Surat had one ruling family which had a tight control over the local area. It didn't have the ability to defend this local area, which was the problem. Surat was isolated. The Maratha cavalry had taken over the countryside, so the Mughal administrators did not have means of subsistence. This was why a great pressure was exerted upon mercantile property within the city. Earlier, the city--in its various groups--could put up resistence, but now this was no longer possible, partly because the pressure upon mercantile property had eroded mercantile strength. The powerful leaders among the merchants had been eliminated. There were no points around which the city could rally. The great Nagarseth family was virtually out of the scene because it had fallen out with its natural allies, the English.

What <u>was</u> happening under the circumstances was the emergence of the European factions. Europeans had not been a significant factor on the scene. But, under these new pressures, European factions were forming themselves, and among them the British were doing better than others. They were developing the trade to China, they were investing in private capacity in the trade to the Red Sea, and they were building up the Bombay marine. It was the Bombay marine that had come to dictate terms under the circumstances.

The situation was simplifying itself. People were gradually getting away from the old check and balance system to the relative simplicity of the new dispensation. The most important development in these ten years was the civil conflict within the city in 1748 over the question of who was going to take over the city? The Dutch East India Company tried its best to keep alive the old system of check and balance, of having two Mughal governors in the city instead of one, in order to prevent the misuse of power. They had several mercantile

225

families in the city backing them. But they lost. The
British managed to put up their own candidate and gradually
came to control the city, which they finally took over
in 1759.

     This Conference has brought out the complexities of
the colonial situation. I do not deny that the colonial
situation was complex enough. But in my case, it was a move
from a complex to a relatively simpler situation in the sense
that it was now possible to make straightforward deals with
the administration. The great distinction between the Mughals
and the British lay in this: the British were a local power
interested in trade, while the Mughals were a distant power
not interested in trade, which made the line-ups within the
city much simpler.

GUSTAFSON - The final paper this morning is by Pauline Milone.

MILONE - I became interested in the subject of this paper because
     of the paradox observable in the former colonial cities: Poor
     and traditional people do not attach high priority to housing
     of permanent materials, while upwardly mobile civil servants,
     army officers, or the highly-paid employees of the multinational
     corporations seek such housing and it has a very high prestige.

     "Entitled housing" means the housing provided by an
employer as one part of the compensation for work performed.
It is a form of housing built of permanent materials characteristic of the colonial port cities. Its antecedents are imprecise. It may have arisen because accommodation had to be provided for newly-arrived Europeans unfamiliar with the local
language and the local system for acquiring necessities. It
also appears to have derived from patron-client relationships
in both East and West, and from the custom of offering shelter
and hospitality to strangers, travelers, and relatives. In
Europe it appears to have been an aspect of royal largesse
offered favorites, members, guests, and servants of the royal
family. It was also customary for artisans to provide lodging
for apprentices, and for merchants to house their clerks. It
was common, of course, to provide housing in the army and navy;
church organizations such as monasteries and seminaries provided accommodation for their membership; charitable institutions such as orphanages provided housing for their staff, as
did the British public, or boarding, schools, prisons, and
hospitals.

     In nineteenth century Europe and America, towns planned
by Utopians and enlightened industrialists offered this type
of housing entitlement related to work as well. However, housing does not appear ever to have been allocated to civil servants within any European country which became a colonial power.

     Furthermore, within European countries that became
colonial powers, almost all housing was constructed of permanent
226

materials, since forests had been depleted early on. In contrast, in Asia almost all housing, whether for commoners or royalty, was built originally of imperanent materials, using principally wood, bamboo, or rammed earth for foundations and a pole and lintel system of construction. The exception was India, which had an indigenous masonry tradition. However, even in India as well as in the rest of Asia, masonry was generally preserved for public architecture or for foundations or accessories, such as balustrades.

Housing of impermanent materials generally was the same for rich and poor, structurally speaking. Ostentation had other outlets--feasts, jewelry, clothing, and keeping an impressive entourage which could serve and transport one in style. There were, however, characteristics that generally distinguish the residence of an aristocrat from that of a commoner. These were spaciousness and height, decoration, color, roof shape, and usually a garden or park designed for enjoyment. In traditional houses there was little room for differentiation. Most people lived in the same undifferentiated type of spaces, except for successful merchants who generally lived in shop-houses. They often had an inner room made of brick or some other permanent material in order to secure their merchandise against fire and theft.

Housing of permanent materials was not an essential status attribute as it was for the aristocracy of Europe.

Traditional Asian society had no formal system of housing entitlement. It was expected that the wealthy would care for their dependents in a befitting manner. In royal capitals, housing was not allocated as much as land. Usually, only the immediate relatives of the royal family--plus servants, palace guards, gate keepers, and *zenana* ladies were housed within the royal *encientes*. Sometimes the relatives of favorites also might be accommodated. This constituted the only true entitled housing in traditional capitals.

Wealthy merchants usually provided accommodation for their clients, clerks, and relatives on an informal basis. There were caravansaries in India and China that offered temporary lodging for travelers; lodgings and space for religious pilgrims were provided in India and in Cambodia; in South China, the Fang lineages had residential compounds set aside for traveling members of their families. The ports often had visitors' lodges, and foreigners staying for long periods were often segregated in their own districts or camps. Foreign specialists may have been offered housing or land as an inducement to stay and perform services for the ruler and thereby invigorate the economy of the port.

The first British and Dutch in Asia fitted themselves into these existing arrangements. The first Dutch who arrived in Java lived in the Chinese camp; in Bantam and Jakarta. The

227

first British factories in India looked, with their interior
courtyards, like the Indian caravansaries. In fact, the
first European factories combined the characteristics of
Asian visitor accommodations with that of Asian shop-houses
since the Europeans lived with their merchandise.

The sixteenth century factories of the Portuguese
in Cochin and of the Dutch in Bantam and Atjeh, that of the
British and other Europeans in Surat, Madras, and Calcutta
in the seventeenth century, the eighteenth century factories
in Malaya and the nineteenth century factories of the Europeans in coastal China, were the first form of entitled
housing. They provided free room and board under collegiate
conditions for their all-male staff. The first factories
were small, but the last factories established by Europeans
in Asia, the Hongs of Canton and Shanghai and of Japan were
relatively spacious.

Entitled collegiate living continued into the twentieth
century for bachelor employees of such institutions as the
Malay civil service , the Chinese Maritime Customs, and those
of the private Shanghai firms. Work and residence remained
combined until Europeans were permitted to build forts in
Asia. Forts were miniature towns within towns. Housing and
go-downs were now in separate structures. Operating from the
secure base that housing entitlement afforded, the first
separate dwellings outside of the fort were built for the
purposes of relaxation and recreation in order to provide relief to the junior factors and merchants from the restrictive
atmosphere that the factories imposed.

Generally, it was the governors-general who first
acquired land for a garden-house. Influenced by the image
of the European aristocrats as sportsmen, they then started
stud-farms and raised horses for riding back and forth and
for hunting and recreation. They also indulged in the fashionable European enthusiasm for gardening that the great landscape architect, LeNotre, had stimulated. They engaged in
botantical experiments in places like Batavia, Penang, and
Bengal as well. Then they began building two-story mansions
in the Georgian and neo-classical style. After wealthy
governors-general, such as Wellesley, constructed palatial
houses with gardens, this fashion became widely emulated.
We see similar trends in Batavia as well.

The move outside of the fort was partly for considerations of health. It was believed in the Europe of that time
that physical hygiene could be promoted by allowing large
amounts of space between dwellings. It was also concluded,
justifiably, that it would be much cooler if residences were
sited at higher altitudes. Therefore, there was a continual
seeking of higher altitudes and more spacious plots for
residences.

The suburban development of impressive mansions took place in the Presidency towns of India as well as in the capitals and port cities of Southeast Asia. Usually, the governor-general, who had a higher salary, allowances, and income from illicit trade, built a country mansion. Then other wealthy officials, army officers and wealthy private merchants followed suit. The first free housing or entitlement for a separate dwelling accorded to governors-general in India as well as in Southeast Asia were built to impress the local people. The local British argued that they had to equal the impressive structures that the Mughals had built in India. Such structures as Triplocaine House at Madras and government houses in Tranquebar and Pandicherry, Penang, Singapore, Rangoon, and Batavia were thus built. The palace built by Daendals in the Weltevreden section of Batavia is another good example.

The next step occurred when the governors-general convinced the East India Company authorities, both the British and the Dutch, that they needed entitlement for houses to relax in. In other words, they required not only a town house but a country house as well. In the case of the governors-general of Calcutta, the first mansions were built in Chowringhi and later at Barrackpore. The Danish Governor of Transquebar, who moved his retreat to Tillaly and called it "Sorgenfri," and the Dutch Governor General who named his high altitutde country seat "Buitenzorg" had coined these mansions' names after translations of *San Souci*, demonstrating the strength of the European aristocratic models.

In both Southeast Asia and India the colonial port cities began to extend to the sites of these retreats. When mansions were abandoned, they became the public buildings of the town. The extension of housing entitlement to a larger group related to administrative reform and the development of the civil service. It started in Java with Daendals, between 1808 and 1811, after the bankruptcy of the Dutch East India Company and the defeat of Holland by France. Daendals converted the company officials into a civil service, forbade private trade, offering as a *quid pro quo* not land but higher salaries and military rank. He also brought the Javanese rulers within the system.

Gradually emoluments or perquisites were increased to include free housing or rent compensation as well as pensions and subsidized schooling for children. The houses allocated were of the type of villa plus extensive garden that had evolved from the original European-style mansions or garden houses. This type of housing also became characteristic of the Europeans who elected to stay in places like Batavia, and of foreign agent officers, Asian Christians, aristocratic and wealthy Asians.

In India, housing entitlement on a wider scale occurred for similar reasons about a decade earlier, with the promulga-

tion of the 1793 regulations. During the administration of
Cornwallis private trade was forbidden to the political
branch of the civil service, salaries were increased, and
free housing was gradually guaranteed. However, in contrast
to Indonesia, the civil service and its emoluments was reserved initially entirely for Europeans.

In India and, later, in Burma, Malaya, Singapore, and
the Netherlands Indies, the technical and educational services also enjoyed housing entitlement. It became policy to
provide attractive emoluments in both the British and Dutch
colonies to civil servants in order to inhibit rapid turn-over,
which proved costly. Military engineers designed and supervised the building of the first spacious residences in a dispersed fashion, leaving open space for parks and connecting
housing by a planned system of streets and roads to squares
and *maidans*, to cantonments, and to the rural retreats of the
governors-general and other high officials and fortunates.

In line with the nineteenth century preoccupation with
modernizing circulation or ventilating the remnants of the
pedestrian-oriented medieval city they planned broad streets
adapted to horse and carriage traffic. Military engineers
also built the cantonments, another large source of housing
entitlement that contributed to the growth of the colonial
port city. The cantonments in both India and Indonesia became
town social centers because of their concentration of amenities.
The public works department built entitled housing for the
railroad, the port, communication department's employees, and
for the government's steamship line workers. Whole sections
of Batavia became identifiable as housing sites of one service
or another.

State-operated enterprises and large-scale private
enterprises similar to present-day multinational corporations
also provided housing. Off-duty public works engineers designed
many of the residences for private business. Most of Singapore's
old mansions are, in fact, the design of one engineer in the
public works department.

In India, Southeast Asia, and the Far East, major areas
of housing entitlement became identifiable as components of the
colonial port cities, the civil lines, the cantonments, the
railway lines. Housing of Europeans stimulated indigenous
rural-urban migration in both a revolving and permanent fashion.
Large numbers of people had to be brought in for land reclamation, for building material collection, for fabrication, the
construction of roads and canals, for transport, and for house
construction. People were brought in also to serve as house
servants, and they often came from far-off areas.

In Batavia, the first slaves were Mardijker Indians and
Arakanese from Burma. Then the West Java Sundanese, the Balinese, and, finally, the Chinese were brought in as workers.

230

In British Bencoolen, Penang, and Singapore, at first Bengali convicts and free men were used and, later, in Malaya, Chinese were brought in to serve as house servants.

High civil servants in British and Dutch colonial port capitals had more servants than others. Staffs of over one hundred were not uncommon up to the beginning of the nineteenth century. They had them for reasons of prestige as well as for functionality because there was such an intense division of labor. By the late nineteenth and twentieth centuries, staffs of nearly a dozen were common. The large country mansions that were the model for entitlement brought in a new concept of housing interiors to Asia, with differentiated, special-purpose rooms and special furniture, however minimal. Space was provided for leisure and for entertainment activities within the housing compound. This was a radical new living style.

Housing entitlement contributed essentially to the creation of a dispersed garden-city of residences, for the most part solidly of one class of people who relied extensively on transport for all their real and status necessities. In contrast, in Europe the development of one-class residential districts--workers' slums, row houses, flats, and elegant neighborhoods--was strongly related to industrialization. The development of suburbs in Asia meant reliance on conveyance, and this dove-tailed with the traditional prestige system whereby those of high status should be carried. Suburbs developed in all colonial ports, and the process created a central business district through extracting housing from trade, government activities and such services as banking and publishing.

In all accounts of colonial Batavia two things are mentioned: the garden-city atmosphere and the tremendous volume of traffic. First it was a stream of carriages and palanquins carrying civil servants and merchants from suburban residences to work; later it was an uninterrupted procession of autos, taxis, trams, and buses.

Suburbanization took place in the port cities of Asia several decades before it took place on the same scale in the mother countries for people of the same social status and salary level as colonial civil servants, army officers, and employees of large-scale business enterprises. It created an unbalanced city, one part dispersed with adequate circulation and open space, another--the indigenous sector--densely populated, with poor circulation. Thus was created the twin problems that characterized the colonial city: The need for intensification of the garden city and the need for deconcentration of the indigenous sector.

How did the indigenous people view this new type of housing? For Indonesians who regarded color and decoration as the hallmarks of aristocratic housing, the startling character-

231

istic was the residence's whiteness. This might have been
inspired by the use of *chunam* on colonial mansions in Indian
Presidency towns. Perhaps also from India came a new style
of European tropical residence which began to become popular
in the nineteenth century, displacing the two-story, neo-
classical mansion: the one-story bungalow with its veranda,
sloping roof surfaces, and open-planned spacious interior.
In Indonesia, the one-story *Indische* house, with similar
architectural elements modified by Javanese influence, began
to displace the Dutch-style, two-story mansions about the
same time.

By the twentieth century, committed and romantic
anti-urban nationalists like Gandhi, Rabindra Nath Tagore,
and European converts to Indian nationalism, like Annie Besant,
advocated a return to a rural, indigenous lifestyle. The same
romanticism permeated Indonesian nationalism and entailed an
active rejection of Western materialism, including European-
style housing and furnishings. But this call proved to be too
Spartan for indigenous civil servants, and entitled housing
has continued to be popular on the same lavish standards up to
the present time. The reason is that Asian civil servants
have demanded the equivalent of what their European counterparts
had enjoyed. They want the increased income that housing entitlement provides. Apart from other benefits, such as free
medical care, retirement pensions, and subsidized schooling,
housing entitlement often increases a man's salary by 25 to 35
percent annually.

Entitled housing has, therefore, endured. A significant
part of the early colonial port city's governing population
only resided in towns for short periods and in rotation. When
they died or had to be replaced, when they went on tours of
duty or on home leave, or when they went home permanently after
their contracts were over, housing constructed of permanent
materials remained, continuing to contribute to the stability
of Asian port cities with a colonial background.

For the poor in Asia, housing of permanent materials is
still non-essential. However, for the well-educated housing
entitlement has provided the means of assured comfort and,
ultimately, of financial security.

GUSTAFSON - Our discussant is Rhoads Murphey.

MURPHEY - Let me begin in the order in which these papers have
been presented and mention a few questions they have provoked
in me. Some of these are straight-forward, factual questions.

Going back to Manila, let me ask how it could ever
happen that the Spanish overlooked the obvious place from
which to try to administer the Philippines and the obvious
place to locate a city whose business was also designed from
the beginning as one of trade? The Bay at Manila is such a

232

superb shelter for ships that it puzzles me how that would
not have been self-evident to even the most purblind, newly-
arrived Spaniard.

Nor do I find it easy to understand the consistent
Iberian difficulty, not only in the Philippines and in Asia
but in Latin America as well, in finding enough to eat.
Obviously, they were under a severe handicap in being unwilling themselves to do much. One gets the impression they just
tucked their napkins into their shirtfronts, pounded the table,
and waited for somebody to come along. It didn't work well
in Cebu or Panay nor, for that matter, in Latin America where
Spanish garrisons came close to starvation---in the middle of
what is now an enormously productive agricultural landscape
where it seems that all that is necessary is to open a seed
packet or take a potshot at something running around in the
underbrush. But this was not considered acceptable behavior
for a gentleman--a *conquistador*.

This Iberian handicap seems to have been severe everywhere. Pearson refers to this in his Goa paper and says that
the Portuguese solution to the problem was simply to conquer
areas surrounding Goa where there was already a productive
agricultural system they could simply siphon off through
threat of force.

I don't understand why the rapid production of surplus
food was impossible in Cebu and Panay, either. I suppose it
depends on what one means by "rapid." These are not sterile
places in terms of agricultural potential. I suppose what
Reed is implying is that the local people were not themselves
surplus-producing agriculturists. Since the Spanish refused
to do anything about it themselves, they had to construct, on
the part of the locals, a surplus-producing agricultural culture. That, indeed, one couldn't do overnight. But the implication that it was "impossible" is puzzling. At this time
there was already a wet-rice cultivation base that could have
been made to produce more effectively in local hands.

A striking feature of the Spanish--and this was Spanish
rather than Iberian because the Portuguese never had the scope
the Spanish had in the Philippines--endeavor was the conception
of an ordered universe with Manila as a cosmic, symbolic center
as Mexico City was in another world. From a comparative standpoint, one may ask why the Spanish mind worked this way?

Most of the papers at this Conference deal with the
English experience, and there are regrettably few that deal with
other than the British-founded, British-managed port cities.
The French conception of the colonial landscape in Saigon or
Hanoi and that of the Portuguese in Macao could make fascinating
studies. Add to this Taipei whose colonial foundation was
laid by the Japanese, which makes it all the more interesting.
But there certainly was a sharp distinction between the Spanish

233

conception of a city in terms of its function and plan and
that of the British who attached little importance to symbolic, cosmic grandeur. The Governor's house was important,
as was the Church, and yet one cannot talk about Calcutta,
Bombay, Madras, Karachi in terms of city planning.

The Secretariat or its equivalent probably represented
a symbol of some kind, but the fort, originally functional
and utilitarian and, later, a conglomeration, grew Topsy-like
and, for the most part, showed little planning. But the
Spanish cities did. I wonder where they got the concept of
city planning? They consciously chose not to learn from the
Moors, who could have taught them much. Does one have to turn
to Augustan Rome, even though the Spanish connection to Augustan Rome was no closer than the connection of the British
through Londinium?

How the Spanish picked up the notion of city-planning
is not clear. The Hispanic-American city as a well-established
model contrasts with what was going on in terms of planned
urban growth in North America, say in Boston and New York.
The one striking exception was, of course, William Penn. Why
didn't the British produce more William Penns? I don't know.
How did they produce him in the first place? I don't know that,
either. It is clear, however, that the notion of a planned
town, of a rational, ordered, super-imposition of human design
on a landscape was not part of the Anglo-American tradition.

Fatehpur Sikri or Jaipur in India showed a cosmic approach,
but the Spanish obviously didn't get it there. If one starts
casting around for other approaches, one might end up in Imperial China where, too, there was a conviction about the rightness
of an existence or order in the universe based on rules and laws.
Man's affairs would prosper only if they could be put in a context of rules and order and rationality and, hence: the city!
Its function was seen as the establishment and maintainance of
order--by this I don't mean the absence of muggings but of a
rational design in the management of human affairs. It was
reflected in the plan which this rational order super-imposed
on a landscape with a rectangular grid, with walls of a regular
and even design, which was also the heart of the Spanish conception. I am not suggesting the Spanish learned it from the
Chinese, although some may say so.

At any rate, I'm a bit startled to learn of the proposition that the Spanish law required the Spanish to live in cities
and, hence, they could not engage in agriculture. I wonder
where this originated?

REED - It was born of the Hispanic experience in the Americas and
then transferred to the Philippines. The purpose was to reduce
direct contact between the indigenous peoples and those who
were there to exploit them.

MURPHEY - No fraternization?

REED - Right. Some tried to break it, but they were disciplined.

MURPHEY - It didn't, apparently, carry over to the Portuguese who were intermarrying and reproducing freely.

REED - That's right. I'm dealing only with the first hundred years of the Spanish situation which, by the nineteenth century, had changed remarkably.

MURPHEY - Perhaps that's why the Portuguese Empire lasted so long. There are other features to Reed's paper that deserve further discussion, but I would leave it here at this point and turn to other papers.

Despite the fundamental differences among them, the three papers are not devoid of connections. The next paper deals with Surat--which was not even a colonial city--as Das Gupta has made clear. Yet it was a city in which there were merchants engaged in trade between Asia and Western markets, and who were acting as intermediaries between two totally different economic and cultural systems. They were, therefore, playing a role similar to that played later on in our colonial port cities.

Das Gupta has given us a glimpse of a traditional Asian cluster of merchants trading in a city caught in the change of the tide, between a situation in which Asians were managing their own affairs and a situation in which external trade and major commercial networks were increasingly being taken over by outsiders. These were a new group of outsiders, I should add, because, after all, those people whom we loosely call "Arabs" were outsiders, as were the Parsis originally.

Surat was caught in the middle, in a temporal and chronological sense and is, therefore, especially useful to look at as one tries to understand the genesis from which there subsequently grew the other port cities dominated by Westerners, attuned to a different set not only of institutions and techniques but of values and markets.

I would like to know particularly the extent to which Surat reflected or differed from the other traditional bases of Indian trade, like Malabar, on which Das Gupta is already our authoritative guide, and inland centers like Agra, Patna, and Hughli, to which he is now turning his attention. Was the Surat situation unique? I am inclined to doubt that. To what extent did it replicate or resemble situations in other bases? If it did differ, how and why? I hope Das Gupta, by extending his previous work on Malabar to Hughli, will be able to give us a larger view of which this introduction in Surat is a tantalizing sample.

A couple of small points: Das Gupta gives the impression that we have a paradox in a declining city whose population was nevertheless rising. How do we know that it was rising, and in what way does one measure its decline? Obviously, it was in trouble, but I've learned to be extremely cautious with purported city population figures from almost any period in the past before the late nineteenth century when censuses began to be reasonably comparable from one period to the next, and when there was a reasonable effort at total head count.

Pre-nineteenth century population figures can be disastroubly misleading. It is plausible, however, that, in this increasingly troubled period, people should have moved into Surat as they flocked into other cities that had a wall and that made some effort to defend themselves against chronic assaults. It is, therefore, possible that the population of Surat could have been rising even while the economic base might have been contracting, with the obvious result that per capita incomes or living levels were falling.

One more small point: Das Gupta talks in an interesting way about the protection racket. Yet he doesn't elaborate on exactly what this highly-valued protection entailed. As one sees his characters move on the stage, it becomes clear how important it was to them. But what precisely did this racket involve? Bodyguards, promises of intercession if these people were in jail? (Sometimes that could be important because one could starve to death unless someone from the outside brought in food.) It is tantalizing the way Das Gupta raises these points, but he lets us hope that, when he completes rounding off the coasts from Surat via Malabar to Hughli, he will introduce other actors on a larger stage.

The Milone paper deserves commendation because it is a genuine effort at comparative analysis. The question of entitled housing was common to all these port cities, yet we haven't thought of it as a comparative denominator. Therefore, I find the paper very interesting indeed. I think Milone brings out well the relationship between housing and the expanding, changing morphology of each of these cities.

There are a few things I would like to mention: First, she is quite right in saying that traditional Asia did not pay the same crucial attention to conspicuous consumption in the housing form as did countries in the West. But I don't agree that there was little to distinguish the house of the urban commoner from a palace in terms of the materials of construction or size in traditional Asia. There were some distinctions in the use, for example, of tiles, which she mentions. Furthermore, mud and wattle construction ought to be distinguished from monasteries, temples, and palaces. These were able to manipulate timbers with occasional uses of stone or brick which simply weren't available to the masses. However, whitewash could cover up a lot, making it look similar.

I suspect the reason why conspicuous consumption didn't become an Asian habit in the way it did in early and late modern Europe was because it was just too dangerous. The individual who displayed his wealth risked having it taken away. Bernier, in his letters to Colbert from India mentions, as some of you may recall, the behavior of wealthy merchants wearing "the garb of indigence" for protection against the revenue collectors and the squeezers.

The second point I wish to make relates to the reason why housing, as a form of consumption manifesting itself in a suburban sprawl, developed earlier in colonial Asia than in Europe. The Europeans in Asia were indeed much richer than their equivalents in Manchester, London, or wherever. They saw themselves as having a much higher status relative to the local people and felt compelled to demonstrate that status by having a grander house and moving out to the country. There was a "pecking order" among the colonialists themselves, but it was more important to demonstrate that theirs was a superior order of humans to that of the locals. They had to keep up appearances in order to maintain that distinction alive in everyone's mind, and they had the means to do so. This is why I think the expression of conspicuous display got established sooner in colonial Asia than it did in the metropoles.

REED - I would like to respond to some of the questions that Professor Murphey has raised while discussing my paper.

First, Why didn't the Spaniards sail straight into Manila Bay when they arrived in the Philippines? A summary answer follows: When Legazpi reached the Visayas, he had never heard of Manila. By the second year of colonial contact, the Spaniards had received rumors of a Muslim settlement of between eighty and one hundred thousand people (a great exaggeration) somewhere to the north, and they probably began to consider a move to Luzon. But the *conquistadores*, who were debilitated because of inadequate food and insufficient supplies from Mexico, hesitated to abandon Cebu. Legazpi knew well that four earlier expeditions, involving thousands of men and dozens of ships, had ended in disaster. He was unwilling to take unnecessary risks. Furthermore, the Portuguese, who controlled most seas in Southeast Asia, were attempting to dislodge the Spaniards from the Philippines. The port of Cebu with its substantial fort was, in fact, under Portuguese seige for much of 1568. During this period, the beleagured Spanish forces found themselves reduced to eating rats and leather. Accordingly, Legazpi, even while considering the transfer of his colonial headquarters from the Visayas to Manila, postponed the final move until substantial reinforcements arrived from Mexico in 1570. Early the following year, the Spaniards prepared to move northward.

Secondly, the question about food: Not enough has been written on this subject. The Spaniards faced a complex and

237

difficult problem when they encountered a society where
there were no surpluses, where shifting cultivators could
abandon agricultural plots at will and reestablish fields
dozens of miles away in the security of the mountains and
where Spanish troops operating in rugged and heavily forested areas could not readily apply the ultimate sanction of
military might.

Initially, the Spaniards responded by planting their
own crops, but they didn't understand the changing seasons
and failed as farmers. They even sampled randomly gathered
plants and were sometimes poisoned in the process. The
Spanish colonists also failed as fishermen. The widely-shared
vision of abundance in such a green, lush, tropical environment simply could not be translated into food surpluses without the assistance of the Filipinos. In their frustration,
many Spaniards responded by systematically plundering Filipino
villages. Naturally, their rapacious activities drew strong
opposition from Church authorities and produced an intense
dialogue within the ruling class.

When stressing the "impossibility" of quickly creating
a food surplus in the Philippines, I attempted to underline
the fact that this fundamental transformation did not occur
in only a few seasons. Though the *encomienda* proved a powerful
instrument of colonization and economic change, it took time
to bring forth fruit. Moreover, some *encomenderos* severely
abused their wards by initially demanding excessive tributes
and, in so doing, stimulated hostility that endured for generations. In fact, this may have somewhat reduced their long-
term gains. And, even when the Filipinos began to expand their
agricultural acreages, locusts and other pests often destroyed
a significant portion of the potential harvest. Not for several
generations were the Spaniards sure of adequate food supplies
for Manila and other regional capitals in the provinces.

Thirdly, the question of Manila as a sacred center: I
am here considering two interrelated notions. The first concerns the role of the city in "cosmosizing" space. Mircea
Eliade develops this idea in his book, *The Sacred and the Profane*.
Wherever the Spaniards founded a town or city in the New World,
the first thing they did was implant a Cross in its physical
center, around which the plaza was developed and near which
the church was built. Through such means, they not only conferred a sacred character upon the urban center but also introduced the divine order of Catholicism into newly-conquered territories. A second notion concerned the role of the Christianized
town or city as the proper arena of human activity. The Span-
iards--both lay and priestly--firmly believed that only "under
the bells," or within the precincts of an urban center served
by the Catholic clergy, could men and women achieve their full
potentials as individuals and communities.

MILONE - I would like to re-emphasize that not enough research
has been conducted on entitled housing as yet. I did investi-

238

gate the Dutch cities, which were strongly influenced by
French concepts of city planning. That the grand form of
housing was for prestige reasons, I have no doubt. But the
point I am trying to explore is, Why this particular kind
of housing?

The allocated housing was of a villa-type with an
extensive garden which had evolved from the original rural
European style mansions or "garden houses" constructed pri-
vately on extensive landed estates. The Utopian collegiate
model, Fourier's *phalansteries* didn't present itself to a
visionary like Daendals when he was planning Welteverden.
Neither did the model of the contiguous two or three-story
townhouses of Paris and Amsterdam, demonstrating how well-
entrenched the European aristocratic rural, manorial model
was and, hence, its obvious appeal to the colonialists.

DAS GUPTA - The general question that Professor Murphey has
posed is, What were the other Indian cities doing when Mughal
Surat went under as it did? All the traditional cities like
Calicut, Masulipatnam, Hughli, were in a state of decline, but
not in the same manner as Surat was declining. The two important facts about Surat were that it was part of a Mughal
system, and that the system had been established there one
hundred and fifty years before the crunch came.

Hughli, also a Mughal city, was declining, but its local
hinterland was much better organized and was in a better shape
in the early eighteenth century than Gujarat's was. This made
its ongoing process of decline not as perceptible as that of
Surat's. As my research on Hughli is still incomplete at this
stage, apart from saying that it was also declining, I am unable to suggest imaginative processes as to how it happened.

Masulipatnam was not a Mughal city, as the Mughal system
in the Deccan was not established until the 1680s, as John
Richards has recently shown in his book. By 1710, however,
Masulipatnam was experiencing a pressure similar to Surat's
and Hughli's but, since the system that supported Masulipatnum
was much weaker, its decline seemed to have occurred faster.

Calicut was a different kettle of fish. It didn't belong
to any continental system at all. It was a coastal principality
where its major detriment was not political disruption but political consolidation. As Travancore transformed itself into a
centralized state capable of establishing a monopoly in the
interior, the southern merchants lost their occupations and
turned into officials of the state. A distinction ought to be
drawn in Calicut's case where there was no decline of trade,
but there was a decline of the mercantile community.

How do I know that the population of Surat was growing?
No figures nor any statistical tables appear in the records
but, throughtout the 1740s period, I come across such statements

239

as "on this day a large number of people came in," and "the city is now over-crowded." This gives me the impression that the city was growing in its population. Not all cities, not even all walled cities, were growing. Much depended on whether the Maratha had a say inside the city or not. Ahmedabad was well-protected, but the Mughal-Maratha struggle there encouraged the migration of weavers to Surat. The ensuing struggle destroyed Gujarat's internal trading networks. Under the circumstances, if there was a coastal city as well-defended and fairly well-administered as Surat was in the 1740s, it is not surprising that people flocked to it.

How do I know Surat was declining? Mainly from shipping and trade, which can be traced. Surat had, in 1701, one hundred twelve ships; in the 1740s, there were no more than twenty in operation. Namewise, I have been only able to track down about twelve. The trade figures dwindled from sixteen million rupees for 1698-99 to five million rupees in 1746.

What was protection? It involved taking a man out of the arena of the Mughal local government so that it couldn't interfere with his functions. These functions refer to his ability to extract things from the weavers and the cultivators in a manner in which he couldn't have done earlier. Under the Mughal system, the weavers and the cultivators were free to sell to the highest bidder, but a man enjoying English company's protection enforced contracts that denied his freedom. In the place of the Mughal legal system, we see "protection," the emergence of a different concept of law which, in practice, implied that somebody who did not have the protection at the other end of the stick knew the negative side of it.

MITTER - I wish to comment on the difference between Spanish and British cities. Founded around 1570, Manila was a planned city based on a grid-plan, whereas other colonial port cities in Asia, especially those built by the British, singularly lacked central planning.

It is interesting that, little before Manila was founded, the Renaissance and the Baroque arrived in Spain and, with them, the concept of the central plan. Madrid and Barcelona wouldn't benefit from this as they were both already developed cities, but the colonial sites probably seemed good testing grounds for such grid plans. The practice and tradition of this conception of the city filtered down to Britain much later where some examples of this could be seen, perhaps in the ordered street patterns which were also replicated to some extent in the colonial port cities.

REED - You're probably right. There is some confusion as to the direct and indirect routes by which ideas of the Renaissance might have reached Spain and its colonies. It has been argued that French and Italian priests, who were involved in overseas enterprises both in America and in the Philippines, played an important part in developing the integrated and carefully planned Spanish colonial city. By the same token, many writers feel that the contemporary form of the "plaza complex," so common today in Iberia, first appeared in the New World and was then transferred back to Spain.

CONLON - The impact of Robert Reed's paper has been much more than our discussion has revealed so far. He has brought us back squarely, among other things, to confronting geographic theory and the role of cities. It seems to me that we have to confront this inter-relationship between the outside, the "colonial" system, and the indigenous one from a different perspective. As he points out in the case of the Philippines, there wasn't an indigenous urban tradition.

If there was no indigenous urban tradition in the sense that the pre-existing conditions of Manila were those of trade wherein a few Chinese came down each year, the place of the Philippines in the triangular trade between Mexico and China strikes me immediately as important. Under this triangular system, was it an important indigenous trading system that emerged? To the extent we've seen in other cities, collaboration between an indigenous Asian initiative and a European initiative, Manila with no pre-existing indigenous tradition poses a serious exception we ought to explore from a comparative standpoint.

Secondly, on the question of planning, I don't think there is anything else to what Professor Reed has shown in the Philippines in the Indian context. After all, it was English merchants, not English *conquistadores* or self-conscious Renaissance men, who went to trade in India. Spanish and British colonial architecture reflected their respective value systems. I will mention--for what it is worth--that the East India Company in London did take the time out to send the charter of the City of London to the Bombay Council for guidance as to how housing should be arranged and how property should be settled. It does not mention anything about the center of the universe. Perhaps the English were confident that the city that was the center of the universe was London.

Thirdly, regarding Pauline Milone's interesting paper: I think house-building and ownership have to be considered not only in the context of entitlement but also as rental income from house-building which became a new area of investment for indigenous capital. Not much work has been done on this, but we know from Jim Masselos's work that the house-owning interest had become an extraordinarily important element in municipal politics and in local affairs during the nineteenth century. While we have talked about the ethnic components of the neighborhoods, the fact to keep in mind is that the color of the money was the same in all cases. It appears that the growing field of housing was not a purely ethnic, or an ethnically pure, function--that, indeed, house rentals were not strictly limited to families and retainers.

241

There were exceptions to this. But these exceptions relate primarily to charitable organizations such as the ones that the wealthy Parsi families built to provide housing for the poor Parsis. During the early twentieth century, the Saraswat Brahmins established a cooperative housing society that was quickly copied by Christian communities, by Muslims, and then by other Hindu organizations. The cooperative housing society, then closely equivalent to the entitled housing of the lower orders of the administrative elite, was made available, not on the basis of participation or particular occupation but on the basis of being a member of the community and having sifficient money to buy into a cooperative, a house-owning society.

Lastly, I shall dissent a bit from Rhoads Murphey's comment, based on a quote from Bernier, about the lack of conspicuous consumption in housing among merchants as being due to Oriental depotism and squeeze. It is difficult to counter this proposition in the absence of sufficient research, but I think in their own special way Indian merchants consumed conspicuously. In terms of housing, one has to turn to the old Gujarati quarters of Ahmedabad where one finds elaborate construction in which a family, its attendants and caste fellows held together.

This pattern was broken by a movement to the suburbs in the early twentieth century. If these merchants didn't make their conspicuous consumption obvious, it might not have been because of political oppression of a visceral kind but could have been due to the accepted code of conduct and professional ethos. If I were a merchant and saw one of my compatriots splurging on an elaborately decorated set of housing and other sundry things that attempted to mimic a kingly lifestyle, I would assume he'd be a pretty poor risk to be in business with.

GUSTAFSON - I wish to make one remark on the question of cosmic design of cities, whether the British had a completely different notion of the cosmos from that of the Spanish. My undergraduate philosophy professor, John William Miller, once said-- and I memorized it at the time because I thought it was so significant--"While Westminster Cathedral does not exactly deny the existence of God, it does seem to make Him a part of the British Empire!"

ANDERSON - I'd say that, in any discussion of what constituted ideal morphology, we have to take into account several variables. I wouldn't say that one was necessarily dominent over the other in the conception of the ideal grid plan in the early urban development in the Philippines, but one has to consider, I think, the consequence of the power of Utopianism. As in Mexico, one can see in the Philippines a transplanting of Sir Thomas More's *En La Casa*, which was an attempt at setting up Utopian forms. Spaniards went out to give the heathens something they

242

didn't have at home, namely, grid cities.

Another variable to consider was the incidence of Moorish influence which probably carried some of these ideas through from earlier Western European traditions. Yet another factor would be contemporary Hispanic formalism, the concern for order, for form, and for structure.

Furthermore, we should note that the siting of churches became a foci of other kinds of activities. For example, near every major church in Manila was a major marketplace so that, after Mass, people could join the market.

I would like to raise, in an altogether different con- text, the question of the rise and decline of the Asian port city. What does the decline of Surat mean? Was there an alter- native authority competing with the authority of the port cities? Here I especially have in mind the idea of rebel bands. In suggesting this as a factor, I am probably raising a red herring, but I am fascinated with the problem of *dacoitry*, which appeared not only in India but also in Burma and other parts of Southeast Asia. Whether we call them rebels, pretenders, proponents of de-centralized authority trying to compete with the central authority, one possible impact of their activity might have been a stimulus to the migration of people from the hinterlands to the urban centers. Was the phenomenon of *dacoitry* in any way connected to the loss of the hinterland? In other words, were they so threatening to the trade system that roads were closed, that rivers were not serving their function to move goods into the port city?

In our papers we touched upon the role of rising piracy in Dutch times. It had grown to a phenomenal proportion, threatening all the European powers until they beat it down with the gunboat around the middle of the nineteenth century. Also, the Dutch had to feed themselves by developing local bases to support themselves. But they had to set up a punitive fleet to punish the pirates; they had to set up convoys to protect the ships, to try to make them come in to Melaka. In the southern and central Philippines as well, piracy affected the trade to the extent that it was falling apart. On the West Coast we also hear of the terrific rise in piracy at Goa and other places.

Finally, one can perhaps say that the decline of the port city, like a life-cycle, was inevitable. In Southeast Asia as well as in South Asia, chronic siltation doomed many ports. Bangkok was once on the water, as was medieval Tamralipti in Bengal. Now they're way into the interior. Rivers change their course, which means that we have to attribute a crucial role in some cases to the basic geographical factors in the decline of a port city.

REED   - I've often wondered whether the willingness of the Spaniards to allow alien Asians to settle in Manila's suburban

quarters derived from their experience with the Moors. In
the Middle East cities grew by accretion, through the gradual
incorporation of "squatters" who had settled outside the
walls of Muslim urban centers. Through this process the
Muslim city in Moorish Spain and in other parts of the Islamic
realm grew gradually and embraced outsiders without great conflict. Such experience probably had a marked influence on
the Spaniards in the Philippines.

The question of piracy is an interesting one. In the
Philippine archipelago today there are hundreds of fortifications made of brick and stone that still stand. Some of these
marked the centers of cities that failed; others testify to
the impact of the Muslim pirates from Mindinao who ventured
into Manila Bay and even beyond in their continuing effort to
subdue the Spaniards. Fortifications of this kind were certainly not part of the Renaissance ideal.

Even the churches of the Philippines had extremely
heavy walls, from six to fifteen feet thick, with steps carved
into them so that they could quickly be converted into forts
if and when the Muslims arrived.

MORRIS - In all our discussion on the context of Reed's paper,
we have ignored a grand and old-fashioned theme which is the
growth of international commerce and how it was decisive in
the appearance of these towns.

Western trades in Asia had to learn how to organize
totally new activities. The British and the Dutch learned
from the Spanish and the Portuguese experience, but it was the
change in the character of technology in international commerce
that finally made it possible to organize the trade on a considerably different scale in the nineteenth and twentieth centuries. It's an old story from which the dramatic element of
barbarians beating at the gates has been taken out. Instead,
what we see is a learning process of adaptation to an environment.

BROOMFIELD - I'd like to follow up on this. I think we can all
benefit from Immanuel Wallerstein's revolutionary work on the
origins of the World Capitalist System. Wallerstein asks the
question, How come Europe burst its boundaries in the way it
did? He looks at Western Europe and the New World, comparing
them with China explicity and asking why the Chinese couldn't
have done this. It's asking old questions that Morris just
alluded to, but Wallerstein doesn't engage in the grand cultural
explanations that Weber led us to quite creatively while leaving
us among some red herrings. Wallerstein emphasizes fundamental
things like climatic periods and, more importantly, agriculture.
As to Murphey's point about the Iberians going out to the Philippines and being such clutzes, Wallerstein's argument is that
the Iberians were led out into the Atlantic by very limited
objectives. They were seeking timber, which had virtually

244

disappeared from Western Europe as well as more agricultural land which they found in the Canary Islands and the Azores. He points very convincingly to the way in which the Spaniards came to terms there with the problem of dealing with "heathens." Previously, they had been used to dealing with Moors and now they had to deal with people who had no Great Tradition.

The Iberians were thus propelled into the Atlantic in search of more resources which soon included human labor, slaves, and, finally, minerals. As to Murphey's question about the lack of interest among the Iberians in agriculture, I would point out that they brought back potato, Indian corn, tobacco, and, more fundamentally important than any, alfalfa which changed, because of its nitrogen content, the input to the soils of Europe.

STREET IN BOMBAY.

TOPIC III: THE RISE, GROWTH, AND MORPHOLOGY OF THE COLONIAL PORT CITY

(continued)

Session 6

CITY STATE TO CAPITAL CITY: AN EXPLORATION INTO

THE URBAN STRUCTURE OF BOMBAY CITY

by

Jim Masselos

        This paper examines the main stages in the development of Bombay
city from the time it first came under Company control in 1668 until the
present.   Each stage represents different kinds of phenomenon and epi-
tomizes different periods of history.

        Factors unknown in 1668 affected the changed shape of twentieth
century Bombay.   Yet early and late Bombay were each part of a chain of
processes and, at least chronologically and locationally, one derived
from the other.   Thus, while, in one sense, Bombay constituted a field
upon which a wide range of external forces operated, in another sense,
cumulatively, it had an identity in its own right, a continuing existence
and a dynamic of its own.

        What, then, were the elements involved in producing this urban
entity, in providing the underlying similarities between earlier and
later Bombay?   Perhaps, like the biologist's double helix with its
determining effect upon the growth of the living organism, there is a
similar, underlying structure in the urban organism?   If so, the paper
argues, it is located in the inter-relationship between the location of
the city and the nature of authority working within and upon it.

        The inter-relationship between these elements is easiest pinpointed
in the first stage, from 1668 to the time when the East India Company
acquired the neighboring island of Salsette in 1775.   It was then that
authority in and over the town was most clearly vested in a single body,
the Company, and one whose general objectives in the use of the harbor and
the islands of Bombay was equally clear.   With trade and profit as an overall motivation, a fort and factory were established, docking facilities
developed, and traders encouraged so that Bombay might become the "grand
mart" on the western coast of India.   In the process, in 1687, the center
of Company administration was moved from Surat, along with other sections
of Gujarat,   and gradually relegated during the following century to part
of Bombay's informal hinterland.

        If the combination of harbor and the possession of a very limited
amount of territory gave Bombay a range of advantages not available elsewhere on the coast at the time, it almost axiomatically made it the logical place for concentration and ensured that, in order to promote trade,
there should be a number of specific developmental undertakings.   The
primary one centered around the need to ensure security since the possession

of the seven Bombay islands did not even ensure control of the harbor. Security had to be maintained by prevention of attack and by defense. Hence, the Company's continuing rounds of diplomacy and, hence, its emphasis on forts at strategic points on the islands and the development of a main fort and walled town on the main island. Within the walls business activities and settlements were concentrated and the affairs of the Company conducted. And it was on the Fort that defense of the area rested.

This was so important that military engineers in theory determined the pattern of settlement, limiting, for example, the height of structures within the walls and determining the clear space around it. Despite some shanty settlement on the peripheries, the formal authority of the Company was accepted by the leading Indian merchants of the town as were the Company's levies for the improvement in the town's facilities and fortifications.

In this first period, then, the forms and functions of the town derived from the interaction between the peculiar location of the settlement with the particular kind of authority wielded by the Company. Both implied trade and a marine bias in productivity; both demanded defense expressed in terms appropriate to the times, and both called for the exploitation of a limited hinterland (the other islands of Bombay) for food, labor, and finance.

The second period, from 1775-1818, was one in which Bombay became a city-state *par excellence*. Its locational significance had altered with the acquisition, in 1775, of the adjoining Salsette Island which gave the town control of the harbor. In addition, by the end of the century, the informal economic hinterland of Gujarat had come formally under direct British rule. Concurrently, the authority pattern over the town had also altered. At one level there was an increasing separation of administrative and trading functions in the Company, exemplified in the Governor-General in Calcutta and the Board of Control in London, and by a similar administrative pattern in Bombay while, at another level, some formal control over the town was ceded to a non-official British element when British merchants were admitted to the Bench of Justices and the Court of Petty Sessions. These, jointly, had some relatively minor municipal functions.

Such changes paralleled a further expansion in dockyard facilities and in shipbuilding. Improvements were made to the forts on the islands and to the town walls (although their strategic need was less and less great) while the breaches between the Bombay islands were filled in so that the seven had become two by 1818. Finally, the Sion causeway was built, linking Bombay with Salsette and enabling a more efficient exploitation of Salsette as a reservoir for food and labor.

Nevertheless, the bulk of population still clustered within the walls of the town. In 1803, after a fire that destroyed a third of the town within the walls, an attempt was made to replan what had become an over-congested area and to relocate populations outside. The efforts of the formal body charged with this function, the Town Committee, were largely negated by the informal--but organized--opposition from the

250

wealthier Indian merchants who refused to be relocated even though a
new town was established outside the walls for those trading in inflammable goods.

Thus, the two elements--location and authority--coincided in
nurturing defense, trade, shipbuilding, and associated production and
services; in addition, the one acted positively upon the other in changing
the physical form of the territory and in extending its effective environs.
But this was the the cost of increased tension within the official authority structure between the interests of trade, defense, and administration
which it represented. Simultaneously, Indian merchants had emerged as a
force sufficiently important to challenge the official authority structure over its plans for the town.

The beginning of the following period was determined by the
acquisition of a Marathi hinterland in 1818; its conclusion in the mid-
1850s related to the altering economic base of the city with the beginnings
of industrialization. It was marked by the assumption of the rich mercantile or *shetia* group in the city's affairs of a *de jure* role in the
authority structures. They were admitted to the Bench of Justices in
1834, to the Board of Conservancy in 1845, and to an elected Municipal
Corporation in the 1870s.

The further expansion of trade with the breaking of the Company
monopoly and control of a Marathi hinterland promoted enormous increases
in population and further overcrowding both in the Fort and in the New
Town (which, by the 1850s, had a density of population greater than an
English equivalent average). The changed locational significance of
Bombay Island now meant that the need for fortifications had disappeared;
moves to have the Walls pulled down began in the 1820s, although this did
not begin to happen until 1848 and was not completed until 1862. There
was further reclamation of low-lying lands in the centers of the Island
but, by and large, the pattern of settlement followed east-west circles
around the fort area rather than a north-south axis.

The logic of these trends was pursued in the following years
through to independence. Most of the low-lying land was reclaimed and
further land won from the sea. (Thus, the land area of the Island was
expanded from 18 to 22 square miles between 1860 and 1872.) There was
considerable expansion to the north of the New, or "Native," Town after
the 1860s, with the spread of cotton mills and the need for dormitory
suburbs for their workers. This highlights the diversification in the
functions of Bombay. It was also becoming an educational center as well
as fulfilling a role as capital of the Presidency, in addition to developing its earlier trading and commercial functions.

The diffuse identity of the city was reinforced by the multipli-
cation of authority centers: A Port Trust was established in 1873, a
City Improvement Trust in the late 1890s, a Development Department after
the first World War. Various service supply companies emerged while
the functions of the Municipal Corporation were expanded considerably.
Thus, the centers of authority grew as did their constituent membership--
officials, Europeans, and Indians.

After Independence there was some consolidation and re-organization of the formal elements wielding authority over the form and functions of the city, while its locational significance again altered with the creation of Pakistan and the consequent influx of refugees and with the division of the Bombay Presidency into Gujarat and Maharashtra in 1960.

In consequence, population expanded enormously, again highlighting an institutional inability to cope with the ensuing problems. A plan to cut the Gordian knot was adopted at the end of the 1960s with the decision to establish a twin city on the mainland opposite Bombay. All planning was left to a City and Industrial Development Corporation (CIDCO), thereby obviating the contradictions that had emerged between the diverse authority centers and the interests they represented. Symbolically, the plan suggested Bombay's closer ties with the mainland, the establishment of a different concept of Bombay's place in the Republic.

SOURCES

Some of the basic accounts of Bombay are in *The Gazeteer of Bombay City and Island*, 3 Vols., (Bombay, 1909); *Materials Towards a Statistical Account of the Town and Island of Bombay*, 3 Vols., (Bombay, 1894); S. M. Edwardes, *The Rise of Bombay, a Retrospect* (Bombay, 1902); S. T. Sheppard, *Bombay*, (Bombay, 1932); J. Douglas, *A Book of Bombay*, (Bombay, 1883); J. Douglas, *Bombay and Western India, a Series of Stray Papers*, (London, 1893); M. D. Morris, *The Emergence of an Industrial Labor Force in India. A Study of the Bombay Cotton Mills, 1854-1947.* (Berkeley and Los Angeles, 1965); J. Masselos, *Towards Nationalism; Group Affiliations and the Politics of Public Associations in Nineteenth Century Western India*, (Bombay, 1974); M D. David, *History of Bombay, 1661-1708*, (Bombay, 1973); R. P. Masani, *Evolution of Local Self-Government in Bombay*, (London, 1929).

Of the numerous articles, see, for example, Ujagir Singh, "Bombay, a Study in Historical Geography, 1667-1900 A.D." in *National Geographic Journal of India*, VI, I (March, 1960), 19-29; B. Arunachalam, "Bombay City, Stages of Development," in *Bombay Geographical Magazine*, III (1955), 34-39; C. B. Joshi, "The Historical Geography of the Islands of Bombay," in *Bombay Geographical Magazine*, IV, 1 (1956), 5-13; C. Rajagopalan, "An Ecological Analysis of the Growth of Bombay City," in *Geografia*, II, 2 (1963), 99-105; J. E. Brush, "The Growth of the Presidency Towns," in R. G. Fox (ed.), *Urban India: Society, Space, and Image* (Duke University, 1970), 91-96; V. G. Dighe, "Modern Bombay," in Indian History Congress 10th Session, Bombay, *Book of Bombay*, (Bombay, 1947), 31-47.

The paper has also drawn on material in the Govt. of Maharashtra Secretariat Record Office, Bombay, and the India Office Records, London, as well as from the printed *Selections from the Records of the Bombay Government*, the *Reviews of the Administration of the Presidency of Bombay*, and from contemporary newspapers like the *Bombay Chronicle*, *Bombay Gazette*, and the *Times of India*.

URBAN AND SUBURBAN PROPERTY IN EARLY

NINETEENTH CENTURY MADRAS CITY

by

Susan Neild

The development of a city can be traced through changes in the use
and ownership of its land. In a colonial city the distribution of landed
property also clearly reflects the political and economic relationships
between the indigenous society and the colonial rulers. An examination
of such property holdings can provide us with important insights into
the impact of colonial domination on the structure and growth of such
cities.

In the British colonial city of Madras, changes in property holdings during the late eighteenth and early nineteenth centuries had a fundamental effect on its morphology. The present spatial organization of this
city, in fact, had its origins in the developments of those years when
Madras was evolving from a relatively small and compact trading center into the administrative, economic, and cultural capital of South India.
During this period, the expanding population and functions of the city
could no longer be contained within the old settlement. The growing demand for space by the colonial government and European residents altered
old property relationships and reorganized the spatial outlines of the
city. By the mid-nineteenth century the colonial presence, once confined
mainly to the old European White Town, was now felt throughout the entire
settlement.

From its founding in the mid-seventeenth century until the late
eighteenth century, Madras was a divided city. Around Fort St. George
the East India Company had created a small European town for its own officials and other Europeans living in the settlement. Outside the walls of
this "White Town," the Company distributed land to different groups of
local artisans, merchants, and laborers in order to encourage the growth
of a useful Indian settlement. Much of the land in this "Black Town" was
either granted freely to the new inhabitants or leased on very liberal
terms. The Company retained some land in the Black Town and its adjacent
suburbs of Peddanaickenpet and Muthialpet, but much of this was quietly
lost through illegal encroachments by local residents and fraudulent property transactions. The streets in this Indian quarter were organized
along the caste and occupational groupings which structured South Indian
society. While the Company maintained a close control over the European
White Town, it left the effective governance of the Indian section to
caste leaders and influential local merchants.

During the seventeenth and early eighteenth centuries, the East India Company extended its territorial possessions around Fort St. George to include fifteen nearby villages. These villages, granted to the Company by local Indian authorities, became known as the Home Farm villages and became an important source of land revenue for the colonial treasury. Until the late 1700s, the Home Farm villages retained their agrarian character. They were controlled by the local agrarian elite, called *mirasdars*, a body of communal share-holders in each village who possessed superior rights over cultivable and non-cultivable land in their communities. They received fees from the occupants of the non-cultivable land and, from the tenants who cul-tivated, part of the agricultural land. The remaining productive land was owned directly by the village proprietors under a communal form of tenure, each *mirasdar* possessing the right to cultivate a prescribed share of this land free from any revenue demands or fees.

During the mid-1700s, the old Black Town was demolished to improve the defense position of Fort St. George. The new Black Town now consisted only of the former suburbs of Peddanaickenpet and Muthialpet. Here also the different Indian castes had built their neighborhoods around their temples, markets, and occupational pursuits. But, by the end of the eighteenth century, the term "Black Town" had already become a misnomer. The Indian neighborhoods, until this time separated by space as well as culture from the colonial settlement, now found themselves partly surround-ed by an expanding European community.

The increasing political and military involvements of the East India Company in the affairs of South India during the second half of the eighteenth century led to a dramatic growth in the European population of Madras and to a search for new space for colonial residences and busi-nesses. The Company government chose the Black Town as a desirable and profitable site for further colonial development. It evicted unauthorized occupants from certain tracts of land it had managed to retain in the town and opened these for sale to private European developers and mercantile houses. A long strip of land running through the middle of the Black Town was cleared, drained, and divided into streets with English names and separate plots for private residences and European shops. By the turn of the century this area, centering around Popham's Broadway, the China Bazaar, and the Esplanade, had become the nucleus of a new European commercial and residential quarter.

The expansion of European property in the Black Town continued during the early 1800s, following the Company's decision to shift the port facilities from the Fort area to the beach opposite the Black Town. Com-pany-owned land along the beach was sold primarily to European mercantile concerns which had a large stake in the activities of the port. Within a few years the entire commercial sector of colonial Madras had shifted from the Fort area to the Black Town. Europeans now owned property in the most highly valued sections of the town—down along the beachfront, the south-eastern corner of the town, along the Esplanade, and around Popham's Broadway. Their demand for land resulted in rising property values through-out the town and forced many poorer Indians to settle in cheaper suburban neighborhoods. The growing European intrusion into the Black Town, however, did not dramatically change the social and spatial composition of the exist-ing Indian neighborhoods. Rather than merging together, the two communities

254

retained most of their cultural and spatial separateness in spite of their close physical proximity.

Outside the European sections, land in the Black Town was owned primarily by Indians during the early 1800s, with the exception of extensive Company-held property. Much of it remained in the form of small house plots and shops owned by individual proprietors. But, from the late 1700s, certain well-to-do Indians had acquired significant amounts of urban property as investments. The Nawab of Arcot, a deposed Indian prince living in Madras, had purchased numerous buildings and plots of ground in the town. Prosperous local merchants extended their possessions through defaulted mortgages, bankruptcy sales, and purchases. Among the largest urban landholders were the Indian *dubashes*, or agents, of Company officials who used their wealth and broad influence within both the European and Indian communities to expand their urban possessions.

The most dramatic shift in property holdings occurred outside the Black Town in the old Home Farm villages which surrounded the original colonial settlement. As some Europeans looked to the Black Town for commercial and residential space during the late 1700s, others looked to these villages for sites for spacious suburban houses. The possession of suburban land, large gardens, and impressive houses soon became an obsession among colonial officials and prosperous European merchants who believed that the growing political authority of the English Company should be reflected in the affluent lifestyle of its representatives.

They purchased land from the local *mirasdars* at prices that seemed low enough to them but were very generous to the village landlords who could hardly resist the increasing pressure to sell village property. Their decision to sell dealt a fatal blow to the structure of these rural settlements. By 1800 hardly any cultivable land remained in certain villages close to the Fort and Black Town. Only the *mirasdars*, their servants, and their dwelling sites, and the village temples survived as reminders of the former agrarian communities. Other villages, however, managed to retain sufficient cultivable land to support the landlords, a few cultivating tenants, and some village servants even well into the nineteenth century. However, by the 1830s only a fraction of the land once possessed by the Home Farm villages still belonged to the hereditary village landlords.

The main purchasers of suburban land up through the turn of the century were Europeans. A list of grants of suburban land made between 1774 and 1803 showed that Europeans owned 60 percent of the land included in these grants. European holdings predominated in the western and southern suburban villages. But most of the land in the suburbs to the north of the Black Town was purchased by Indian merchants, *dubashes*, and government servants after 1800.

The transformation of village land into suburban estates was accompanied by the creation of a new network of roads throughout the area connecting the suburbs with the colonial administrative and commercial centers in the Fort and the Black Town. By the start of the nineteenth century, suburban Madras had become an integral part of the spatial and administrative organization of the city as a result of the acquisition of land by colonial Europeans. This was most clearly reflected in the redefined boundaries of the city which now included ten of the original fifteen Home Farm villages and an area of 27 square miles. Yet less than one-fifth of this immense area, including the Black Town, Fort, and the suburban town centers of Triplicane, Mylapore, and Chintadripet could be called urbanized. The remaining area within the city's boundaries was occupied by suburban residences, the old agrarian villages, the modest hamlets of laborers, fishermen, servants, and various low-caste groups, and a growing number of Indian suburban neighborhoods.

The expansion of colonial commercial and residential sites from the old White Town into the Black Town and the suburban villages obliterated the dual settlement pattern that had characterized Madras since its establishment in the mid-seventeenth century and that continued to shape many other colonial towns in British India. By the early 1800s, Europeans had acquired land throughout much of the area within the city's bounds. Their business houses could be found adjacent to Indian neighborhoods in the Black Town, and their suburban houses juxtaposed with agrarian villages and semi-rural Indian hamlets.

The old dual pattern gave way to an overall impression of spatial integration aided by the creation of new administrative and judicial institutions which, for the first time, had jurisdiction over both the European and the indigenous populations. However, underneath this official unity, there continued to exist in nineteenth and even twentieth century Madras a profound distinction between the colonial and Indian communities. Though spatially partly integrated, the two communities remained socially and culturally apart.

SOURCES

The primary sources for this paper include H. D. Love, *Vestiges of Old Madras, 1640-1800*, 4 Vols., Indian Record Series (London: John Murray, 1913): Madras Board of Revenue Proceedings; Madras Public Consultations; and the Madras District Records.

In addition, the relevant secondary sources and works have been consulted.

TOPIC III: THE RISE, GROWTH, AND MORPHOLOGY OF THE COLONIAL PORT CITY

(continued)

Session 6 - DISCUSSION

257

Moderator - Thomas Metcalf

Discussant - Robert Reed

James Masselos, *City-State to Capital City: An Explora-tion into the Urban Structure of Bombay City*

Susan Neild, *Urban and Suburban Property in Early Nineteenth Century Madras*

METCALF - Later, I would like to summarize some of the general trends and themes we have discussed during these last few days. It is important that we come to grips with the three themes of morphology, merchants, and hinterland in some fashion as well as the question of what is "colonial" and what is "a port," and what is "a city," and their interaction. Before doing this, let us start out with the two papers of Mr. Masselos and Ms. Neild, followed by brief discussion on the morphology question. We can then take up, in an extended session, the general ques-tion of colonialism and the port city and its role in the whole system. First, Jim Masselos.

MASSELOS - While listening to the discussion the past few days, I was constantly reminded of Australia--the country I come from--which is full of colonial port cities. I've been trying to work out in my own mind what distinguishes Asian colonial port cities from their Australian counterparts, because Sydney, Brisbane, Melbourne, Hobart, and Perth are also colonial port cities.

     A basic distinction is fairly clear: There was no interaction in Australia as there was in Asia, with a large indigenous, highly-developed population and civilization. The nature of interaction between the two socieities, Asian and Western, in the port city context has, indeed, been a key issue at this Conference. One point that has underlain much of the discussion relates to viewing the cities as transfer points, as areas where traders came and transferred goods from one country to another, where merchant communities developed, and where an interchange of value systems took place in the form of temples, municipal institutions, housing styles, or, alternatively, as Neild shows, even in land systems.

Generally speaking, the papers have looked at the process of the transfer of goods <u>out</u> of, rather than into and within, India, the mechanisms <u>of</u> the transfer of goods inwards being largely ignored. In terms of value systems, the process of interaction has also been widely stressed.

The focus of my paper is somewhat different. Essentially, I'm trying to see the city as an entity in its own right, not merely as a junction point, although I do not deny the interchange role of the city. My model for change in the city attempts to give it an independent quality of its own while allowing for change in terms of decline or growth. I've tried to avoid forming a determinist model that only fits the structure of an ongoing, successful city.

First, I look at Bombay over a number of periods and attempt to work out common features. I build a structure common to each period even though, in each period, variables changed quite significantly. In order to accomplish this, I have developed a double concept of location and authority which I argue provides a basis for understanding the interplay of the variables that are clearly important in a city's growth-- trade, defense, migration, labor supply, cultural factors.

During the first period, Company authority was great, both in the determining of trading patterns, of the siting and form of the city, and in control over population. In the following periods, the official authority of the Company lessened, due largely to the rise of elite groups: to merchants of various kinds and, in the nineteenth century, to Western educated groups, professional men of various sorts. These were absorbed into, or pushed to find, their places in the city's authority structure.

At the same time I argue that these authority locations were limited in their ability to control either the shape of the city or its functioning. The specific examples that support my argument are: the rise of shanty-town settlements around the wall of the fort or, after the fort was pulled down and settlement expanded, on the outskirts of these areas. Here formal authority institutions were ignored as new shanty-town locations were established. The pattern, of course, follows right through to present-day Bombay.

In my model, I focus on how the social components of the formal authority institutions changed over time, how new groups were brought in, and how--in all stages and times--there was constant tension between power that was being exerted and the population on which it was exerted and which, at times, accepted and at other times did not accept it.

With regard to the concept of location, I view it as an organic element in that, in Bombay, the nature of its location

260

changed. It altered from a small township hugging around
a castle to a town trapped within a fort to one that broke
through the walls and expanded. Each time changes occurred
the locational significance of the area altered. Within this
concept I also try to allow for changes in strategic significance of the city in various periods.

For example, I argue that the first period was a
time in which the Company's basic strategy was one of defense
rather than offense in military terms. This was reflected,
functionally, in the shape of the township. In subsequent
periods, the locational significance was to alter as the Company moved to an offensive military posture and acquired territory, thus altering the nature of its hinterland.

Specifically, for Bombay the city had an expanding
hinterland, both of a formal and informal kind. I try to
distinguish between the areas immediately under Company rule,
initially the seven islands that were Bombay, and then, later,
neighboring Salsette Islands as well. It had, by the end of
the eighteenth century, a direct administrative hinterland
combined with an informal trading hinterland in Gujarat and
some limited trading hinterland contacts into Mahrashtra.

From this expanding nature of the hinterland I try to
pull out the idea of the city-state, using it in the sense
Hicks describes in his book, *Theory of Economic History,* drawing
upon analogies with ancient Greek city-states. I would push
strongly Hicks's view of economic change, the role of credit,
the nature and use of hinterland, and so on. I have found
this book particularly provocative, partly because it allows
for changes in mercantile, monetary, and economic systems.

Finally, I provide a brief account of the nature of
authority in present-day Bombay which had developed a complex
authority structure along with an equally complex locational
pattern. Dramatic action was required to cut the Gordian Knot:
This was the movement towards establishing a twin city. It
marked a transfer and a change in the whole nature of Bombay
city, aligning it far more with the wider hinterland of Maharashtra, giving it a sense of identity with the Republic of
India in a way that the former city-state character of Bombay
had previously lacked. To achieve this a single authority
institution was established, something akin to the kind of
authority once wielded by the Company over Bombay Town in the
earliest days.

METCALF - Now, Susan Nield:

NEILD - My paper deals with a far more limited topic than many
of the other papers at this Conference. But the questions I
raise are not without some importance to our understanding of
the growth and morphology of the colonial city: the question
of who owned property in the city, how they acquired it, valued

it, used it, and what effect their property holdings had on the local environment and on the existing settlements. These are questions basic to the study of any community that must be answered before general trends and comparisons can be made.

I chose to focus on the question of property in Madras because in the course of my research I observed that changes in the use and ownership of land during the late 1700s and early 1900s had, in fact, very important effects on the later morphology of the city. Some of these changes illustrate ways in which certain spatial features, common to several colonial cities, were actually imprinted on Madras. Among these were the concentration of colonial commercial activities along the waterfront of the city and the dispersed pattern of spacious colonial residences in the suburbs.

The paper also raises the issue of how one colonial government attempted to deal with the segmented nature of its urban territory as well as with problems of defining city boundaries and property rights. For reasons of space and time, I omitted mention of several important features of the morpho-logical growth of Madras city, including a discussion of urban centers in Madras other than Black Town.

Madras--as you may realize--was a conglomeration of several different types of indigenous urban and rural settle-ments. I also, perhaps, do not emphasize here sufficiently the underlying pluralistic nature of the city, a feature common to most colonial cities. In Madras there existed not only a division between European areas and Indian areas but also a high degree of social and cultural segmentation in the Indian areas of the city, as Mr. Frykenberg reminded us yester-day. My map of the towns and villages of Madras illustrates the segmented nature of the Indian parts of Madras.

I have divided the paper into three sections. The first contains a rather brief review of property holdings up to about the end of the eighteenth century. The main point I make here relates to the clear, dualistic structure of the city, the distinction between the Black Town and the White Town, and be-tween these town centers and the agrarian settlements outside which acted as the hinterland for the Fort.

The White Town during this early period included property largely owned by the Company in and around Fort St. George proper, plus land leased or sold to various Europeans for houses and shops. In the Black Town, property holdings were less clear-ly defined.

In its enthusiasm to encourage settlers to Madras during its earlier years, the Company granted land to various artisan and merchant groups. In some cases land was sold to Europeans and Indians for gardens. Many of these grants, sales, and leases were not recorded. In other cases, land was simply occupied without official sanction. By the mid-1700s the Company really didn't know who owned what land in the city. In fact, it discovered to its dismay that it had very little control over the actual distribution of land.

Outside the town boundaries but under the Company's jurisdiction were the Home Farm Villages. These were villages near Madras that had been granted to the Company during the seventeenth and eighteenth centuries by various local rulers which provided a steady source of revenue to the government at Fort St. George. I have included a discussion of their land structure because the villages were later included within the boundaries of the city at the end of the eighteenth century. These villages were an integral part of the local agrarian order, dominated by a landlord elite called *mirasdars*, holding superior proprietory rights over the land. Different kinds of tenant cultivators possessed limited rights in land they cultivated. The villages also included the usual array of functionaries and village servants. Until the later eighteenth century, the structure of these villages seemed to be very little affected by the proximity of the Fort and the Black Town.

The second part of my paper concerns the changes that occurred in property holdings in the Black Town during the late eighteenth and early nineteenth centuries, in particular the growth of European holdings and commercial activities. My purpose here has been to describe the way in which European commercial activities and some residential areas were transferred from Fort St. George into the Black Town area, partly as a result of the expanding European population of the settlement during the late eighteenth century and partly as a result of deliberate Company policy. The Company wished, by this time, to reserve the Fort for its own military and public purposes. Thus, it decided to evict European merchants who had property in the Fort and to re-settle them in the Black Town. In order to do this, it had to reclaim a lot of land in the Black Town which, throughout the years, had gradually been lost to the Company through illegal claims and encroachments. The Company was thus forced to come to terms with the question of property holdings and property rights. It undertook a mammoth survey of the land holdings in Madras, hoping to recover a great deal of property that it had formerly claimed as its own. But the holdings were so complex that it had to give up the plan and satisfy itself with determining merely who, in fact, occupied Black Town and in issuing certificates to the people who occupied the land at the time. However, the Company was able to recover a strip in the middle of the Black Town, dividing the two older Indian settlements. This it sold to some European developers who created in this strip a thriving commercial center called "Popham's Broadway" and "China Bazaar."

The Company was also able to recover land along the beachfront which it decided would be a perfect place for the relocation of European commercial activities. Part of this land was sold to some Indian merchants who stored their goods in small warehouses along the beach. But most was sold by the Company to Europeans.

By the early 1800s there had developed in the south-eastern corner of the Black Town a small European enclave which, as time went on, became the center of European commercial activity in Madras. In spite of European encroachment on the older indigenous settlements in the Black Town, however, the Indian neighborhoods seemed little affected, even though European agency houses were often situated quite close to the homes of Indian merchants and temples. The Indian neighborhood continued to be concentrated around the markets and caste neighborhoods.

The third part of my paper focuses on the development of suburban Madras and the question of suburban land-holdings. During the late eighteenth century, not only did the Europeans shift their commercial houses and sometimes their residences to the Black Town, they also shifted their residential localities to the suburbs. This process actually had begun in the early eighteenth century but, after 1750, the pace quickened.

The growth of suburban property had a fundamental effect on the existing village communities. The *Mirasdars*, who controlled the village land, came under tremendous pressure to sell their property to Europeans and some Indians with Company ties. They were offered prices far beyond the amounts they would receive even after several years of cultivation. When some landlords resisted the attraction of high prices, political pressure was often applied. As a result, in the villages closest to the Fort and to the Black Town, agricultural land declined dramatically during the last quarter of the eighteenth century and the first quarter of the nineteenth century.

At first, the *Mirasdars* hoped to sell just wasteland and then, if necessary, to sell the cultivatable land their tenants had occupied. But, finally, they found themselves forced to sell even their own private plots. In several of these villages, where such conversion of village land into private suburban holdings occurred, the natural result was the decline of the village community. The tenant cultivator class disintegrated. Many among them went to the Black Town to serve as laborers while many artisans found new employment in the Black Town as well. In these villages all that remained were the village elite who still hung on to a few privileges, still had a few servants and, perhaps, a few plots of land.

In the most distant villages, however, substantial amounts of cultivatable land continued to exist throughout the nineteenth century. Along with cultivation, the agrarian order remained fairly strong in villages like Mylapore, Nungam-bakkam, and Vyaserpady.

The extension of suburban holdings to the villages of Madras forced the Company government, by the early 1800s, to come to terms with two basic issues of urban organization: defining municipal boundaries and developing a consistent policy regarding land in the city. It may have been a more logical decision to limit the boundaries of Madras to the areas that were clearly urbanized, such as the Black Town, the Fort, or, perhaps, to Triplicane or a few other smaller urban centers around there. But pressure from Europeans and some Indian suburban garden holders led the colonial government to extend the boundaries of Madras far beyond these areas. In fact, ten of the original fifteen home-farm villages were included within these boundaries, giving Madras a total area of 27 square miles in 1800, a considerable size for a nineteenth century city and one that led many observers to call Madras "The City of Spaces," "The City of Gardens." Even now, visitors to Madras are struck by the spacious and low-density appearance of the city.

In addition to re-defining the boundaries of the city at this time, the property rights in both suburban residential and village communities were also re-defined. Not only new suburban landowners but also village landlords were required to possess Company grants as proof of ownership. The Company, after a century and a half in Madras, only now asserted its authority as the final arbitrator of property rights. This policy of establishing a uniform system of land holdings led the government to overturn the old communal village land tenurial system in favor of a system of individual and full proprietary rights. This was, indeed, a radical change for the village communities within Madras that transformed their traditional views about landed property and facilitated their absorption within the growing colonial suburban structure.

In conclusion, I must emphasize that the change in property tenures was not merely a shifting of ownership of land but also a change in the way property was valued within the city, especially in the suburban villages where land was no longer valued as a productive commodity. To the colonial European and to the new Indian elites who acquired land there, it was valued as a symbol of authority and wealth.

As space in the Black Town was shared by Indians and Europeans and as Europeans gained suburban property, the clear-cut divisions between what I call Indian and colonial space became muted by the nineteenth century. If you superimpose one map on the other, you can see how the European suburbs overlay the existing village of communities in Madras. By the early nineteenth century, the spatial development of Madras was, perhaps, different from that of other cities in that, underneath the overlay of colonial space in Madras, there were thriving indigenous settlements. The strict division between European and Indian space had become more subtle in Madras by the early nineteenth century but continued to exist throughout that century and into the next.

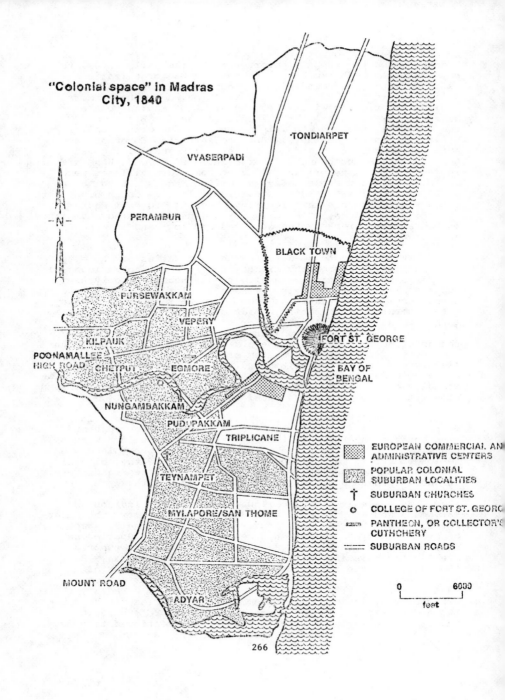

"Colonial space" in Madras
City, 1840

-N-

TONDIARPET

VYASERPADI

PERAMBUR

BLACK TOWN

PURSEWAKKAM

VEPERY

KILPAUK

FORT ST. GEORGE

POONAMALLEE
HIGH ROAD   CHETPUT   EGMORE

BAY OF
BENGAL

NUNGAMBAKKAM

PUDUPAKKAM

TRIPLICANE

TEYNAMPET

MYLAPORE/SAN THOME

MOUNT ROAD

ADYAR

EUROPEAN COMMERCIAL AND
ADMINISTRATIVE CENTERS

POPULAR COLONIAL
SUBURBAN LOCALITIES

† SUBURBAN CHURCHES

○ COLLEGE OF FORT ST. GEORGE

PANTHEON, OR COLLECTOR'S
CUTHCHERY

SUBURBAN ROADS

0   6000
feet

266

METCALF - Thank you. We now have about half an hour that
I would like to aim at a general discussion of the morphological question. Morris?

MORRIS - I am puzzled by one fact: By the middle of the
seventeenth century, the British had very clearly developed
private property in England when they reclaimed land or made
it available in England. Now, when they gave these grants
away, Neild says they didn't have any notion of private
property that they were introducing in Madras--Why not?

NEILD - Well, in some cases they did--at least, initially.
My feeling is that they were dealing with intermediaries and
that they were more eager to gather communities of settlers
to the area than perhaps getting a concept of private property
across.

MORRIS - You know, the British brought with them an intellectual
baggage of private property. The Company itself was an instrument of private property that shared and understood the baggage. You don't have any feeling about it?

NEILD - No, I don't, except that they were, perhaps, eager to
replicate in Madras the existing ideas about property in order
to attract settlers.

LEWANDOWSKI - I think Susan is right about the role of the intermediaries. Perhaps a certain area was given over to an inter-
mediary and then, as people settled, they remained in the area
and claimed the area in their own right.

NEILD - And perhaps it reflected the Company's own sense of
instability and insecurity in the area. They didn't come with
an idea of creating a permanent settlement, at least not at
the very beginning.

METCALF - I'll ask the third question, which has to do with the
dispersal of the city. It seems to me that we do have a curious
morphological pattern in Madras that is quite different from
that of Bombay or Calcutta. I'm thinking of the discussion we
had about the north-south sort of narrow-strip quality. There
is a north-south quality about Madras, but it also bulges out
in the middle. Very markedly. And the whole garden suburb
question: why garden suburbs in Madras and not elsewhere, or,
conversely, why did they not stick to the established pattern
in the settlement of Madras? It does seem curious.

NEILD - I think that was partly due to local and topographical
causes. By the time Europeans developed an interest in suburban gardens, many of the closer areas had already been claimed
by indigenous groups. For example, the Black Town had been
settled by Indians. South of Fort St. George, Triplocane was
developing in the mid-eighteenth century. A lot of the town
directly to the west of the Black Town was rather marshy, not

congenial to the development of suburban gardens. So the
best land happened to be somewhat further away.

MASSELOS - In Bombay, although there is clearly a north-south
    axis, there is also very much an east-west axis. I think
    one should look rather at the east-west axis in Bombay since
    it goes far toward explaining the land reclamation movement
    right up to the present day.

METCALF - What about Back Bay--?

MASSELOS - Bay Bay--that whole movement is on the east-west
    axis--

MURPHEY - In Calcutta, the reasons are obvious.

FUREDY - It's not so obvious that the pattern of Madras is
    different from Calcutta's because, if you turn the map around
    so that Madras is on the east, it looks very much like the
    shape of Calcutta. The scale may be different but, at least
    after the Calcutta municipal boundaries were expanded in 1888,
    the shape is very similar.

MURPHEY - Impressionistically, one gets the feeling that Madras
    is all over--it's a garden city, green and open, and it sort
    of spreads like a blob over the landscape in a very pleasant
    way. One does not get that sense in either Bombay or Calcutta.

BASU - I'll support what Chris Furedy has said. There was a
    mushrooming of garden villas in Calcutta suburbs, especially
    along the river banks as one approached the port city by boat.
    During the nineteenth century, Garden Reach was especially
    noted for its garden houses. Later, the northern and the
    eastern fringes of the city also developed an impressive array
    of such houses. Many among them were owned by the newly-rich
    Bengali families. The Tagores, for instance, had a fabled
    villa at Belgachhia.

BROOMFIELD - I was going to make the point that Basu has men-
    tioned about the gardens around Calcutta. My question to Neild
    is, What did the gardens consist of in Madras? Vegetables?
    Rice? Mango? Nice trees? Flowers?

NEILD - In the eighteenth century there were fruit groves, perhaps
    some cultivation as well. By the late eighteenth century, how-
    ever, the situation had changed. These had become primarily
    residences, consisting of a bungalow, a few other buildings,
    some trees, shrubs, perhaps a small vegetable garden, all with-
    in an area ranging from half an acre to ten acres. They were
    generally non-productive.

ANDERSON - A quick point, one we discussed this morning that fits
    in nicely here and with Jim Masselos's paper, too. It relates
    to possible dynamism within morphology, to the question of

permanent buildings and impermanent buildings--permanent
buildings being the civic or public buildings and impermanent buildings being the private ones. I'm speaking primarily
for Southeast Asia, but I would like to reflect on this more
generally. Light, impermanent buildings in Southeast Asia,
which were the dominant forms, performed some interesting
functions.

Climatically, on a manifest level, they accommodated
well to the climate. The air moved through them, and people
were cool. They were, however, built of light materials--
sometimes built on stilts above the waters where they could
take flooding, built in such a manner that they could take
typhoons. The roof might blow off, yet one could put it right
back on again. The point is that one made little capital investment in such buildings. In fact, as capital goods go--
even among peasantries in Southeast Asia today--the caribou is
worth five to ten times what the house is worth.

On a latent level, there were some interesting aspects,
too. It was possible to move these easily, and it was possible
to shift the capital. It was possible for someone to move the
treasury, as somebody made the point this morning, and the dependents would follow suit since it was so easy to dismantle
houses. In the Philippines, one could actually see a house
moving across space, people underneath it, carrying it, literally moving it from one site to another.

Finally, another point that relates to urban, or *kinyan*,
living: Bob Reed and I have talked about this for many years.
"Kinyan" means "shifting cultivation" or "fire agriculture."
It's the use of fire to burn off areas to establish planting.
We see it regularized in reports of regular fires, in markets,
in sections of the city where, inadvertently or intentionally,
cities are burned off to restructure or reorganize "urban development." It gives possibilities for real urban redevelop-
ment, for the imposition of urban planning, and for change.

Coming back to Susan Neild's point about the changes in
areas for different kinds of use, Jim Masselos gives us a nice
example of a fire that took place and of a committee of the
city using it as an opportunity to replan.

MURPHEY - As in 1666 in London, or 1906 in San Francisco--

MORRIS - There are some real differences. As an authority on
the bombing of London in 1944, I was impressed by the difficulties of the planners in recreating the city in a more efficient
way because of property rights. Everybody had his place on the
street and wanted it restored. Now, when you're getting re-
structuring, you have quite a different set of rights. Then
the value develops in <u>land</u>, land expressed as a common denominator, that is, the money value at which land transfers. And
values go up. Or down.

269

REED - I think there should be some comparative work on the
impact of fire in the traditional city in Asia. In Southeast
Asia houses were consumed so frequently in general conflag-
rations that people often kept valuables in small iron safes
or in little stone boxes within their highly flammable houses.
These could occasionally be seen, even in the early part of
this century.

Were fires always of accidental origin? Was fire used,
perhaps, to prevent the spread of diseases? Or by authorities
to clear sections of cities that were plagued by particularly
virulent illnesses?

Another question: Many societies in Southeast Asia and,
I suspect, in parts of India where shifting cultivation occurs
(which, incidentally, today still supports about five hundred
million people in the world, directly or indirectly), share
notions of "transitory right" to space. These ideas were
carried from rural situations to the city. Accordingly, we
must think, in some cities at least, of the suburb or the village as something ephemeral or something not always tied to
place. Such patterns of transitory rights die hard, even when
systematically neutralized by European ideas of private property.

FUREDY - Can I say here that this last discussion has fired my
imagination? I find Masselos's attempt to see a relationship
between location and authority very fruitful, applicable to any
number of cities. It brings me back to something we were discussing earlier, when we talked about the dichotomous notion
of the organic city and the planned city that traditional urban-
ologists have tended to operate with.

Now that seems rejected by the latest position, that
there is no such thing as a planned city, no such thing as an
unplanned city, no such thing as organic growth. Organic
growth is not unplanned, because for any structure to arise in
the city, someone has to make a decision for it to appear.
Planning is, after all, only decision-making, and it occurs
at different levels. Instead of talking of just centralized
planning, one tries to separate out the levels of decision-
making that result in the appearance of city structures, whether
they are roads or drains or houses or institutions.

In his paper, Masselos seems to have gone to the crux
of urban planning. He not only looks at the relationship between authority, or decision-making, and physical structure,
but also at a certain type of authority and a certain level of
decision-making. I'd like to suggest that the relationship
between the physical structure and authority could be applied
to any number of levels. Of course, one has to sort out which
are the levels of decision-making that result in the shaping of
a city? Who makes the decisions? Who else tries to assert
authority? There may be, there surely are, several levels of
decision-making as well as several levels of authority. Perhaps

the conflicts and tensions that Masselos has identified in making decisions about physical structure in Bombay would be better understood if we begin to sort out the levels of decision-making and understand with what sort of power, with what sort of authority, with what sort of legitimacy, did people make certain decisions? How were they able to make the ideal decisions, the planning decisions, and what sort of tensions arose in the attempt to bring those into reality? I think that opens up vast possibilities for exploration in the study of colonial port cities.

MASSELOS - I accept the point about looking at various kinds of levels. Perhaps one also needs to look at the different purposes of decision-making. One is struck by a whole series of inter-actions among a number of different authorities, all working on the city, and each with different concepts. This multiplies down the line, becoming increasingly complex, so that the danger is that one may lose sight of the total pattern in the mass of detail.

BAYLY - I'm interested in the same thing. What strikes me is that Masselos is defining authority largely in terms of the city itself. It seems to me that another dimension emerged among people in authority outside the city who wished to trans-late themselves into an authority position within the city, as it were, by obtaining property.

For instance, a suburban landholder who wished to asso-ciate himself more directly with the colonial power might well buy up urban land and settle on it in order to buy himself _in_ to the urban authority situation. So, it's a question of access to authority as well as of existing authority. For instance, the Talugdars of Lucknow, wishing to associate them-selves more with the Nawab's Court, obviously moved the loca-tion of their political activity from the hinterland progressively into Lucknow during the nineteenth century.

MITTER - I quite agree, and what I wish to emphasize is the extent of planning done and to ask, ultimately, how does it emerge out of conflicts of interests? As regards the question of fire, London was much easier to plan after it was destroyed in the Great Fire.

METCALF - But it didn't change the street pattern--

MITTER - Right, but I was thinking more of the wider streets and better organization. I think it changed quite a bit in these respects.

METCALF - This is the question we should wonder about--whether Bombay, after its fire, changed more or less.

MITTER - It never did change much.

METCALF - The authority in Bombay was more paternalistic and
authoritarian as compared with that of London of 1666 or San
Francisco of 1906 where the inhabitants had an input into
the system which meant that they had to be taken into account.
But I'm not sure that was true in Bombay.

CONLON - Morris's point about the limits of British power was
revealed best in the tentative way in which the British dealt
with hutments, when one compares recent news from Delhi as to
the creative propensities of purification by fire. I know
that the Bombay police were doing that with slum dwellers over
the last twenty years. I don't know if it goes back before
Independence or not.

METCALF - The removal of unauthorized hutments by police action?

MASSELOS - I think this has been over-exaggerated in Bombay.
I have watched the growth of one particular hutment area over
the past fifteen years. Every time I go back it has become
more of a lower-middleclass suburb, although highly and densely
packed, and far less of a squatter's lumpen proletarian shanty-
town.

I agree that one of the significant things in Bombay
has been the constant fear of fire. Fire is surrounded by
other features, including fire insurance, which was one of the
first formal insurance institutions that operated indigenously.
As the urban structural pattern changed, the role of fire en-
gines and fire service arrangements also altered. Fire came
to be used, also, as a method of protest. If one looks at
strikes in the twentieth century, one is impressed by the number
of mill fires that occurred during the period of strike agitation.

METCALF - We almost had a paper at this Conference on the question of hutment planning and relocation in contemporary Karachi
which we finally ruled out because it was, technically, post-
colonial. Keith Sipe gave a paper on this at the Toronto
Association of Asian Studies Conference this year to which I
would like to call your attention. I wonder whether Neild
would wish to add anything on this question of fire relocation
from the Madras point of view?

NEILD - I'm not aware of fires in the early period of Madras,
although certainly in recent years it is a common problem.

METCALF - How about hutments?

NEILD - Combinations of huts often appeared in unauthorized areas
in the Black Town and other sections of Madras, and the colonial
government was in a quandary as to whether to remove these huts
from the land which it claimed as its own. It knew that if the
huts remained, well-established communities would soon evolve.
Often these hutments were built by lower castes who had the re-
putation of being quite inflammable at times, especially during

272

periods of caste conflict. So, sometimes the government removed them, and sometimes they left them alone.

LEWANDOWSKI - Municipal records from the late nineteenth century through the early twentieth century on the removal of
huts in Madras show that there were constant attempts at removing them, but they continued to reappear. The hutments
that were torn down were rebuilt.

REED - It has been observed that fire was sometimes used by
Europeans to discipline alien Asian communities within certain
Southeast Asian cities. During periodical uprisings of the
Chinese in Manila, the Spaniards and Filipinos found fire a
very effective weapon in both defensive and offensive maneuvers
against the alien Asians.

Furthermore, through the occasional threat of fire, the
Hispanic colonial officialdom gained an important measure of
control over the especially restive Chinese. On the other
hand, by "guaranteeing" some degree of protection against fire,
the Spaniards could better command the loyalty of many Chinese.

BASU - I have a question for both Susan Neild and Jim Masselos:
In Calcutta, money was raised for building roads and other muni-
cipal improvements, through holding lotteries under a Lottery
Committee. Was there something similar in Bombay and Madras?

NEILD - Yes. That was the major way of building suburban roads
in Madras. These lotteries were mainly patronized by the European inhabitants, although Indians often participated in them,
too. But the roads that were chosen to be built from these
funds were usually defined by the European community.

MASSELOS - The evidence I've seen on Bombay doesn't indicate
that lotteries were held to build roads. But lotteries were
used to build the Town Hall. There was also a spate of sub-
scriptions to Calcutta lotteries. Lotteries in Bombay became
popular around the beginning of the nineteenth century but,
to my knowledge, most of these were commercial ventures.

FUREDY - In Calcutta, private lottery also became popular first.
Then the municipalities got the idea of financing improvements
by lotteries. In press advertisements, you can see several
lotteries going on in Calcutta at any one time up to about 1840.

MASSELOS - They're still used in some areas, to build opera
houses--

FUREDY - --and to finance the Olympic Games!

SIPE - I was wondering if either of you would care to speculate
on notions of social ranking and the allocation of space within
your respective cities? Does the port city, in part, differ
from other cities in this respect?

MASSELOS - If I understand you correctly, you are trying to
relate high status with geographical areas and the degree
of space that each family possesses in these areas. In
Bombay there were certainly "status" areas. For example,
in the first half of the nineteenth century, the Fort area
was a status area.

METCALF - Were there class, or ethnic-based, neighborhoods?

MASSELOS - Both. Some were class-based and, within that,
were often ethnic as well. By the end of the nineteenth
century the Malabar Hill area had become very upper-class.

METCALF - Pure class, without any ethnic overtones?

MASSELOS - Yes, pretty much so.

NEILD - The development of the suburbs in Madras was, indeed,
a part of the process of defining property according to class
status. First of all, the garden suburbs were generally occupied by the higher-level Europeans, higher-level civil servants,
rich merchants, the tradesmen of the town. The European artisan
generally lived in the Black Town, even in the nineteenth century.
In certain sections of the suburbs, one could see class distinctions among the Europeans who lived there, as was also the case
among the Indians who acquired suburban land during the nineteenth century. They were defining themselves as an elite
class by acquiring suburban property. Even within the Black
Town there were areas that certainly were identified as upper
class and combined, or included, a number of castes. One particular street, the Mint Street, in the western part of the Black
Town had very much the character of upper class, though traditional Hindu locality. So, in both the Black Town and the
suburbs there did develop, in the nineteenth century, a notice-
able degree of class differentiation.

METCALF - But you also make the point, don't you, that class
differentiation does not wholly override ethnic considerations?

NEILD - That's so. One finds areas of the city defined primarily
by caste, occupational and ethnic identitites co-existing with
other--mainly newer--areas influenced by class identities. This
coexistence of ethnic and class groupings is an important and
characteristic feature of colonial cities and one that accounts
for their particular kind of plural, spacial, and social structure.

BROOMFIELD - While we were talking about country houses, it
occurred to me that once, when I was visiting Puri, I was told
by a local resident that either Jagannath or his sister is
taken to a country house where he or she dwells for the summer.
It was explained to me that this is his or her summer residence,
and it was explained in terms of a garden house in the country.
Is it Jagannath?

MITTER - Yes.

BROOMFIELD - And is it like a villa? A garden villa? Is it he or she who stays there for the summer?

MITTER - The two of them go there together; actually, there are three of them.

BROOMFIELD - But the interesting thing is, then, where does this idea of the country house come from? Is it pre-colonial? Is it borrowed?

BASU - I would like to add a comment on this question of garden-villas: In Calcutta, a distinctive new type of garden house started to emerge in the late eighteenth century. It was a combination of lavish Mughal and European style, with furniture imported from France or Italy, a big dancing floor, and a banquet hall. Entertainment included nautch girls. Both Europeans and Indians among the newly rich took part in such junkets and parties.

CONLON - That fits what Susan Lewandowski was saying earlier. A lot of this has to do with the colonial port city and the "security" it created. It permitted people to think in terms of moving out of the security of traditional mores.

MURPHEY - --which never happened in China . . .

METCALF - But it did happen in seventeenth century Agra. There was security in other places at other times, so it's not wholly a colonial phenomenon.

METCALF - I shall now make an attempt to summarize the discussion on the problems we have looked at and then open the floor for general discussion.

First, we had the Conference organized in three topical sections: morphology, merchants, and city-hinterland relationships. We endeavored to develop a certain amount of ideas and generate a body of shared factual information on each of these three subjects. The question we now have to ask is, What can we do with all of this? How can we bring it to bear on the problems of the Asian colonial port city?

Looking at the three elements of the title of the Conference one asks, Why cities? What is it that is important about dealing with a city, not just a port? Is the fact of the city significant? The question we looked at during the first afternoon session was, What is distinctively colonial about these cities and, indeed, which are the cities we have in mind? Then, of course, we have to face the question of the role of Asian cities and European dominance. What forms of dominance are required to make cities colonial? Further, there is the question of why the port city is distinct from some

275

other kind of city, such as an administrative or cultural
capital? In the same vein one may ask, Why are port cities
the locale for certain kinds of urban commercial activities?
Why should we study entrepreneurs in port cities rather
than, as Morris suggested in his paper, entrepreneurs in
general? Why should we discuss planning in port cities
rather than planning in general? Perhaps, if we're talking
about planning, New Delhi, say, may be more relevant than
Bombay.

          The question still nags, What about the port? What
about the colonial context? What about the urban context?
These are the three elements we have to keep in mind as we
try to pull our thoughts together.

          Various themes and ideas have been generated during
the course of the Conference that call for further discussion.
I made a quick list--some themes are more obvious than others.
There is the question of extraction of goods for Europe, the
role of the port city as the devise or funnel for colonial
exploitation. One can generalize this, as Masselos did in
the beginning of his remarks: These cities can be looked on
as transfer points for goods and values. There is the mutual
reciprocity between European attitudes and values, and indigenous values and attitudes.

          We have had some discussion, not as much as one would
have liked perhaps, on the role of neo-classical architecture,
the role of traditional patterns of temple and kingly patronage, and other themes in the cultural interchange area as
well as the more straightforward economic interchanges of
goods and services and the social responses of people to the
colonial context.

          On the social side, we have tried to play with themes
of migration, segmentary communities, of separate groups of
people who acted in certain fashions, perhaps floated even, as
we discussed in relation to western India. There is also the
notion of cosmopolitanism. Are we dealing with cosmopolitan
centers, metropolises, or are we dealing primarily with the
centers for the exchange of goods?

          There is also the question of phases and periods.
Harking back to our first morning discussion: What are the
phases we wish to delineate in the process of the rise and
development of the colonial port city in Asia? Are there
pre-colonial cities? Proto-colonial cities? Full-blown colonial cities? Are there stages? If we wish to delineate phases
in the process of growth, what is it that demarcates one phase
from another?

          Questions of overseas trade and its volume, the Indus-
trial Revolution and steamships, political dominance in the
inland empire, as against simple maritime fortifications,

surface time and again. Finally, there is an epilogue of
the post-colonial phase, the extent to which these patterns
persist after the coming of Independence, the extent to
which cities remain in their "traditional" colonial role as
time goes by, after 1947 and 1949, as the case may be.

        This is a jumbled attempt at summarizing questions
that have surfaced, and throwing some of them on the table.
Let me now open the discussion and hope that you will try
to raise some of these issues and problems.

BASU - I would like to say a few things on morphology first.
Professor Anderson has mentioned the question of possible
changes in the siting of the port city, historically, over
a period of time as well as spatial movement of merchant and
other social classes.

        In my work on Calcutta and Canton there are two striking
things I've come across which relate to the evolution of the
morphology of these two cities. Both cities changed in terms
of their locus as the river courses changed historically.
Calcutta was referred to as late as the fifteenth century
in a literary source as, "The Land of Kilkila," or water land.
In 1956, Communist historians discovered some archeological
sites which show that what is now Canton's central district
was under water probably only a thousand years ago.

        The point that emerges from this is that, due to the
nature of their techtonic and geological structures, the Calcutta and Canton regions had undergone considerable shifting
and change. Economically, the role of the river system
changed with a more "outward," or "seaward," orientation
which the Western traders tapped. Little indigenous marts
and market centers, themselves creations of physical changes
in the river system, developed into larger, colonial hinter-
land-type towns and urban centers.

        Another point is that merchant and other social classes
followed faithfully such changes and the opportunities they
brought. Thus, the growing Calcutta commercial networks
attracted merchants from the declining traditional port towns
of Satgaon and Hughli, as did the Canton networks from Amoy.
I submit that the role of the Portuguese in the early phases
of such development was crucial--a fact that doesn't seem to
have received sufficient attention in the recent revisionist
literature on Portuguese trade.

REED - Our basic problem in understanding morphology is filter-
    ing out those elements of genesis that are indigenous and those
    that are of European derivation.

METCALF - A distinction ought to be made between geographically-
    imposed indigenous elements of the land, perhaps, and those
    that were imposed by social structures, adaptations, and res-
    ponses.

277

From the European side one has to keep in mind the ideas of different European peoples, or the ideas of European peoples at different times: It may make a difference that the Spanish came in the sixteenth century with full-blown Renaissance notions, and the English later on, in the eighteenth or nineteenth century, with differently defined ideas.

REED - The actual changes in site were not only a result of activities in the immediate hinterland of the city but also in regions beyond.

METCALF - You can't change the basic physical structure--

REED - That's right. Sometimes, for instance, changes were a result of deforestation upriver. Obviously, one has to consider many elements here that have not yet received sufficient attention.

METCALF - Once settled in, the site itself was subject to change, both directly and inadvertently, by human action.

CONLON - I think that one has to consider the relative difference in technologies between the cities in the 1600s and cities in the 1900s. Changes in public transport had effects in Bombay--to argue from the exotic case of the development of the *dabbawallah*.

METCALF - The who?

CONLON - The men who collect lunch buckets in suburban housing developments and deliver them to offices each day. It permits a reorientation of the work schedule away from the old pattern of staying home, eating your meal, and then going to the office at 11:00 a.m. And it permits--not a very impressive technological chore--considerable reorientation of the population.

METCALF - The commuter train can be advantageous only if a lunch system has been worked out.

CONLON - They come in on the baggage compartments of commuter trains with headloads of lunch buckets--

METCALF - Why couldn't people carry their own lunch buckets?

CONLON - It would be beneath their middle-class dignity. It's like civil servants in Vienna, carrying their lunch in their attaché cases.

METCALF - Yes, the general question of technological change and the way in which it could facilitate a larger scale of operation in general is important. But there is no peculiarly colonial or port city aspect to that. This goes back to the question that Susan Neild remarked about--the difficulty of getting around

278

in a far-flung city like Madras. Was Madras's leisurely
lifestyle a product of the eighteenth century garden-house
development?

MORRIS - It wasn't easy to get around in any eighteenth
century city. The reason why suburban development has
taken place in a substantive way in modern times is because
of reduction in travel time by commuter trains and bicycles.

FUREDY - Someone should do a study of the impact of the bi-
cycle in India.

MORRIS - I would like to bring up two points: We have neglected
here the role of the city as an industrial development and the
role of the city as a political center.

METCALF - We did have a brief reference in Chris Furedy's
paper to political forces and in Bob Eng's to silk-reeling as
an enterprise within the city. Rather tangential in both
cases.

ANDERSON - In our paper, we were aware of the political implications in the sense that personalistic, economic, extractive
forms of marketing relationships were political in nature--
"embeddedness," as we call it. With reference to hinterland,
a range of possibilities existed which we staked out by linking city and hinterland. Das Gupta's paper also spells out
some of these linkages.

FUREDY - I would say, in defense of the Conference, that there
were three topic areas specified for the Conference, and politics and political structure was not one of them. That is
why politics seems tangential in most papers. We never expected this Conference to be comprehensive in its coverage
of the colonial port cities.

METCALF - The question still remains: To what extent are the
three specific considerations of this Conference either colonial or port city? They can, perhaps, be asked of any city,
or, indeed, of any countryside. The questions that Anderson
and Reed have raised about ecological or morphological considerations can be connected with any habitation. Questions of
commuter trains, or lunch- *wallahs*, are part of the process of
urbanization and industrialization, and not particularly either
colonial or port city.

   The same is true, surely, of industrialization and politics. Their connection to the port city, one might argue, is
at best coincidental or happenstance in the sense that a port
city is a convenient place to carry out these enterprises.
One could, however, ask why should so many of India's or China's
industries, why should the loci of their political activity be
in Bombay and Calcutta, Canton, and Shanghai and why, curiously,
not in Madras or Amoy?

These questions are relevant, but one can't, obviously, answer all of them. In defense of the Conference, I would say that we tried to pick out the critical areas which defined the colonial port city as a distinct species--although one can argue whether there is, indeed, such a species and whether we can define it in any meaningful, useful way.

MORRIS - Why did "colonial port city," then, come to your mind as a Conference topic?

BASU - Because some of us have worked on that subject.

(Laughter)

FUREDY - But why did some think they're working on cities and some on a colonial port city?

METCALF - The whole thing is fortuitous. Basu just let the cat out of the bag!

MURPHEY - I don't think that's bad.

METCALF - A few of us were into what could be broadly and historically defined as Asian colonial port cities, which doesn't mean we're trying to produce a mirror of the cosmos at this Conference.

MURPHEY - But one must ask whether this is a useful or relevant analytical tool. Does this tool get us anywhere that the concepts of urbanization or industrialization or modernization would not have achieved just as satisfactorily?

METCALF - It's not quite fortuitous that certain individuals just happen to be interested in working on Asian port cities. Ideas didn't come from the mind of Zeus: some topics are locally specific, dealing also with a relatively limited period of time rather than with the entire 1498-1970, or 1949, period. To this extent, there are some discontinuities between Portuguese time in Melaka and contemporary Karachi. That is not a tragedy. It would have been very strange if it were otherwise.

MURPHEY - We must try to make it more explicitly and consciously comparative and less exclusively locally specific, limited to a particular time and place. We should be more concerned with phenomena that stretch over a long period of time, over a great variety of cultures and, in the hands of different sets of colonial masters, between the Philippines on the one hand and a highly urbanized, commercialized India-China on the other.

It is rather striking that, apart from processes and phenomena that we've been given some examples of, we've looked almost entirely at British establishments. Manila is an exception, of course; so is Melaka. But, for the most part, we are looking at the British *raj* in its various manifestations. Even then, we left out Rangoon because nobody's working on Rangoon; nobody means to leave it out, but we don't know anybody who is working on Rangoon. Penang isn't here, and Singapore is an obvious lack. China is represented in Hong Kong, Canton, and Shanghai, but not as part of the generic treaty port system.

We've left out the French, the Dutch, and what survived of the Portuguese, namely, Goa and Macao. Goa isn't any longer the kind of interesting, still-breathing fossil that Macao is. Somebody might like to play with that sometime. And we've left out the Japanese, who were the other great colonizers. I suppose the Americans, who used to own Manila, were colonizers in this system, too. It may be interesting to look at the particular qualities of American colonial imprint, as seen in what they did with what they had inherited from the Spanish.

MASSELOS - I don't think it's a matter of what we leave out. We aren't, hopefully, producing a textbook covering every aspect of colonial port cities. Rather, what we are aiming at is a series of insights.

Clearly, we've got three kinds of phenomena: the colonial, the trading, and the urbanization issues. We're attempting to bring together these three circles where they intersect in the focus of the city. It isn't merely a matter of bringing out material from different areas, but rather in finding the similarities, in trying to determine whether the patterns are common. And the only way we can do this is through case-study techniques and in generalizing from these specifics. Colonialism is, of course, the key variable in that it led to dominance over most of Asia. We are right in calling this "Colonial Port Cities in Asia."

I would, however, like to see some material which would link the trading patterns and the relationship with the environment in which they're situated, connected with the international trading systems. One of the things this Conference has brought out strongly is the way in which we've moved from the view of an extractive, exploitive picture of colonialism to one that has emphasized the resiliency and role of indigenous factors, such as the rise of mercantile groups and the interchange of values.

We've moved away from simplistic, exploitative, political, and economic dominance theories to a typology of complex interaction.

BASU - I wish to comment on the Conference themes. Some of the glaring lacks are at once intentional and fortuitous. We planned on focusing primarily on South and Southeast Asia, with

281

a comparative component from East Asia, principally China. With the limited resources at our disposal, we had to lower our sights, both from the point of view of the number of people we could have invited as well as the topics and foci we wanted covered. Some scholars we had expected would come finally didn't, but on the whole we landed a balanced group. We limited the scope of the Conference to three specific themes intentionally, believing that a larger and more general focus would have diluted the quality in addition to being unwieldy and unmanageable.

MORRIS - Even though you picked certain elements, there is the general overriding fact of colonialism. It seems to have gotten less attention than it deserves as a moving force behind port city development.

METCALF - We believe the role of colonialism as a general force to be central and beyond dispute. Assuming that, we have attempted to zero in on interactions and interconnections within the colonial framework, with special emphasis on social exchanges and value changes, the flow of goods and persons.

MILONE - An answer to, Why the colonial port city? In contrast to other orban situations, a unique feature of the colonial city is that it reversed the polarity. When the Europeans arrived on the scene, the administrative and economic power of Asia was at inland capitals. With the colonial port city, the economic and adminstrative power shifted to the coasts. And, then, this power was controlled externally by Europe. This was unique.

BROOMFIELD - I agree with Milone. I wouldn't, however, go as far as to say that, with the arrival of DaGama, power shifted to the coast. I think that is where K. M. Panikkar went wrong. But I do think there is no need to defend the impor- tance of colonial port cities, even though Goa of the sixteen- th century is very unlike Calcutta or Hong Kong of the 1940s. We have to look to the fundamental developments in Europe: European commercial domination and military innovations of the seventeenth century, with ripples across the world. Some recent explorations fit well with what we're doing here. For instance, Athar Ali, in his article in *Modern Asian Studies* on the collapse of the Mughal Empire, points out that, as yet, no one has linked together the crises that came upon a number of Asian empires and the Muslim world around this time. He is underlining a crucial problem in South Asian history: Did the Europeans pick up the pieces of the Mughal Empire already in a state of decline, or were they involved in the shaking, pushing, and toppling of that Empire?

One can, perhaps, combine Athar Ali's suggestive question with Niels Steensgard's recent book on the decline of the cara- van trade and come to the conclusion that, during the period between the intrusion of the Portuguese and the end of the eighteenth century, when the Europeans had not yet captured power in Asia, the port cities of the Europeans in Asia were critical. They were the touchpoints on Asia which re-directed the economic system of the world progressively towards Europe, damaging severely the internal Asian trade routes, the Persian Gulf trade, and the Red Sea trade.

This should be viewed alongside the increase in the cost of military organization in Europe with the formation of the small platoon operating with lighter artillery and tactical cavalry, resulting in a bureaucratic hierarchy that linked armies together. This bureaucratized army and navy were brought to India and Asia in the seventeenth century. The cost of the military ran ahead of actual conquest, and I believe this was one factor that helped topple the great Asian empires which were organized patrimonially and could not (or were unwilling to) adapt, although some small states like the Sikh state in the eighteenth century developed the capacity. The port cities were crucial because they brought the military technology and organization to Asia, forcing Asian states to respond.

METCALF - Are you arguing, then, for a proto-colonial phase in the process of colonialization over the long run?

BROOMFIELD - Yes. A proto stage which had political, economic, and military consequences _before_ direct imperialism.

CONLON - Much depends on the extent to which we want to emphasize the exploiting or the enabling aspects. The papers of this Conference in general don't provide a clear fix in which there was definitely an exploitative arrangement without enabling some Asian group to make new gains or achievements.

A colleague at the University of Washington, working in the area of ethnicity, has used the term "the cultural division of labor." I think the expression can be applied appropriately to the colonial port city in terms of internal colonization where a dominant colonial power played off one interest group against another. Of course, it depends on the extent to which, as scholars, we need not grind particular political axes.

METCALF - We are not simply grinding our political axes but dealing with relevant and essential questions. We cannot push colonialism aside and pretend it didn't exist. We have to face up to the structure of the colonial relationship, the question of extraction and exploitation on one hand, and the enabling or modernizing features on the other. It is clear from these papers as to who made disposition of property in Madras, as to whether "sub-wheeling" in silk could prosper in Shanghai or Canton. There is no way to get around such questions. Yet the enabling aspects must be squarely faced, too. It's some-

283

thing we don't like to consider squarely because it leads us into the charged atmosphere of Marxist analysis versus Imperialist apologetics, but I don't think that it's feasible to completely ignore this.

ANDERSON   -   It's not merely an emotional subject. A large number of theories have been developed around it.

METCALF   -   Right.

FUREDY   -   Yes, on that topic--and, since we're talking about theories of dominance, does anyone think that the metropolitan satellite model of André Gunder Frank for Latin America, the relationship of Latin American cities to the mother country, is pertinent to South and Southeast Asia? Is that a theory worth discussing in this context?

       The colonial city was not a city in its own right, according to Frank, but only a satellite of the metropolis of the mother country in terms of the extraction of primary produce from the colony and the absorption of manufactured goods in the satellite. This is, of course, a simple way of putting it.

METCALF   -   Our great success is that we've gotten away from that kind of simplistic analysis. Morris?

MORRIS   -   Once we discuss the fact that colonialism existed and that it was a meaningful phenomenon we don't have to take sides. This Conference has shown how complicated the colonial relationship was, which Frank has not. It would have been helpful, however, if, at the beginning, it had been laid out like this: that there was an imperial expansion that had something to do with world trade and the transfer of power, but that this wasn't a one-way phenomenon.

METCALF   -   The reason it wasn't laid out at the beginning is because I believe we have to work our way through to reach it.

SIPE   -   Evidently, we are dealing with a closed topic in the sense that, at some point, the colonial relationship ends. What about carry-overs in the post-colonial phase? Is the role of port cities diminishing in importance? Already recent developments suggest that ports, in a general way, won't have a life much longer. Japan estimates that 85 percent of its trade within two more decades will be airborne into dry ports. The ex-colonial ports' role may be reduced to handling only grain and bulk merchandise.

DAS GUPTA   -   At the beginning, around 1500, there was the establishment of European dominance at certain ports. These ports didn't link with the hinterland; there wasn't much they controlled except oceanic trade. I believe this phase lasted well into the 1700s, followed by the second phase when the port was linked with the hinterland. During the third phase, a definite political control altered the character of the hinterland. So, one does have, indeed, a colonial port city from 1500 onwards but, in its relationship with the hinterland and control of the hinterland, the colonial port city changed character. The three distinct phases must be brought out in discussion.

BAYLY - It's important, first of all, to set up the type of hinterland that existed before the European arrival in the Indian case. Then arises the question of the relationship between economic and political factors in the h interland and the question of embeddedness. Was there a point when the economy, as it were, became disembedded from society? Or, as in the case of eighteenth and early nineteenth century India, are we talking about a form of economic organization that was still structured fundamentally around the relationships of power?

METCALF - I presume Das Gupta's phase had an economic hinterland that was more or less on a basis of equality, without overtones of a dominant political situation vis-à-vis the hinterland.

DAS GUPTA - I learned this from Chris Bayly's paper. One might have had political control and access to hinterland, yet it took a long time to change the hinterland by political control.

METCALF - It is the changing of the hinterland that produced the full-fledged colonial relationship. We may go back to the point we made earlier, at our very first session, about the 1500 to 1780 phase, when there were implications outside of the walled city. But, as Das Gupta has shown, it was a limited situation. During phase two, political dominance was in but the full transformation of the hinterland, the re-direction of it, was a much longer and slower process.

Another break-point was in 1860 or thereabouts, with railways and steamships and the onset of full economic relationships. The tapping of the hinterland by railways and steamships had, I believe, a considerable impact on the social structure of the port city. For, if one stayed inside the port city, obviously the inter-action among new migrants with each other was bound to be much more substantial than was the case in hinterland towns like Mirzapore, Kanpur, and what have you.

MURPHEY - There's a certain amount of unnecessary self-flagellation going around the table on, "Why didn't we think of this?" and "Why did we do that?" That's precisely the point of having a Conference where people can, indeed, confront and communicate with each other. Somehow, the vision of the whole emerges. We learn individually and collectively. That's why I talk about hauling up our drawers and making the next assault, which I hope we will all do soon.

BASU - I don't know when and where "the next assault" will take place, but it was, indeed, a great pleasure having you all at Santa Cruz. Thank you.

BAZAR AT CABUL, IN THE FRUIT SEASON.

286

EPILOG: WHAT REMAINS TO BE DONE

Rhoads Murphey

The colonial or semi-colonial port cities which acted as the tips of the Western wedge in the effort to penetrate Asia have been acknowledged since early in the nineteenth century as playing a key role. They were seen by their founders or by the early pro-consuls as potentially powerful agents, not only for the establishment of Western power but for the re-making of Asia along Western lines.

A score or more of them did, indeed, rise under Western management, from relatively humble origins, to join the ranks of the world's great cities in the space of little more than a century, spread from what is now South through Southeast and East Asia, displacing the indigenous cities in both size and new functions. In each country with a seacoast, the largest cities were, by the twentieth century, those originally founded or dominated by Western colonialists. * Even with independence, they continued to act, as they had through the preceding century of colonialism, as the chief centers of new national life and of the gathering force of what is referred to as "modernization," often difficult to distinguish from Westernization.

As these cities grew in size and influence after about 1800 (in East Asia, after about 1850), their special and fundamental role was accepted as a truism as long as the special Western position in Asia lasted. Their transforming power, by example and by direct agency, was part of the mystique of colonialism. But colonialist perceptions and assumptions did not end abruptly in 1945 or in 1950.

Perhaps it was this almost axiomatic assumption that was partly responsible for the absence of any major body of scholarly analyses of these cities themselves or of the impact they actually made. Most of the literature that dealt with them took the form of personal accounts of social life (Busteeds, *Echoes of Old Calcutta*, Love's *Vestiges of Old Madras*), promotional tracts, and diplomatic adventures (Alcock's *The Capital of the Tycoon*, Denys's *The Treaty Ports of China and Japan*), or lurid journalistic pastiches (Hauser's *Shanghai: City for Sale*). Nearly all of the serious scholarly work on the port cities has been done since the early 1950s, and most of it in the 1960s and 1970s. In this sense, it is still a relatively new field. The conference papers in this volume reflect that in a number of ways.

It is common and understandable that exploration of a new field begins with separate monographs centered on relatively small and, hence,

---

* Tokyo is a qualified exception, given the single-minded effort at Westernization that fuelled its post-1870 growth under the treaty port system, albeit in Japanese hands, and the even more direct Western role in Yokohama.

287

workable aspects of a larger but still imperfectly seen or understood pattern. Construction and comprehension of the larger whole and of the inter-relationships among its parts rests, necessarily, on the accumulation of such smaller monographic building blocks. Scholars must also begin with what they know or can encompass and, in the absense of fully relevant studies in the past to build on, each must work with his or her own separate skills, interests, training, circumstances, and familiarity with particular materials or situations.

This conference is probably the first occasion when a group of scholars concerned with different aspects of the colonial port city in Asia assembled to share and discuss their recent work. The conference formula was appropriate, coming after monographic work had been begun and bringing together previously scattered people who were already involved in pursuit of a common interest to the point where a sharing of findings and an occasion to try to put some of the pieces together could advance the development of the field. There seems little doubt but that this has, indeed, happened, quite apart from the usual gains derived by each scholar from exposing his or her work to group criticism and, at the same time, learning from group discussion of the work of others.

One measure of how this conference may advance the growth of the field is the occasion it provided to see what has been neglected and what remains to be done. It is hardly surprising that some twenty people working independently and following their own lines should have provided spotty, or even haphazard, coverage of what, partly as a result, one can now see more clearly as a larger integral whole.

Most scholars work primarily or entirely with the cultures/societies and situations they know best, following their own specialist or disciplinary inclinations. Most also assume that the best way, at least to begin with, to advance knowledge is to focus on a topic that is small enough to permit new basic research and detailed analysis based on it. Circumstantial factors—preservation and availability of materials—have also tended to make such research easiest and, hence, more scholars devoted to it in certain parts of colonial Asia. Thirteen of the nineteen papers written for the conference were on South Asia, three on China, three on Southeast Asia, and no others—although the paper by Milone was to some extent pan-Asian. Some of this distribution doubtless reflected other chance factors, including the differential possibilities for field research but, whatever the reasons, the result is still primarily an incomplete and probably unbalanced set of pieces from which to begin constructing the larger pattern.

The greatest single lack, although an understandable one at this stage, is probably the comparative and cross-cultural dimension. The colonial port city was a pan-Asian phenomenon, varying surprisingly little, at least in its avowed goals and in its own internal institutions and values, from one Asian country to another. A complete and balanced understanding of these cities and the role they played must rest on an effort to compare them, to discern both common and disparate features, to trade inter-connections, and to relate them and their impact, collectively and singly, both to their separate Asian contexts and to the far more uniform context of the Western imperial-colonial drive.

288

Some of this kind of analysis is now being pursued, although not yet published at the time of this conference. The conference itself may stimulate further such comparative work, if only by calling attention to the need for it. Another shortcoming of the papers as a whole is that, for reasons already suggested (including the chance availability of participants), many important colonial port cities were not represented at all, some of them important or different enough, perhaps, to affect any general schema: Rangoon, Penang, Kuala Lumpur, Singapore, most of the China treaty ports (and that system as an integral whole), Bangkok, Batavia (except, tangentially, in Milone's paper), Soerbaja, Saigon, Hanoi, Yokohama, Kobe, Taihoku [Taipei], Seoul, Macao, and others. At the least, it would seem essential to examine the port city bases of French, Dutch, and Japanese colonialism in Asia, to compare with the dominantely British scene dealt with in these papers.

Most of the papers also dealt--again, appropriately, given the beginning stage of work on this large topic--with a relatively short period of time and not necessarily one that is representative of or includes all important aspects of the centuries during which the colonial port city existed in Asia. Most are, hence, temporarily as well as locally specific and represent an early building-block stage toward a larger understanding of this major phenomenon.

There was, in particular, a major watershed in the mid-nineteenth century, as Western power and influence increased rapidly and enormously over the relative insignificance of Westerners on the Asian scene in the three centuries following DaGama. Surat in the eighteenth century, Manila in the sixteenth, or Melaka in the seventeenth, have little in common with nineteenth and twentieth century Bombay, Manila, Hong Kong, or Singapore, and yet all are part of the larger phenomenon which needs to be seen as much as possible whole. To do that one must first assemble and examine all the pieces: This conference has begun that process most encouragingly. It is hardly to be expected to have completed the job. Some of the papers do attempt successfully to look at a large urban or commercial _system_, as opposed to a single city, and over a longer period of time. One suspects this may be the most promising line for further research.

The conference was wisely planned from its early stages to center primarily on three major topics (among the many recognized as part of the problem): merchants, urban morphology, and city-hinterland inter-relations. While this was, in part, a function of who was already working on what and on who was available to prepare a paper, it served effectively to help focus what might otherwise have been an unworkably diverse and diffuse mishmash, especially at this stage.

As a result, our understanding of these basic aspects of the colonial port city has been enhanced, but, to some extent, at the cost of the comparative dimension. We have learned a lot about particular merchant groups and activities in particular times and places. But we have not, in most of these papers, reached the stage--although we now have a number of useful building-blocks for it--where we can sketch a more general, comparative, and analytical picture of the kind of environment the colonial port city offered for the fundamental changes in merchant roles and functions that took place there, differing from country to country and even from region to region as

289

well as from period to period, but still part of a larger pan-Asian phenomenon.

Urban morphology received somewhat less emphasis on the whole, although several of the papers did address it, and a few pursued it in some detail--but, again, mainly in the context of a single city. There, too, one senses a missing comparative dimension and one that should be relatively easily pursued. To mention only two obvious aspects, orientation to navigable water was a necessary universal among all of these cities, as was varying degrees of racially-based, residential segregation. But the more locally and temporally specific treatments of morphology and ethnicity in particular cities, and the lively discussion they generated, made an important contribution.

The third topic of city-hinterland inter-relations is, of course, basic to the assumed role of the colonial port in transforming the areas it served. In the smaller countries this came to include most of the national area, while in the larger ones, such as India, the country as a whole was, in many respects, blanketed by commercial services and other influences radiating out from several colonial ports, spaced so as to draw separate regional sectors into the hinterland of each, as Hindustan and Assam to Calcutta, the Indus watershed to Karachi, etc. The port-based process of commericalization/transformation of the hinterland and city-hinterland inter-actions was directly addressed in only four of the papers. It clearly needs a vast amount of further work, some of it already begun elsewhere or by others but most still to be done.

The four papers here make an important contribution, the more important, perhaps, for the magnitude of the task and the smallness of the beginning. Part of the colonial legacy referred to earlier is surely the persistence, to some degree, of what were once wishful or, at least, untested assumptions about the impact of the influences toward "modernization," Westernization, commercialization, or, simply, changes which were clearly generated in the colonial ports. To what extent, in what ways, and in which areas, did these influences spread? Most scholars would resist the notion that such influences resulted in anything like complete transformation; but how far short of complete was it? In what ways, which areas, and why? Most would also agree that the impact differed widely, not only from area to area within any one country but on a larger scale as between countries, states, and major cultures. There is also an important temporal dimension and clear consequent distinctions to be made, different in each area.

Finally, the interactive effect of hinterlands, traditional socio-cultural and economic systems, and migrants, on the character, morphology, and role of the port cities was clearly of major importance, but this remains inadequately studied, both in its effects on particular ports and in helping to shape their different roles and influences in their hinterlands. The contrasts between the two largest cases, India and China, in all of these terms, is especially striking. They, and the similar differences between each Asian colonial area in the role and effects of the port cities, need to be further pursued, especially through more pointed efforts to examine the dynamics of city-hinterland inter-actions, with all that this involved.

Among many other things, measures need to be found or designed that can help to indicate the nature and extent of colonial port-based change as it spread into each port's supposed hinterland, and similar measures need to be devised to show how each port's character and function reflected the multi-faceted nature of its hinterland. Each hinterland itself needs more precise spatial delimitation, resting in turn on more sophisticated definition. This will also require the refinement of better criteria and of quantitative measures to make optimal use of what data are available or can be uncovered or extrapolated.

All of this--and much more--represents a huge task still ahead. But the conference demonstrated that important work has begun, some of it very recent, some over the past decade or two, and that we are already at a point where we can begin to put some of it together. Most significantly of all, the conference attracted and then magnified or re-kindled in its own sounding chamber--as good conferences are supposed to do--a sense of the immense importance and equivalent excitement of the Asian colonial port city as a seminal theme, significant for its own sake simply by its scale and role but, still more importantly, as an endlessly revealing window onto the dynamics of half the world during its modern centuries of Western influence, Asian response, and changing interactions.

That most of the job remains to be done merely adds to the excitement, as the conference has also shown.

SELECTED BIBLIOGRAPHY

Allen, G.C. and Donnithorne, A.G., Western Economic Enterprise in Far Eastern Economic Development. New York, 1954.

Bagchi, A.K., Private Investment in India 1900-1939. Cambridge: At the University Press, 1972.

Banerjee, P., Calcutta and Its Hinterland. Calcutta, 1975.

Bastin, John, Essays on Indonesian and Malayan History. Singapore, 1961.

Batley, C., Bombay's Houses and Homes. Bombay, 1949.

Blair, Emma H. and Robertson, James A. (eds.), The Philippine Islands, 1493-1898. Cleveland, 1905.

Bose, N.S. (ed.), Calcutta: People and Empire. Calcutta, 1975.

Boxer, C.R., The Portuguese in the East 1500-1800. Oxford, 1953.

Boyd, Andrew, Chinese Architecture and Town Planning. London, 1962.

Breese, Gerald (ed.), The City in Newly Developing Countries. Englewood Cliffs, New Jersey, 1969.

Burger, D.H., Structural Changes in Javanese Society: The Supra-Village Sphere. Ithaca: Cornell University Press, 1956.

Busteed, H.E., Echoes from Old Calcutta. Calcutta, 1897.

Chang, Hsin-pao, Commissioner Lin and the Opium War. Cambridge: Harvard University Press, 1964.

Chaudhuri, K.N., The English East India Company. London, 1965.

Chaudhuri, Keshab, Calcutta: Story of Its Government. Calcutta, 1973.

Chaudhuri, Susil, Trade and Commercial Organization in Bengal, 1650-1720. Calcutta, 1975.

Cunningham, Charles H., The Audiencia in the Spanish Colonies as Illustrated by Audiencia of Manila. Berkeley: University of California Press, 1919.

Das Gupta, A., Malabar in Asian Trade. Cambridge: At the University Press, 1967.

Dobbin, Christine, Urban Leadership in Western India: Politics and Communities in Bombay City 1840-1885. London, 1972.

Dwyer, D.J., The City as a Centre of Change in Asia. Hong Kong: Hong Kong University Press, 1972.

Elvin, Mark, The Pattern of Chinese Past. Stanford: At the University Press, 1973.

Elvin, M., and Skinner, G.W. (eds.), The Chinese City Between Two Worlds. Stanford:
    At the University Press, 1974.

Endacott, G.B., A History of Hong Kong. Hong Kong, 1958.

Fairbank, J.K., Trade and Diplomacy on the China Coast. Cambridge: Harvard
    University Press, 1969.

Farmer, B.H., Pioneer Peasant Colonization in Ceylon. London, 1957.

Feldman, H., Karachi Through a Hundred Years. Karachi, 1970.

Furber, Holden, Rival Empires of Trade in the Orient, 1600-1800. Minneapolis:
    The University of Minnesota Press, 1976.

Furber, Holden, John Company at Work. Cambridge: Harvard University Press, 1948.

Geertz, Clifford, Agricultural Involution: The Process of Ecological Change in
    Indonesia. Berkeley: University of California press, 1963.

Glamann, K., Dutch Asiatic Trade, 1620-1740. The Hague, 1958.

Greenberg, Michael, British Trade and the Opening of China. Cambridge: At the
    University Press, 1969.

Hao, Yen-p'ing, The Comprador in Nineteenth Century China. Cambridge: Harvard
    University Press, 1970.

Hirth, F., Rockhill, W.W. (trans.), Chau Ju-kua. New York, 1966.

Hou, Chi-ming, Foreign Investment and Economic Development in China, 1840-1937.
    Cambridge: Harvard University Press, 1965.

Hughes, Richard, Hong Kong: Borrowed Place, Borrowed Time. Hong Kong, 1968.

Jacobs, Norman, Origins of Modern Capitalism and Eastern Asia. Hong Kong, 1958.

Kincaid, Denis, British Social Life in India. London, 1938.

King, Anthony D., Colonial Urban Development: Culture, Social Power and Environment.
    London, 1976.

King, Frank H.H., Money and Monetary Policy in China, 1845-1895. Cambridge:
    Harvard University Press, 1965.

Kling, Blair B., Partner in Empire: Dwarkanath Tagore and the Age of Enterprise
    in Eastern India. Berkeley: University of California Press, 1976.

Kulke, E., The Parsees in India. Munich, 1974.

Lach, Donald F., China in the Eyes of Europe. Chicago: University of Chicago Press,
    1968.

Lach, D.F., Southeast Asia in the Eyes of Europe, The Sixteenth Century. Chicago:
    University of Chicago Press, 1965.

Le Fevour, Edward, Western Enterprise in Late Ch'ing China: A Selected Survey of Jardine & Matheson Company's Operations, 1842-1895. Cambridge, Mass., 1968.

Leach, E., Mukherjee, S.N. (eds.), Elites in South Asia. Cambridge: At the University Press, 1970.

Love, H.V., Vestiges of Old Madras, 3 vols. New York, 1968.

McGhee, T.G., Hawkers in Hong Kong. Hong Kong: Hong Kong University Centre of Asian Studies, 1973.

McGhee, T.G., The Southeast Asian City. London, 1967.

Masselos, J., Towards Nationalism: Group Affiliation and the Politics of Public Associations in Nineteenth Century Western India. Bombay, 1974.

Maunier, Rene, The Sociology of Colonies: An Introduction to the Study of Race Contact. Edited and translated by E.O. Lonimer, 2 vols., London, 1949.

Meilink-Roelofsz, M.A.P., Asian Trade and European Influence in the Indonesian Archipelago Between 1500 and about 1630. The Hague, 1962.

Mendis, G.C., Ceylon Under the British. Colombos, 1948.

Moorhouse, Geoffrey, Calcutta. New York, 1971.

Morris, M.D., "Private Investment on the Indian Subcontinent 1900-1939: Some Methodological Considerations," Modern Asian Studies, vol. 8, part 4, October, 1974.

Moulder, Frances V., Japan, China and the Modern World Economy. Cambridge: At the University Press, 1977.

Mukherjee, N., The Port of Calcutta: A Short History, Calcutta, 1968.

Mukherjee, S.N., Calcutta: Myth and History. Calcutta, 1976.

Murphey, Rhoads, Shanghai: Key to Modern China. Cambridge: Harvard University Press, 1953.

Murphey, Rhoads, The Outsiders: The Western Experience in India and China. Ann Arbor: The University of Michigan Press, 1977.

Murphey, Rhoads, "Traditionalism and Colonialism: Changing Urban Roles in Asia," Journal of Asian Studies, XXIX, November 1969, pp. 67-84.

Nightingale, Pamela, Trade and Empire in Western India, 1784-1806. Cambridge: Harvard University Press, 1970.

Nilsson, Sten, European Architecture in India, 1750-1850. London, 1968.

Parry, J.H., The Establishment of the European Hegemony. New York, 1961.

Pearson, M.N., Merchants and Rulers in Gujarat. Berkeley: University of California Press, 1976.

295

Perkins, Dwight H., China's Modern Economy in Historical Perspective. Cambridge: Harvard University Press, 1975.

Phelan, John L., The Hispanization of the Philippines: Spanish Aims and Filipino Responses, 1575-1700. Madison: The University of Wisconsin Press, 1959.

Polanyi, Karl, The Livelihood of Man. (Edited by Harry W. Pearson), New York, 1977.

Polanyi, Karl, Arensberg, C.M., and Pearson, H.W. (eds.), Trade and Market in The Early Empires. Glencoe, Ill., 1957.

Raychaudhuri, T., Jan Company in Coromondel, 1605-1690. The Hague, 1962.

Rozman, Gilbert, Urban Networks in Ch'ing China and Tokugawa Japan. Princeton, New Jersey: Princeton University Press, 1973.

Ryan, Bruce, Caste in Modern Ceylon. New Brunswick, New Jersey, 1953.

Schricke, B., Indonesian Sociological Studies. The Hague, 1955.

Schurz, William L., The Manila Galleon. New York, 1939.

Simkin, C.G.F., The Traditional Trade of Asia. London: Oxford University Press, 1968.

Singer, Milton (ed.), Entrepreneurship and Modernization of Occupational Cultures in South Asia. Durham, North Carolina, 1973.

Sinha, Pradip, Nineteenth Century Bengal. Calcutta, 1965.

Sinha, N.K., Economic History of Bengal, 3 vols. Calcutta, 1956-1970.

Sinha, Surajit (ed.), Cultural Profile of Calcutta. Calcutta, 1972.

Sjoberg, Gideon, The Preindustrial City: Past and Present, Glencoe, Ill., 1960.

Skinner, G.W. (ed.), The City in Late Imperial China. Stanford: Stanford University Press, 1977.

Spencer, Joseph E., Shifting Cultivation in Southeastern Asia. Berkeley: University of California Press, 1966.

Szczepanik, Edward, The Economic Growth of Hong Kong. Hong Kong: Hong Kong University Press, 1958.

Thorner, Daniel, Investment in Empire: British Railway and Steam-shipping Enterprise in India 1825-1849. Philadelphia: University of Pennsylvania Press, 1950.

Timburg, Thomas, "A Study of a 'Great' Marwari Firm: 1860-1914," Indian Economic and Social History Review, VIII, 1971.

Tripathi, Amalis, Trade and Finance in the Bengal Presidency. Calcutta, 1956.

Ucko, Peter J., Tringham, Ruth, and Dimbleby, G.W. (eds.), Man, Settlement and Urbanism. London, 1972.

Van Leur, J.C., Indonesian Trade and Society: Essays in Asian Social and Economic History, The Hague, 1955.

Wakeman, Frederic, Jr., Strangers at the Gate: Social Disorder in South China, 1839-1861. Berkeley, University of California Press, 1965.

Wallerstein, Immanuel, The Modern World System: Capitalist Agriculture and the Origins of the European World Economy in the Sixteenth Century. New York, 1974.

Weber, Max, The City. New York, 1958.

Wertheim, W.F., The Indonesian Town. The Hague, 1958.

Wheatley, Paul, The Golden Khersonese: Studies in the Historical Geography of the Malay Peninsula before A.D. 1500. Kuala Lumpur: University of Malaya Press, 1966.

Wheatley, Paul, Pivot of the Four Squares. Edinburgh: University of Edinburgh Press, 1971.

Wiekberg, Edgar, The Chinese in Philippine Life. New Haven: Yale University Press, 1965.

Willmott, W.E., Economic Organization in Chinese Society. Stanford: Stanford University Press, 1972.

Wilson, C.R., and Carey, W.H., Glimpses of the Olden Times: India Under the East India Company, Calcutta, 1968.

Wright, Arnold (ed.), Twentieth Century Impressions of Hong Kong, Shanghai, and Other Treaty Ports of China. London, 1908.

Yeung, Y.H. and Lo, C.P. (eds.), Changing Southeast Asian Cities. Kuala Lumpur: Oxford University Press, 1976.